P9-BZH-811

SMALL ANIMALS

PARENTHOOD IN THE AGE OF FEAR

KIM BROOKS

FLATIRON
BOOKS
NEW YORK

Certain names and identifying characteristics have been changed, whether or not so noted in the text, and certain characters and events have been compressed or reordered.

www.flatironbooks.com

Earlier versions of some portions of this title were previously published by *New York* magazine.

Designed by Donna Sinisgalli Noetzel

Library of Congress Cataloging-in-Publication Data

Names: Brooks, Kim (Author and essayist), author.
Title: Small animals : parenthood in the age of fear / Kim Brooks.
Description: First Edition. | New York : Flatiron Books, [2018] | Includes bibliographical references.
Identifiers: LCCN 2017061165 | ISBN 9781250089557 (hardcover) | ISBN 9781250089564 (ebook)
Subjects: LCSH: Parenthood—United States. | Mother and child—United States. | Fear—United States. | Child welfare—United States.
Classification: LCC HQ755.8 .B753 2018 | DDC 306.874/3—dc23
LC record available at https://lccn.loc.gov/2017061165

Our books may be purchased in bulk for promotional, educational, or business use. Please contact your local bookseller or the Macmillan Corporate and Premium Sales Department at 1-800-221-7945, extension 5442, or by email at MacmillanSpecialMarkets@macmillan.com.

First Edition: August 2018

10 9 8 7 6 5 4 3 2 1

For my children

CONTENTS

AUTHOR'S NOTE

In March of 2011, a person I didn't know, and would never meet, tried to have me arrested for what she viewed as criminally irresponsible parenting. The consequences of that action played out slowly over the course of two years, and ultimately motivated me to begin writing about the experience, and about the broader subjects of parenthood and fear. To learn about these subjects and their points of intersection, I spoke to other parents, psychologists, social workers, historians, sociologists, legal experts, parenting rights' advocates, safety advocates, medical professionals, and writers. My goal in initiating these discussions was not to justify my actions or to establish myself as a parenting expert. My goal was not to gauge my own success as a mother, or to arrive at any consensus about how much freedom parents should be allowed in the choices they make for their children, or how much independence children need to thrive. My goal, in fact, was not to provide any particular answers at all but, rather, to pose questions that were not being asked with the frequency or urgency they deserved.

Why, I wanted to find out, have our notions of what it means to both be a good parent and to keep a child safe changed so radically in the course of a generation? In what ways do these changes impact the lives of parents, children, and society at large? And what, in the end, does the rise of fearful parenting tell us about our children, our communities, and ourselves?

Inevitably, some will argue that my recollections of anxious motherhood, the story of what happened to me, and the path of inquiry down which it led me are not representative, or that they represent only one woman's unique experience. They may argue that my experience of motherhood would not have been what it was if I had had more money or less, a more high-powered career or no career at all, a more supportive network of extended kin, a different group of friends and neighbors; or if I were a single mother, a woman of color, an older or younger mother, a mother who needed, wanted, and expected something more or less from motherhood. I'd like to concede the point from the start. I'd argue only that the subjectivity of one woman's or, specifically, of one mother's experience does not render it irrelevant any more than the subjectivity of one soldier's experience, or one lover's experience, or one critic's—or any of the individual experiences more commonly deemed suitable for serious discourse.

This problem of diminishing or demeaning women's experiences by challenging their universality—to insist that if you can't speak for everyone then you can't speak for anyone—reminds me of a recent encounter I had during a panel discussion on motherhood and creativity. During the question-and-answer portion, a woman in the audience raised her hand, then made an incisive and thoughtful remark about the multitude of practical and artistic challenges mothers face as writers. She followed up her comment by adding that she wasn't any sort of expert but "just a mom." The idea that being "just a mom" was both an admission of a form of amateurism and a justification for disregarding a person—and all of her experiences, observations, knowledge, and so on—saddened and infuriated me. There is an extended musing about the inherent problems of perspective in Doris Lessing's masterpiece *The Golden Notebook* that I wanted to share with her. I'll share it with you (and, if she's reading this, that so-much-more-than-just-a-mom) now:

Nothing is personal, in the sense that it is uniquely one's own. Writing about oneself, one is writing about others, since your problems, pains, pleasures, emotions—and your extraordinary and remarkable ideas—can't be yours alone. The way to deal with the problem of "subjectivity," that shocking business of being preoccupied with the tiny individual who is at the same time caught up in such an explosion of terrible and marvelous possibilities, is to see him as a microcosm and in this way to break through the personal, the subjective, making the personal general, as indeed life always does, transforming a private experience . . . into something much larger; growing up is after all only the understanding that one's unique and incredible experience is what everyone shares.

With this in mind, I share with you the story of the day I left my son in the car and the journey I embarked on in its aftermath. It is "just" my story. But it belongs to you as well—as yours belongs to me.

You had a Dame that lov'd you well,
That did what could be done for young
And nurst you up till you were strong
And 'fore she once would let you fly
She shew'd you joy and misery,
Taught what was good, and what was ill,
What would save life, and what would kill.
Thus gone, amongst you I may live,
And dead, yet speak and counsel give.
Farewell, my birds, farewell, adieu,
I happy am, if well with you.

—ANNE BRADSTREET,
"IN REFERENCE TO HER CHILDREN, 23 JUNE 1659"

In his late sixties, Herman Melville took a four-year-old granddaughter to the park and then forgot her there.

—DAVID MARKSON, *READER'S BLOCK*

Oh, honey, you're not the world's worst mother. What about that freezer lady in Georgia?

—HOMER SIMPSON

PART I

FEAR ITSELF

1

THE DAY I LEFT MY SON IN THE CAR

It happened in the parking lot of a strip mall during the first week of March 2011, my last morning in Virginia, at the end of a visit with my parents. The day it happened was no different from any other: I was nervous, and I was running late.

I was thirty-three at the time—a young mother, a frazzled woman, an underemployed writer, a mostly stay-at-home mom, secretly wishing I was something more, something else. I had a husband, a son, a daughter, and a dog. We lived together in a town house in Chicago. But all of this happened in Virginia, in the rural-suburban community south of Richmond where I'd spent most of the first eighteen years of my life. I'd taken my children there to visit my parents for the week, and now the week was over. Back to Chicago. Back to life.

The morning it happened, I was packing and planning. Packing is utterly transformed by becoming a parent. There had been a time when packing had been fun and easy. For an entire summer in Israel, I'd once packed nothing but sundresses, a pair of Birkenstocks, a few Edith Wharton novels, and a package of oral contraceptives. For a semester in France, I'd packed a few pairs of jeans, black shirts, an English-French dictionary, and an asthma inhaler in case I decided to take up smoking. When my husband and I traveled in the days before having children, we mostly packed books. Travel was for reading, walking, eating, seeing. It was for sex and sleeping in. I remember once being out at dinner with a friend who said, "I have to go home early to pack." I'd wondered what she meant. "Don't you just open up your suitcase and throw some shit in?" I'd asked. That was how I thought about packing until the age of twenty-nine. Then something changed: The something was parenthood. When you have small children, there are no vacations; there are now only trips. When you have small children, packing is a challenge, a project, an ordeal—or if you're me, and you spend hours thinking about every worst-case scenario and how you might prevent it and what you might need if it comes to pass, a destination as exotic as Massachusetts seems impossibly inhospitable simply by virtue of not being the place where you have all of your shit.

"Mom!" I yelled across my parents' house. "Mom! Have you seen Felix's headphones?"

She was in the backyard, pulling up weeds, watching him jump on the trampoline. "Your phone?" she called back. "Have you looked in your pocket?"

"Not my phone. His headphones . . . for the plane."

"Look in your purse," she said. "Look on the kitchen counter."

They were not in my purse. They were not on the kitchen counter. They were not in the diaper bag. They were not in my backpack. "Fuck," I said, though not loudly, because the baby was sleeping and the doors in my parents' house are cardboard-thin. "Fuck, fuck, fuck," I whispered, then looked at the clock.

I'd divided the items to be packed into two categories. First were things I might possibly need during a flight with my four-year-old and two-year old—the category of contingency items. This category was infinite. It had no beginning and no end and grew larger with every trip I took with them. I tried not to think too much about this category. Then there was the category of things I would almost definitely need. Felix's special headphones—the padded kind that were the only kind he'd tolerate wearing as he watched a movie on my iPad, leaving me free to do things like feed the baby or change the baby or bounce the baby up and down, trying to keep her from annoying the other passengers—were on the column of essential items. They were nonnegotiable, on par with diapers, wet wipes, bottles, a packet of unmixed formula, snack food, storybooks, water, a sippy cup, a stroller, a change of clothes, a changing mat, crayons, paper, stickers, suckers for popping ears at takeoff and landing, and my bottle of lorazepam—a lovely controlled substance also known by the brand name Ativan, a member of the lovely class of drugs called benzodiazepines, whose main indication is the treatment of anxiety disorders—to keep me from having a panic attack during turbulence or any of the other in-flight moments when the irrational portion of my brain sent a message to my body that, by the way, you and your children are currently hurtling miles above the earth at five hundred miles per hour in a manmade cylinder resembling a large, aluminum coffin. Yes, a low dose of lorazepam was as essential for flying as my four-year-old's special headphones.

I had the lorazepam. I didn't have the headphones. This was what I was thinking as I slid open the screen door and told my mother I was running to the store.

Felix had hopped down from the trampoline and was pushing a toy lawn mower around the yard when I made the announcement. "Can I come?" he asked.

"You hate going to the store," I reminded him. "Why don't you stay here with Grandma?" It wasn't really a question and yet I phrased it as a question. This was a habit I'd later learn to identify, of mistakenly turning a command into a choice. What I meant to say was, *You stay at home with Grandma, Felix. Mommy will be right back.* A very clear order. And yet, without ever consciously deciding to do so, I'd become a parent who associated empathy for my kids' feelings and discussion and consensus-building with enlightened parenting. *Are you ready for dinner? Should we clean up your toys? Can you apologize to your sister for drawing on her feet?* Parents such as myself didn't give orders; we made suggestions, negotiated, took things under consideration.

I had ample love, endless good intentions, and absolutely no confidence in my own authority. And often I'd wonder why, in the time I passed with my children, did I feel so anxious and overpowered and out of control?

"No Grandma. I want to come with Mommy. I go too," Felix said.

I should have seen what was going on—my parents had been letting him play with the iPad in the car, and he was trying to score the extra screen time. My parents let him do all kinds of things I didn't let him do at home. I let them let him. My children saw their grandparents three or four times a year. Felix knew the system. I was too busy rushing and worrying to think about his motives.

I was busy thinking—thinking about the security line, the boarding process, how there were few things I enjoyed less than flying, and how flying with my children was one of them. I was thinking about the quiet rage I would feel as I struggled barefoot with my thrashing children through the metal detectors or body scanners while other passengers sighed behind me at our slowness, the impatience I'd feel at their impatience, at my own clumsiness, and at the security procedures themselves, procedures that would surely not prevent a determined person from blowing our plane out of the sky but that we'd all submit to in a choreographed act of security theater.

"Pleeeeeaaase?" Felix said.

It seemed heartless not to let him come along. Also, and maybe more important, I was weak. I equivocated and wavered. As a mother who was also trying to work and write, stealing time away from one pursuit to feed the other, I was uncertain, second-guessing, skeptical of my own instincts. These were useful qualities to have as a writer. They sharpened the critical eye, staved off complacency, urged redoing and redoing again. They were not great qualities for a parent. Whatever that quality is that gives people the confidence to say to a child or an electorate or an army, "I know the answer; do as I say!" I didn't have it.

"Kim," my mom called to me from the laundry room. "Just let him stay here. It'll be faster. Stay with Grandma," she said to my son.

"Noooo!!!!! Want Mommy. I want to go with Mommy. Mommy, don't leave me."

For about two seconds, I tried to think of a good reason why he shouldn't be allowed to come along, why my convenience running this errand should be prioritized over his desire to spend time with me, his mother. Children needed time with their mothers. So much time. Endless time. When I couldn't think of such a reason, I folded.

"All right," I said. "But hurry up. We have a plane to catch. Quick, quick. Let's go."

I remember other details about that morning. I remember it was overcast and cool enough that we both put on our jackets before we left—Felix's neon orange, mine pink—and that I was thinking how in Chicago, though it was already March, it would probably be snowing.

I took Felix's hand and led him into my mother's minivan. The garage door was open, which was how she left it if she was inside or around the neighborhood. "What do I have that anyone around here wants to steal?" she'd ask. She was probably right. There were more squirrels per square acre than humans; it just wasn't the sort of place where someone was going to walk into a garage and steal a bike. There would be nowhere to go with it, no place for people to hide from each other.

We got in the car and drove two miles along the winding two-lane parkway, past the side streets where kids rode bikes in cul-de-sacs and plenty of people didn't bother to lock their doors, and then we parked in the recently erected, nearly empty strip mall. I had two hours to get the headphones, to get home, to get my two-year-old daughter up from her nap, to get her fed and changed, to get everyone to the airport, through security, and onto a plane. Halfway to the store, Felix noticed Grandma's iPad, which was sitting on the seat beside him. Like an air pressure gauge, the owners' manual, a box of Kleenex, an iPad was just something you found in a minivan. Felix started to play with it. I said nothing.

He was still playing when we pulled up in front of the parking lot.

"Ready?" I said.

"I don't want to go in," he said.

I turned around to look at him. "Felix," I said. "Come on. You said you wanted to come with Mommy."

He was tapping animals on a screen, dragging them from one side to the other. "I don't want to go in. I changed my mind."

I tried to make my voice both calm and firm.

"Felix," I repeated. "If we don't get your headphones, you won't be able to watch a movie on the flight. It's a long flight. If you can't watch a movie on the plane, you're going to be a very, very, very unhappy boy. It will just take a minute. Now come on. We're running late."

He glanced up at me, his eyes alight with what I'd come to recognize as pre-tantrum agitation. "No, no, no! I wait here," he said.

I took a deep breath. I knew what I was supposed to do. Set a limit. Be firm and consistent. Communicate my expectation calmly but with authority. But I was tired. I was late. I was nervous about flying. I didn't want, at that moment, to deal with the full-scale meltdown of my spirited, forty-pound four-year-old. Also, just beneath these reasons was something else, something more serious. It was a voice, this small, quiet voice I'd been hearing more and more lately. "Why?" the voice asked. "Why?" Why did I have to do it? Why did I have to have this discussion, this confrontation, this battle? It wasn't as though he were asking to smoke a joint or to rollerblade in traffic. He just wanted to sit in the car and play his little game for a few minutes. Why did I have to drag him inside? It was cool outside, hardly fifty degrees. The parking lot was safe. There were four or five cars around, a couple of middle-aged women in festive sweaters unloading their carts. It was the middle of the day. Cloudy and mild. Felix hadn't yet figured out how to undo his car seat buckle. Nothing was going to happen to him in the four or five minutes it would take for me to run into the store. I could lock the doors, crack the windows. If anyone tried the handle, the alarm would sound, but no one was going to try the handle. Hadn't I grown up waiting in the car while my own parents ran errands? What could possibly happen, here of all places, in just five minutes? Why couldn't I leave him, just this once?

I looked at the clock. I looked back at my son. Then, for the next four or five seconds, I did what it sometimes seemed I'd been doing every minute of every day since having children, a never-ending, risk-benefit analysis. I noted the mild weather. I noted how close the parking spot was to the front door, and that there were a few other cars nearby. Mostly, though, I visualized how quick, unencumbered by a fussing four-year-old, I would be, running into the store, grabbing a pair of headphones, checking out, and coming back to the car. So I let him wait there. I told him I'd be right back. I opened the windows halfway to ventilate the car. I child-locked the doors and double-clicked my keys so that the car alarm was set.

I went into the store to get the headphones.

The store I visited that day might have been newly constructed, along with all the other mega-chain big-box stores spurred by an influx of families and professionals to central Virginia, but the space itself, the place where I left him that day, was familiar. I'd grown up about two miles from where I stood. I knew the sky, the flat, hazy horizon, the local people, their accent, more twang than drawl. My parents still lived in the same subdivision down the road where we'd moved when I was one. They lived on the same street and in the same house where I grew up. How I hated Brandermill, that subdivision, when I left it at eighteen, that street, that house, its planned-development stupor, its inaccessibility to all things meaningful and cultural, its lack of sidewalks, its sprawling golf course, its painful faux pastoralness that had obliterated a genuine pastoralness for the purposes of God knows what, making nature seem less threatening, less necessary to explore (which was extra work), less *unknowable*.

"Why did you move here?" I asked them at least once a month throughout my teen years. "Why would anyone choose to live here?"

"Oh, come on, Kimmy," my dad answered. "If you think this is the worst place, you haven't seen much of the world."

Of course, in many ways, he was right. In this rural-suburban, 1980s, American subdivision, my childhood was largely free from the hardships children have faced throughout much of human history, and continue to face today in much of the world. There was no starvation, no lack of sanitation, no outbreaks of deadly, communicable diseases, no war or mass violence. Crime was low. Neighbors knew or at least recognized one another. My mother seldom locked our door.

Occasionally, of course, even in such an idyllic setting, bad things happened to children. When I was twelve, a girl named Charity Powers, who lived in an adjacent county, disappeared outside a fast-food restaurant near a roller-skating rink late at night while waiting for her mother's friend to pick her up. There was a massive search effort, her grainy, photographed face appearing on the six o'clock news. People in supermarket aisles wondered what a little girl was doing alone in a parking lot so late at night. Where was the mother? It was the mother's boyfriend, some said. He never showed up. But these grumblings faded four months later when her body was found in a shallow grave on the property of a man who was later found guilty of capital murder. It really happened. She really died. But I remember it now, almost thirty years later, because it was so unusual, so exceptional in its horror.

Still, there were other, awful things from time to time. A carful of teenagers crashed into a tree in our neighbor's yard, killing three and maiming the fourth. A high school sophomore's truck was struck head-on by a drunk driver. Another teen dove from a rocky ledge into a swimming hole and snapped his neck. But I remember these incidents precisely because they were anomalous. Bad things happened to children, even in Brandermill, but only on the rarest of occasions. And so when they happened, you remembered them. Surely similar tragedies struck other communities around the country, but when they did, with the exception of the rare, high-profile case, we didn't hear about them. This was pre–internet age, pre–Amber Alert; we knew when terrible things happened within arm's reach, but not beyond.

Usually, life was peaceful. The days came and went with the easy stupor they were supposed to have. Safety, security, health, and prosperity were what we expected; we were white and middle-class. "I think it's a fine place to live," my father declared. As a teenager, and then a young adult, I would roll my eyes. I was too young to conceive of choosing a home for what it lacked. I hated it.

"You're out of your mind," my mother would tell me. "I love it here. I loved it the moment I saw it—the trees, the quiet, the people—and I never want to live anyplace else. When I die, scatter my ashes on the back porch so I can stay here forever."

"You're a Jew, Mom. Jews don't do cremation."

"Then bury me beneath the trampoline out back. Or find a nice spot near the magnolia tree. Whatever's easiest."

I gazed at her with that particular mixture of love, repulsion, amazement, and horror so many daughters reserve for their mothers. How was it possible that I was made from this person? "Who *are* you?" I would ask her. She would listen, smile, answer automatically.

"You know who I am."

That spring, when I visited my parents in Virginia, I knew them as well as I'd ever know them. I knew my children to an equal degree, having incorporated their every need into my muscle memory, my intuition. And yet somehow, as a thirty-three-year-old wife, writer, and mother of two, I didn't really know myself. I didn't know who I had been before children, much less who I had become, how I had changed. Worse still, I didn't know how much I didn't know. Only one thing was clear: My days of reflection and self-discovery were indefinitely on hold. That March, the spring that I returned to Virginia to visit my family, I was deep into the phase of life my therapist would later call the All-Hands-on-Deck, Every-Man-for-Himself, Just-Trying-to-Survive phase of parenting, the phase Judith Warner writes of in *Perfect Madness*, the phase when, if you are a college- or graduate-school-educated working woman in her late twenties to early forties, you realize that every skill you have learned and perfected over the previous one to two decades of your life is of little to no use to you now.

To put it another way, before I had kids, my dream had been to become a mother and to write my first novel while the little ones napped. At the height of this All-Hands-on-Deck phase, my dream was to take a nap. I had a draft of a novel, but I wasn't writing or revising much. Most days, I was barely reading. Felix had been sick on and off for the first three years of his life, moving from one respiratory infection to another, each one bringing with it a flare-up of asthma or an icky secondary infection. The ensuing marathon of antibiotics, nebulizer treatments, and oral steroids of those early years left me shell-shocked. And now, even as his health seemed to be improving, I found it hard to relax whenever he or his younger sister, Violet, had so much as a sniffle. With all the crud circulating in their preschools and playgroups, it sometimes seemed as though I was living out my life in the waiting rooms of doctors' offices.

When I wasn't worrying about fevers and mucus, there were plenty of other uncertainties to keep the cortisol flowing. For every one of my children's needs—food, sleep, affection, discipline, socialization, and education—there'd be at least a hundred different ways of responding, countless methods and approaches for nurturing these little people I loved so deeply. And for every choice that needed making, for every path not taken, I'd feel a tiny tinge of fear, a ripple of anxiety passing through me about the infinite ways it seemed possible to mess up. There were so many moments when I felt inept, when I felt like I should be fired, when I felt, though I loved my children, that motherhood, at least as it was practiced by those around me, was, as the career counselor or later employers would say when they wanted to communicate that you sucked at something, "not a good fit." It required so many skills I never would have associated with parenthood, not just love and empathy and patience, but organization, discipline, foresight. The things that needed doing to be a good mother—there were too many of them, or too few of me, to do them. There were playdates to be scheduled. Birthday parties to be planned.

Preschool applications to be submitted. Appointments and enrichment programs to be prioritized. Being a mother, it seemed, was a lot like being a manager or a CEO of a small company, and there I was, a former English major who'd never learned to make a spreadsheet. So I did the only thing I could do. I winged my way through it. And even as I improvised this frantic state of being that has become synonymous with modern, middle-class parenthood, I puzzled over it. How could something as common as parenthood feel so complicated and so unnatural? Was I going about it the wrong way, trying to squeeze too much out of every hour, every minute, barreling through days and nights of child-rearing as though I were being chased?

When I think back to that March, to my decision to take the two kids and spend a week with my parents in Virginia, I can see this uncertainty beneath the impulse. I wanted a break, a pause, a week or two out of time, free from the unsustainable pace I'd established at home and my chronic, gnawing anxiety about . . . I could hardly say what it was. It had started the morning Felix was born in the sunny hospital room, faded when they brought me my baby, rosy-cheeked and cleanly suctioned of all the meconium in his lungs. Over the next four years it resurfaced, again and again, a virus that went dormant but never died. I felt it every time I read an article about the significance of a particular developmental milestone my kids hadn't yet achieved. I felt it when I'd stand at a birthday party with thirty other parents, watching for two hours as our children played, chiming in with encouragement and managing their every social interaction. I felt it at the beach one afternoon when a lifeguard told me I couldn't let Violet (not yet two at the time) play topless in the sand because "any creep might snap a photo." I'd felt it at the park the week before. Felix was playing, and just at the moment I took out a book to read, he stumbled, bumped his chin, and a woman began shouting across the play lot, "Where is this child's mother? Is this child being supervised?" I'd felt it when my husband, Pete, and I spent every second of our time together debating preschools, or sleep-training, or airing resentments about who was slacking in which domestic duty.

I wanted to get away from them, these voices, this chaos, all the incessant worry. I wanted to sleep and read and have conversations and let my kids play unsupervised in a big backyard or around the neighborhood the way my own parents had. I wanted a short break from watching and worrying and caring so intensely and being in charge of every detail of my children's lives. It seemed to me that there was no better place for this than Virginia, the place I'd grown up.

Four days before I left Felix in the car in front of that Target, my children and I arrived at the Richmond airport, frayed and disheveled after the flight. "My babies, my babies," my mother called when she spotted us making our weary way toward her. She'd parked the car in the hourly lot and came right up to the edge of airport security to meet us. She walked a little past the edge, actually, and a guard kept nudging her back. "Come to Grandma. Come here and let me kiss you a million times. Grandma is here, Grandma is here."

The children hesitated, then inched forward enough for her to scoop them up. Noisy smooches. Hugs and kisses and squeezes. Only after she'd gotten her fill did she glance up at me, her daughter, now more of a grandchild delivery device than a discrete individual. "You look exhausted," she said.

"I am exhausted," I said.

In reality, I was still a little high on lorazepam. I'd tried reading the reassuring statistics on air-travel safety. I'd tried knitting and meditation and counting my breaths, watching movies and listening to music. In the end, only a low-dose benzo was really able to convince me that the jet I was trapped inside was not, at any moment, going to plunge to the earth. This had been a short flight, so I was still swaying a little as I watched my mother squeeze my children as though she were wringing them dry. I was left lugging the kids' jackets, the diaper bag, the in-flight electronics, the snacks and half-empty bottles. The security guard seemed relieved when we started walking. At the baggage claim belt, the suitcase came quickly, the car seats last. We loaded it all onto a cart and dragged it to the parking garage, and then my mother turned on some terrible kids' music and began dispensing cellophane bags of graham crackers, freeze-dried apple snacks, and peanut butter cookies while I went about the business of installing both car seats into the back seat of her minivan. Fifteen minutes later, we were ready to leave.

"Why are those things so hard to put in now?" my mother wondered as I dabbed the sweat off my brow with the bottom of my shirt. "When you were a baby, it was just a buckle and a snap. Now you might as well be launching the kid to the moon."

"Cars are dangerous," I told her. "Kids are more likely to be killed in a moving vehicle than anyplace else."

"Are we going to be killed?" Felix asked.

"No," my mother said. "We're going to Grandma's house. I've set up a tent for you in the living room. I've bought a thousand new toys. You're going to have the time of your lives. You done with your graham crackers already? Thirsty? Want a sip of Grandma's Diet Coke?"

He smiled as she handed him the can.

I thought about protesting, then sighed instead.

She started the car and pulled onto the highway, unwrapped a piece of gum, and put on a visor to keep the sun out of her face. I sank into the leather seat and closed my eyes. March in Virginia. Everything outside newly thawed. Winter there was just for fun. My mom smiled at me as she drove, patted my hand. "I'm so glad you came," she said. "Every day I wish you and Pete would move to

Virginia to be close to us. I don't understand the draw of Chicago. I guess you like to freeze and to have no space."

"Maybe we will move here," I said. "We could move back in with you and Dad. I could try to get a job at that Subway where I worked in high school."

"There are plenty of good jobs in Richmond. Capital One just came here. Couldn't you get a job writing for Capital One?"

"Maybe," I said.

"It's hard to live far away from family when your kids are little. I remember."

And yet that's what we're doing, I thought. My parents had tried, for eighteen years, to give me everything I needed in order to make me a successful human, and the mark of their achievement toward my success would be my not needing them anymore, not even now, with small children of my own to raise.

Margaret Mead wrote, "A society that cuts off older people from meaningful contact with children, a society that segregates any group of men and women in such a way that they are prevented from having or caring for children, is greatly endangered." *Bullshit,* I'd thought when I read this in college. *If I ever have kids of my own, I'd sooner let a stranger on the street help me care for them than the lunatics who raised me.* But the stranger on the street, it turns out, doesn't want to help you. Only the lunatics want to help. And parenting without a full brigade of boots on the ground is lonely, grueling business.

"We manage okay," I replied.

The highway opened up as the van gained speed. Four lanes and hardly that many cars in sight. I'd ridden down this road so many times in my life. I had a feel for every curve and turn, yet now it was new because I was new, no longer a kid, no longer a teenager or a student. I was a mother now. How could this place, which had made me, be exactly the same when I was so different? The landscape of wet trees, open sky, exit ramps, and nothingness slipped by, all of it both familiar and foreign.

"Well," my mother said, "this week will be a nice break for you. You look so tired. You don't still take those drugs when you fly, do you?"

"No," I lied. "Not anymore."

"Why don't you close your eyes now? Take a little rest."

The kids loved being in Virginia. Felix loved the fact that he could play in the backyard without an adult hovering over him, that he could ride his scooter around the cul-de-sac without my yelling, "Car!" every ten seconds. Violet liked that my mother spoiled her with dolls and stuffed animals, let her eat Froot Loops for breakfast and binge-watch whatever pseudo-educational abomination they were into at the moment. And though I quietly disapproved of all this, there was a part of me that loved it too; that felt relieved by this temporary retreat to the mind-set of my upbringing, a mind-set where everything you did with your kids or let them do didn't matter so much. It was a mind-set Pete and I had consciously rejected as parents. Think of all the things we could have accomplished with the hours we each spent sitting around watching reruns of *Full House* and *Diff'rent Strokes*, or playing Nintendo, or walking around the mall, we'd mused in the early years of our marriage. We could have learned Mandarin or mastered the cello. We'd have done things differently from our parents. We'd be better. And yet, watching my own kids on my parents' home turf was a little bit like watching myself back then, the kid I had been. It was a peculiar, but not an entirely unpleasant, déjà vu.

The week passed quickly. By the last day, as I thought about going back home, I grew anxious and restless. My mother, trying to raise my spirits, invited some of her friends over for their social gathering of choice: an evening of bridge, gossip, heavy hors d'oeuvres, and goblets of Chablis. I'd never learned to play bridge myself, but I sat among them on a pleather barstool, sipping pink wine and listening to them discuss me as though I weren't in the room.

"Is it good to have Kimmy home?" one friend asked. "And the babies?"

"Heaven," my mother said. "Especially the babies. I can't get enough of them. I wish I could keep them all to myself for a couple of weeks. She needs a rest. She's so anxious," my mother announced to the group as she dealt the first hand. "She worries constantly."

"Prozac," suggested her friend Dana. "I couldn't get out of bed without it. It's a miracle drug."

My mother glanced at me, then back at her cards. "Are you kidding? She's already on it. Aren't you already on Prozac, Kimmy?"

"Zoloft," I said. "Should I go get my full medical file, Mom?"

"It is what it is. She gets it from me. The women in our family, our brains are short on serotonin."

"They're short on something," I said.

"What are you worried about, Kimmy?" asked Priya, another friend. "And what's the opening suit? Hearts?"

"Spades."

"She worries about the kids," my mother answered for me. "She obsesses over them. Speech therapy, occupational therapy, social therapy. If they had any more therapy, they'd be in an institution. And that's just the beginning. After that there's the baby sign language, the breastfeeding on demand, the co-sleeping, the mommy-and-me classes. Baby monitors all over the house. I'm afraid to fart. Then she's schlepping them to calculus for two-year-olds, baby language immersion, yoga. Yoga! Because it's good for them. Why does a three-year-old need to take a yoga class?"

"This is what they're all doing," said Priya. "The same with my grandchildren. Enrichment. Lots of enrichment."

"Why does a two-year-old need to be enriched? Can't they be enriched by digging in a sandbox the way we were?"

"It's good I'm old," said Dana. "Just hearing about this makes me anxious. I wouldn't have made it. I think I was an A mother in the eighties. Now I'd be like a C. It's different than when we were doing it. We were involved. We were invested. But there were limits. It's changed now."

"Changed from when we were children too," said Priya.

My mother laughed. "I don't think I saw my parents that much. When I was ten, they bought me a moped and I used to ride around Albany with my little brother on the back. That was that."

"In India, we had servants," said Priya. "It was a special treat to see my parents. Holidays. Birthdays. Jack of spades."

I watched my mother as she stuck a cracker into a bowl of whitefish salad, nibbled, shuffled, dealt. She'd gotten her nails done. Her hair too. I had to admit it: She looked good. Having her two daughters all grown up and living in distant states had done wonders for her mood and health. She'd lost weight, started exercising, gotten her blood pressure down and her spirits up. It struck me for the ten millionth time in my life how strange it was, how wildly unlikely, that this particular woman, this distinctive human sitting before me of all the humans on earth, should be my mother, the woman from whose body and soul I sprang. She ate more whitefish, brushed a crumb from her mouth. The round of bridge was over, so she got up from the table, carried a tray of veggies to the counter to be replenished. "You like the kitchen's new backsplash, Kimmy?" she asked as she passed.

She pointed to the silver polymer behind the stove. It was plastic, but it sparkled like quartz.

"Sure," I said.

"You could have such a big kitchen if you lived in the suburbs. Why don't you and Pete get out of the city?"

"We like the city."

"You could have more space. A big yard. A garage. Good public schools."

"Maybe," I said.

"An easier life," she added.

"I like things hard," I said.

I dipped a carrot into the bowl of briny mayo, wondering momentarily where my mother managed to find whitefish salad in central Virginia. In a land of smoked ham, we always had smoked salmon. While others ate biscuits and gravy and cobblers and collard greens, our house was stocked with rye bread and chopped liver and borscht. This was not because my mother kept kosher but rather because she was . . . my mother. She'd lived in Virginia thirty years but was still a Jewish girl from Albany who saw no need to change. No wonder I strove to be her inverse, a chameleon who blended into any background.

"It's true," my mother said. "You always have liked to do things the difficult way. You've never trusted anything easy."

"Thanks, Mom."

"Oh, leave her alone," Dana said. "She's a writer. Writers are supposed to be tortured."

"Tortured! What does she have to be tortured about? She worries too much. That's all."

"Is that true, Kimmy?" Dana asked.

"I enjoy worrying. It's my main hobby."

My mother gave me a look, but offered no further comment. "Are you still doing Weight Watchers?" she asked instead. "You look good."

I thought, not for the first time in my life, that every time I came home to visit, no matter how long I stayed, it was always one day too long. "I'm enormous," I answered. "I've never been bigger."

She sighed, patted my shoulder as she walked past me in the kitchen. "It's hard to take care of yourself when you're taking care of everyone else."

. . .

The next day, I drove Felix to Target. It was a few miles from my parents' house, but it was nearly identical to the one in Chicago where I'd been shopping on a biweekly basis since Felix was born. All through our long winter, I found myself lured there by its covered parking garage, its cart-lifting escalator, its enormous family restroom, and the SUV-sized kid-carrying carts. Here was a corporation making life easy on a mom—a mom who wanted to buy its products. Navigating so many of the city's public places and crowded spaces with children and their accompanying equipment felt like walking on the moon. Strollers didn't fit. The babies' cries echoed. Changing tables were broken or fetid or nonexistent. It was only when I got pregnant that I noticed that my favorite neighborhood café had a passive-aggressive sign on its front door: BABIES AND CHILDREN MUST BEHAVE AND USE INSIDE VOICES. When I pushed the stroller up a ramp outside the Art Institute, a woman in a wheelchair waved her fist at me and told me I should be ashamed of myself. I felt awful, but also exasperated. So many places I went with my babies, the message seemed the same: *You're not really wanted here, but if you come anyway, don't expect any help.* But not at Target. At Target, everything was easy. Target loved new mothers, even with our screaming charges and unwieldy gear, even with (especially with) our anxiety and boredom and expendable cash. I'd once shunned chain stores, shopped local, and supported small businesses. By the time my daughter was born, Target was my second home. *I'll be a good person again when I have more time,* I said to myself.

And so, though I was hundreds of miles away from home, nothing about that Target felt foreign. "Be a good boy," I told my son, promising I'd be gone only a minute. I jogged across the parking lot and moved quickly through the store, on automatic pilot, easily orienting myself to the slightly altered layout from the store in

Chicago—kids' merchandise to the left, electronics in the back. *Headphones, headphones, headphones.* I glanced toward the wide, glass-paneled entrance. I could see the car. In my mind, I could see Felix playing. I hurried past groceries and handbags, found electronics.

"Can I help you?" a salesperson asked.

"Headphones?"

She pointed to the next aisle. There were at least forty brands: black headphones and pink headphones, earbuds and noise-canceling devices, top-of-the-line and ten-buck cheapies. But where were the kind I needed? I scanned top to bottom, left to right. I don't wear a watch, but there was a clock on the wall. Or did I look at my phone? Two or three minutes had passed. I tried to find the salesperson who had approached me a moment before, but she wasn't around now. There was a woman behind the display case, talking to another customer. I looked for someone else, considered giving up, then I saw them: the padded kind my son preferred. One pair left on the far bottom corner. I grabbed them, didn't bother to look at the price. On the way to the register, I passed the grocery aisle and picked up two cereal bars to toss into my purse for the plane ride. There was only one customer ahead of me in line. The cashier scanned her items with impossible slowness while I looked at the packages of gum and breath mints and batteries and toys. If Felix was with me, he'd be begging for candy. Through the sliding doors of the store's entrance, I could see the car, could see the blurred outline of my son.

"Sorry, was there a price on this?" the cashier asked the woman ahead of me.

"I'm not sure. Five dollars?"

"You don't remember?"

"I think it was five. I can't be sure."

She picked up the phone beside the register. "I'm going to need a price check."

I took a deep breath, exhaled, craned my neck. I could still see the car.

"You know what," the woman said. "I'm gonna skip it. I'll pick it up next time." I wanted to kiss her.

"Are you sure? It'll only take a minute," the clerk asked. I wanted to hit her.

"I'm sure."

At last I was up. I swiped my Visa, declined the offer to save 5 percent. No need for a bag. Thanks, thanks. Then I was jogging. The doors slid open. The wind blew my hair. A cool March day. My mother's minivan right where I left it. In it, the boy.

"Hi, you little boy," I said as I settled into my seat.

"Hi," he said, still playing his game. I tossed the headphones onto the passenger seat and put the keys in the ignition, took a deep breath, glanced in the rearview, over my shoulder, then backed out slowly, the windows still open.

I've replayed this moment in my mind again and again, approaching the car, getting in, looking, pulling out. I replay it, trying to uncover something in the recollection I hadn't noticed at the time. A voice. A face. Sometimes I feel like I can hear something. A woman? A man? "Bye now." Something. But I can't be sure.

We drove back to my parents' house. My mother was cooking and talking on the phone. My daughter was awake in her crib with a diaper full of poop. I changed her, gave her a bottle, gave her to my mother while I loaded up the car, shoved the headphones and enough snacks for a caravan across the Mojave into my diaper bag.

"All set?" my mom asked.

"Have I ever told you how much I hate flying?" I said to her while I hoisted my suitcase into the trunk.

"You didn't used to," she said. "As a kid, you weren't afraid of anything."

"Yeah," I said. "I remember."

Then we were on our way.

We landed. We deplaned. We schlepped through O'Hare, a place where the only form of movement permitted is schlepping, and eventually, eventually, found ourselves in the baggage claim.

Pete usually picked us up in the carpool lane outside, so I was surprised when we stepped off the elevator between baggage carousels and I saw him waiting. The kids both ran to him. I straggled up behind them, dragging the equipment. Then I came forward and hugged him, pressed my face against his beard and felt pure and genuine relief at the sensation. It was funny, these moments, these flickers of uncompromised feeling. For more than four years, there'd been no more him and no more me. There was only us. And mostly them. But occasionally, coming back from a few days away, I'd notice the kinds of things I used to notice all the time in our childless years—the particularities of his face, his skin, his gestures—small qualities that made me love him.

Felix tugged on our arms, smiling, but Pete hardly looked at him. Something was different. Something was wrong.

"What is it?" I asked.

"Call your mom," he said.

"Why? What happened?"

"Just call her. The kids and I will wait for the bags."

I stood next to the wall and dialed. When she answered, she was crying.

"What is it?" I asked her. "Calm down. I can't understand you."

After a few seconds, my father took the phone. He told me that about ten minutes after my mother arrived home from dropping us at the airport, a police officer pulled into the driveway and came up the porch. When she opened the door, he held up a picture on his phone. "Is this you?" he asked. "The person in this picture . . . it's you, isn't it?"

"It's not me," she said.

"Who is it then? It's your car. Can you identify this person?"

"It's my daughter," she said, and started to panic. She thought something must have happened. An accident at the airport. A bomb.

"Is she here?" the officer asked.

"No, she's . . ."

"I need you to tell me where to find her."

"My husband will be home in an hour. Can you come back then?"

At that point, the officer told her she had two choices. She could tell him where to find me or he could put her in the back of his car and arrest her for obstructing justice. She began to cry. "I'm sorry," she said. "I have no idea what this is about, but if you don't have a warrant, I'm waiting here for my husband." Then she closed the door in his face.

I followed Pete and the kids to the car. We loaded the suitcases, collapsed the stroller, reinstalled the car seats. We didn't talk. I felt like I couldn't move. It was early evening, close to the kids' bedtime. We'd thought the kids would fall asleep, but sensing the tension, they sat wide awake. I don't remember how far we'd driven when I realized there was a voice message on my phone. The message was from a police officer calling from Virginia. "I'm trying to get ahold of Mrs. Kimberly A. Brooks. I need to speak with Mrs. Brooks about an incident this afternoon in a parking lot. Please contact me as soon as you receive this message." By the time we were nearing our exit on the Kennedy, the kids had finally dozed off. Pete was driving and I was shaking, trying not to panic, trying to figure out what to do. I started to dial the number the officer had left on the voice message, then stopped.

I dropped the phone back onto my lap and stared out the window. Car rides were more dangerous than flying, yet I'd always found them calming. When I was a baby, my parents used to drive in circles around our subdivision to get me to sleep. Even now, it was soothing, the soft darkness around the highway, the streaks of headlights and taillights, white on red, the familiar, almost transparent motion.

The phone hummed on my lap. It was the Virginia number again. Pete just looked at me, a look that said . . . I don't know what it said, but it wasn't good.

"I think I fucked up," I said to Pete, without turning away from the window.

He reached out and silenced the phone. Then he asked what he'd probably wanted to ask since the moment he saw me come out of the airport elevator. "What happened?"

Once we were home, Pete carried the kids up to their bedroom, walked the dog, emptied the dishwasher, made tomorrow's lunches—saw to all the domestic minutiae that make up our days—while I tried to piece together what had happened.

Eventually a picture emerged of someone—a man, a woman—who had seen me run into the store, leaving Felix in the car. That person had recorded him there, alone, and called the police. But before the police arrived, I had returned to the car. The person had watched me—us—leave. The person had waited there, explained to the police what had transpired, handed over the recording and the license plate number.

Late in the evening, I reached an attorney. My father-in-law had recommended I call a friend of his, a criminal lawyer. When I reached him, I thanked him for talking to me so late, and explained as best

I could the unfolding of events. He told me that if the prosecutor decided to press charges, I'd need to find a lawyer in Virginia, someone who really knew the local system, but in the meantime, he was happy to return the call to the police officer to explain the situation.

"That would be wonderful," I said. "What is the situation, exactly?"

"The situation is that you're a regular, responsible, attentive suburban mother who let her kid wait in the car while she ran into a store to get one item, which you shouldn't have done. But you weren't thinking, and you did it, and your kid is fine. No pattern of neglect. No history of abuse. No criminal record. No problem with drugs. It was a lapse in judgment. A momentary lapse in judgment. Is that about right?"

"Right!" I said. "A lapse in judgment."

"There's nothing you've forgotten to tell me, is there?"

"Nothing," I promised. "I mean, I don't live in the suburbs, but . . ."

"Never mind that."

He told me he'd call me back in twenty minutes. It was well past working hours, but as a friend of the family's, he wanted to help. Two hours later, I was still sitting at the dining room table, staring at a glass of wine, waiting for the phone to ring. Pete had fallen asleep. The washer and dryer were grumbling downstairs. I sat at the table, folding and unfolding a paper napkin. The living room was messy. It was always messy. I surveyed the objects scattered across the floor without getting up to put them away. There was a purple barrette, a lint roller, a handful of Duplo LEGOs, a tube of diaper cream, a baby nail clipper, a baby blanket, a pillowcase, a *National Geographic Little Kids* magazine, a battery-operated talking globe, and seventeen stuffed animals. I could pick them up, but the next morning, they'd be back on the floor. What was the difference? Why bother? I couldn't come up with an answer, so I just sat there sipping my wine and thinking about every mistake, every oversight, every miscalculation I'd made during my four years as a parent.

At twenty-five, I'd opted to have a breast reduction, though I knew it might one day compromise my milk supply. Three years later, before I knew I was pregnant, I drank two glasses of champagne at a New Year's Eve party, with Felix's little tadpole fetus tipsy inside me. As soon as I knew he was there, I stopped drinking alcohol and coffee, forswore sushi and cold cuts and all things unpasteurized; but after long deliberation, I chose to stay on my antidepressant, prioritizing my own mental health over the risk to his development. And still, there was more. I wanted to have a natural childbirth, to have his entry into the world take place in a candlelit tub of warm water and rose petals, to give him the gentlest, calmest, quietest arrival. Instead, I ended up with my legs half numb and hoisted in the air, feeling him crown as my first epidural wore off and I screamed for someone, anyone, to kill me. I wanted to co-sleep, to bond with this little precious creature all through the night, but he had colic and wailed the first eight weeks of his life, and I, teetering on the edge of sleep-deprivation-induced psychosis, sleep-trained him before the fourth month. I had hoped that the first year of his life would be filled with love and music and long walks in nature and interesting nonplastic toys and baby-mommy swim classes, but he was sickly, so instead the days passed in a haze of nebulizer treatments, antibiotics, oral steroids, and ear tubes. I wanted to be a devoted stay-at-home mother until he started kindergarten, but after only six months, I realized that if I went one more week without working or using my brain, I'd stick my head in the oven, so I put him in day care three afternoons a week to begin work on a novel.

As I sat there at the table that night, it seemed that every hope and good intention I'd had since becoming a mother had crumbled under the slightest pressure. The baby book I wasn't keeping would be a long log of failure, an exhaustive inventory of good intentions gone wrong.

"I'm a terrible mother," I said to my empty wineglass. I wanted to hear how it sounded. "I left my son in the car." Our rat terrier, Liza, trotted down the stairs and looked up at me with clear eyes, as though she understood. The phone rang. It was the lawyer.

"Sorry about the wait. I got caught up in something."

"What did you find out?" I asked.

"This is the funniest thing," he said. "I talked to the officer who called you. It turns out that we went to the same high school in Brooklyn."

"That's so funny," I said.

"So I explained the situation. He seems like a reasonable guy. You know they have to be cautious in situations like these where kids are involved. There are so many terrible parents out there. But I don't think you're the person they're after. You're not the kind of mom they'll throw the book at."

"You think it's fine? They'll drop it?"

"I think that's a definite possibility. I do."

He gave me the name of a Virginia lawyer, someone who would be able to better help me if it went any further. He told me to call the guy in the morning.

I thanked him at least ten times.

"Glad to do it. Glad to help," he said.

He was about to hang up when I said, "Just one more question. After I call the lawyer tomorrow, what happens next?"

I could hear he was distracted, covering the phone while he said something to his wife. I pictured his perfect family, his perfect children, his perfect, happy home. "Next," he told me, "you'll wait."

"Well, I don't understand it," my father said over the phone the next morning. "I just don't understand what in the hell all the fuss is about."

This was him at his angriest, a state I'd seen him in only a few

times in my life, usually when he'd gotten off the phone wi
manager at a health insurance company or had submitted himself
his masochistic ritual of watching Fox News. He'd called me from work, hoping for an update, more information, some explanation or assurance that it was all a misunderstanding, the same thing I'd been hoping to get from the lawyer the evening before.

"What is he saying the problem is? What are they accusing you of?"

I had taken Felix to school, put Violet down for her morning nap, and was now sitting on the living room floor, trying to keep my voice steady as I told him the little I knew. "They're saying that I left him in the car. That someone saw me leave him while I ran into the store."

"And that's against the law? That's a crime?"

"I don't know. Maybe. It varies by state. I'm waiting to hear back from the lawyer. I don't think there's a specific law in Virginia. But they could argue it's child neglect. Abuse. I don't know."

"You've got to be kidding me. Neglect. I've never heard of anything so asinine. Do you know how many times your mother and I left you and Sari in the car for a minute? I'd be serving consecutive life sentences if that were a crime."

"I know. I'm trying not to panic," I said, secretly relieved that he was panicking for me, that he was as taken aback by the whole thing as I was. If he said what was happening was asinine, then it was asinine. I trusted and believed him. Still, my voice was shaking as we spoke. "I guess what they're saying is that someone could have hurt Felix, broken into the car, kidnapped him."

A week earlier, it would have seemed preposterous. Of all the dangers I feared might befall my children, this wasn't one of them.

I hadn't yet memorized the facts that illuminate the paranoia behind our obsession with the occasionally horrific but largely fictional, inanely named phenomenon of stranger danger: the FBI data that show that the number of missing person reports involving d low levels in recent years, that the number llen by more than 40 percent since 1997, and ng person cases (adults and children) in 2014, t were runaways, that only 0.1 percent of missing re what we'd think of as a "stereotypical kidnapping." … know any of this then, but I must have sensed it, because a… uction was simply not on the list of nightmare scenarios I worried about, and the list was long. But I was rational in my hierarchy of fear. Speeding cars, distracted drivers, unfenced swimming pools, asthma irritants, third-floor windows left open too wide: These were the demons that haunted my imagination. Not creepy-looking strangers. I lived in a city and rode public transportation and spent a decent portion of my time hanging out with people who wrote for a living. I felt right at home among creepy-looking strangers. Only now, when I pictured this person in the parking lot, this faceless concerned citizen peering through the window of my car, recording my son as he played, watching him, talking to him, excited (maybe) to have found this defenseless, neglected child, I wondered if I'd been naive.

My father sighed into the phone. "Kidnapped?" he repeated flatly. "Last I checked, kidnapping is a crime. Someone could break into my house and shoot me in the head, but the police aren't showing up to arrest me if I forget to lock my door."

"I don't think they see it the same way when kids are involved."

"The same way," he said. "You mean rationally?"

I waited a moment, then asked what I didn't want to ask, the thing I'd been avoiding. "How's Mom?" I knew the answer by the amount of time it took him to respond.

"She's been better. She's upset by all this, obviously."

"Upset?"

"It's hard for her. It's been hard."

There's an episode of *Fresh Air*, one of Terry Gross's approximately seven million interviews with Philip Roth. They talk about his mother's reaction to *Portnoy's Complaint*, an extended and hilarious rant about the Jewish mother. Gross asked Roth if his own mother had seen herself in the characterization, and if so, whether the likeness had upset her. He responded that another journalist had asked his mother the same question years before and that she replied with Cartesian eloquence, "Every mother is a Jewish mother."

"Your mother worries," my father said. "She can't help it. She feels like it's somehow her fault."

"I understand that," I said. "But you know, not every bad thing that happens to me is about her."

"I understand that."

Softening, I asked if I should call her.

"Maybe hold off a few days. Wait until we have a sense of what's happening so you can put her mind at ease. It will make my life easier. You know how your mother gets. She makes your problems her own."

"Yes," I told him. "I know."

In the years since, whenever I tell people the facts of my case, that I left my four-year-old son in the car for five minutes, that someone recorded me doing so and called the police, that this single decision I made and its ramifications played out in my family's life over the course of two years—when I recount these facts to some new friend or family member, to a reporter or colleague or radio-show host, they all want to know the same thing. "How did you feel?" they ask me. "How did you feel when you realized what was happening?"

It's a simple enough question, yet it took me almost two years to answer it honestly. "I was scared," I used to tell them. Or "I was shocked." I would tell them I was angry or embarrassed or bewildered. And there was truth to all this. But the deeper truth was much worse. The deeper truth was that I felt as though I'd been caught doing something very bad, even if I didn't understand what the bad thing was, exactly, or what the rationale was for its badness. I felt, I think, what just about every woman feels whenever someone attacks or criticizes her mothering. I felt angry. I felt embarrassed. But beneath all that, I felt ashamed.

2

PARENTHOOD AS A COMPETITIVE SPORT

Before the incident in Virginia, when it came to absorbing and integrating ideas about parenting, about what it means to be a good parent, I had simply followed the herd, at least when others were watching. In a way, I was really two different mothers: There was the parent I was in private, and the parent I was in public; there was the parent I was to my children (loving, unstructured, disorganized, and probably overly permissive—my husband once told the children, "Mommy is not a 'yes' machine"), and there was the face of motherhood I projected onto the world, the face of a mother who always knew the best and most enlightened way to nurture and protect her children. This mother was thoughtful and competent and loving in a precise way that neither overinflated egos nor made them doubt their mother's affection. I subscribed to a rational, knowledge-based philosophy of parenthood, a philosophy in which information was elevated above all else. Children drowned in swimming pools not because their parents didn't love them. They drowned because their parents simply hadn't known that an unfenced swimming pool is as dangerous to a toddler as a loaded gun. Children grew fat watching television and drinking juice boxes not because their parents didn't want them to be healthy, but because their parents didn't know that the American Academy of Pediatrics recommends limiting screen time, or that sugary juices are nearly as toxic as soda. And children died in hot cars not because parents were stupid or reckless, but in most cases because they didn't know how easy it is to become distracted on the way to work, to be thrown off by a change in routine and not notice an infant in a rear-facing car seat.

Bad things happened to children not from lack of love but from lack of knowing—knowing what the risks were, knowing the best way, knowing the right method, knowing the latest research—and so I strove to be the mother who was informed and enlightened. I was a writer, after all, a reader, a person more comfortable in my head than anyplace else. I might not be good at holding a job or cleaning my house or organizing my kitchen or making birthday cakes. I might not be the most patient or creative or energetic mother. But I could be the one who always had the answer, who always had the most accurate and up-to-date information. And I believed that if I did this, if I played this part, my kids would be okay. Knowing, as anyone with an anxiety disorder can tell you, is one step away from controlling.

But it's hard to continue to believe that you have all the answers when you find out that someone has called the police to report you for criminal negligence of your son.

In the days and weeks following our return from Virginia, I felt myself slipping through the cracks of the façade I'd constructed. What's more, the incident put in sharp relief the charged and often stressful jockeying for status and approval that lurked beneath so many of my interactions with other parents, a habit I'd never acknowledged but one that became clear to me when I considered doing what I typically did when working through something difficult: talking to people about it.

I've always been terrible at keeping secrets. Pete once asked me if I'd ever *not* told anyone anything. But suddenly, for the first time in my life, something had happened that I realized I would have to keep hidden from as many people as possible, and especially from other parents. I felt this with absolute certainty; to tell people what I'd done, what was happening, no matter how absurd it seemed to me, was out of the question. I felt certain, and yet at the same time, I wondered why this was the case. If I didn't believe that I'd intentionally put my child in danger—if I believed, as I'd said to the lawyer that first night, that at worst, this was a momentary lapse in judgment—then why should the idea of telling other parents about the lapse fill me with shame and dread? We were all friends. Neighbors. Peers. We were all doing the best we could to raise our kids and keep them safe. Why should I have to keep the ordeal to myself? Why shouldn't others lend a sympathetic ear, or even a bit of advice? It wasn't like we were competing at raising our kids.

"Have you given much thought to what kind of pregnancy you'd like to have?" a nurse practitioner asked me during my first prenatal checkup. I was wearing a paper gown, sitting on the plastic examination table of the University of Illinois–Chicago family health center, halfway through my first appointment, when she posed the question. I remember it clearly all these years later for two reasons. First, it was the moment at which I began to understand not just intellectually but emotionally that this was actually happening—that there was a small, fast-dividing cluster of cells embedded in my uterus, hurtling toward humanhood, and that I, Kim Brooks, was going to be the mother of this person. The second reason I remember it is that it was also the instant in which it occurred to me that pregnancy and, later, parenthood, was not just a thing that happened, not just a thing one experienced, but something a person did, an arena in which I in particular would have the opportunity to impose my own preferences and ideas and desires, of which I had many.

This was the winter of 2007, shortly after Pete and I moved to Chicago. We'd gone there without jobs, with few friends in the city, with no clear idea of what, exactly, we wanted out of our lives other than to spend time together, to write, to read, to drink beer, to make enough money to live, and to maybe, potentially, possibly one day start a family. That day arrived sooner than we'd thought it would, about a week after we'd moved into our new apartment. It was not quite an accident. I'd stopped taking the pill a couple of months earlier and was relying entirely on a form of birth control I'd stumbled upon while buying shampoo at Rite Aid. It was called spermicidal film, and it consisted of a flimsy disk of clear, congealed spermicide, kind of like a Listerine melt-away strip. The idea was to fold it in half and insert it into the vagina, where it would dissolve and serve its spermicidal purpose. I was intrigued. Also, and maybe more important, I believed that because I'd always wanted to become a mother, because it was one of the few things in life I was absolutely certain I wanted, I assumed that getting pregnant would require years of temperature-taking, timed intercourse, and prohibitively expensive fertility treatments.

Infertility was a hot topic in the early aughts. You could hardly open a magazine without being swept up by a story of unfulfilled maternal yearning. I read every one of the stories I came across. I knew a few women who had struggled to get pregnant or to carry a pregnancy to term, women who'd been heartbroken by the frustration and disappointment they'd endured. Somehow all of this convinced me that conception would be horribly difficult for me as well.

But a month after relying on what I now believe actually was a

Listerine melt-away strip for birth control, I woke up nauseated, hungry, and intent on guzzling a gallon of grapefruit juice. The next day, a pregnancy test confirmed my suspicion. I called the 800 number of my (about to expire) graduate student insurance and was told by the voice on the line to make an appointment at the campus health center. It was at this center that a few weeks later, as I was sitting on a sheath of tissue paper and examining the chipped purple polish on my toenails, that the nurse posed her perplexing question to me, the question of what kind of pregnancy I wanted to have, which was really a coded way, I later realized, of asking what kind of mother I planned to be. I remember that she had warm, heavily mascaraed eyes, earrings that looked like the gears of a clock. She was friendly, professional, unsentimental in her posture and tone. She spoke as though having a baby were no different from ordering a steak.

"What kind of pregnancy," I repeated, watching as she unpeeled her latex gloves, scrubbed her hands with foam sanitizer. "An easy one?" I said.

She began opening drawers, gathering brochures, thumbing through informational leaflets. When she was satisfied with the materials she'd gathered, she looked up at me and smiled. "Here's my advice," she said. "Take some time and think about what kind of experience you want to have. How much medical supervision during the pregnancy? Are you considering natural childbirth? Are you leaning toward a midwife, an obstetrician, a family doctor? Would you like to deliver in a hospital, an attached birthing center? Are you interested in alternative pain management? Hypnosis?"

She handed me a pile of printouts. "You have time to decide, but in the meantime, this should give you some things to keep in mind. You should be getting plenty of exercise, plenty of rest. But also you should start taking folic acid if you haven't already. It can help prevent spina bifida. You should also be taking a prenatal vitamin to ward off anemia. Let's see now—things to avoid: alcohol, which causes fetal alcohol syndrome and many other problems. No Advil. It can cause bleeding. No smoking, which is associated with low birth weight. No sushi or tuna, because of the mercury. No unpasteurized cheese or cold cuts, which could contain listeria. No caffeine, associated with miscarriage. And do everything you can to minimize stress—cortisol's no good for the baby." She told me all this in a single breath, in a flat, even tone, the same way the flight attendants explain how to put on your oxygen mask if the plane falls out of the sky.

I left the medical center feeling as if I'd just been booked on a trip around the world. I drove home with the pamphlets on the seat beside me, picking them up and skimming them at red lights. *I've been given facts*, I thought. *I've been issued instructions.* There was so much to learn, so much to do, so much to decide, so much to buy. I got home and hurried up the stairs of our third-floor walk-up to pee. Then I sat down at the dining table with these pamphlets, spreading them out before me. I read and reread, making mental notes on all the things I should avoid doing if I loved my unborn baby, all the risks to be minimized or eliminated. I wondered as I read, and continued to wonder for the next nine months, how it was possible that any healthy baby had ever succeeded in being born. Reproduction suddenly seemed as dangerous as nuclear fission, the human embryo a rare and delicate flower tenuously imported into a woman's toxic womb. The literature was unambiguous: Be informed, be vigilant, or you and your child will suffer.

The brochures the nurse gave me at that first appointment were only the beginning of the mountain of literature I would read in the coming years. Even before I laid eyes on my son, my shelves were filled with parenting books, books full of advice on the best ways to feed, bathe, sleep-train, and discipline my kids, books by experts, books by other mothers, books by doctors, psychologists, nutritionists, and every other parent who might have a useful bit of wisdom. In this sense, I was intensely American in my parenting orientation. I wanted to be an informed consumer. Whatever the subject and whatever I thought I knew about it, I believed that there was an expert out there somewhere who knew more and knew better. It was only in the months and years following the incident in Virginia that I gradually began to read a different kind of parenting book, not the how-to kind but the what-exactly-are-we-all-doing-when-we-do-parenting kind—that is, I became more interested in historical, anthropological, and sociological examinations of American parenthood. Much of what I've read has focused on the all-consuming, increasingly intensive, super-pressurized, status-obsessed, safety-fixated world of modern, American, middle-class parenthood. For example, in *How to Raise an Adult: Break Free of the Overparenting Trap and Prepare your Kid for Success*, Julie Lythcott-Haims, a former dean at Stanford and mother of two, describes how competitive overparenting has harmed a generation of children and the parents raising them. She highlights the multitude of ways we as parents engage in some combination of "overdirecting, over-protecting, or over-involving ourselves in our kids' lives; we treat our kids like rare and precious botanical specimens and provide a delicate, measured amount of care and feeding while running interference on all that might toughen and weather them." She describes how easy it is for highly educated and informed parents to be sucked into a cyclone of anxiety and micromanagement, accepting an expanded notion of parenthood that includes not simply loving, sheltering, feeding, and counseling one's children toward adulthood, but managing their day-to-day lives to a degree that would have been unthinkable one or two generations ago.

Likewise, in *Playing to Win: Raising Children in a Competitive Culture*, the sociologist Hilary Levey Friedman describes how many parents speak and think about parenthood as though "it were a giant school project," feeling that if they only "start soon enough, read the right research, and do the right things, [they] can get the particular end product" they desire.

The historian Paula S. Fass echoes these observations in her book *The End of American Childhood*. She examines a generation of mothers—including herself—who are "increasingly fearful that the slightest deviation in oversight will ruin their children's carefully prepared path into the future." According to Fass, parents of this generation "yield to their most directive instincts and attempt to manage all parts of their children's lives."

No wonder that American mothers today spend more hours with their children than ever before in recorded history, even though most have now entered the workforce. As Lisa Belkin describes in a *New York Times* blog post, "Now that parenting has become a verb—an active, measurable, competitive thing—it brings with it an infinitely expanding job description. We create one for ourselves, different from our neighbors' or even our partners', but always broader than the ones our parents used."

Long gone are the days when a woman would be naturally inclined to ask her own mother or grandmother or aunt or neighbor for advice or guidance. My maternal grandmother smoked through three pregnancies, gave birth under ether, and hardly saw her children past the age of eight. I would have asked her for help building a spaceship before I sought her guidance on having a baby. And so, with few of those who have gone before to guide us, we set out to reinvent the wheel of child-rearing, all of us in our own way.

After that first appointment with the nurse practitioner, I tried to learn everything I could on the subjects of carrying, birthing, and caring for a baby. As I read, I'd often share my findings with my other pregnant friend, Tracy. Tracy and I had known each other since graduate school, and while I'd always enjoyed spending time with her, we became especially close that fall when we realized that we were both pregnant and that our boys would be born just six weeks apart. We had lunch whenever we could, bought maternity clothes together, sent each other "stroller porn," images of the high-end, time-travel-looking contraptions that we couldn't afford but really, really wanted. At the same time that Tracy and I were growing closer, so many of my other relationships were feeling more distant.

I was twenty-eight when I became pregnant with Felix. By geo-historical standards, this is hardly young. Many of the girls I'd known in high school became mothers even younger. But among the women I'd grown close to in college and graduate school, feminists with advanced degrees and career ambitions and various forms of domestic ambivalence, I was the first to think about having kids, the first to want them.

"You're really odd," my friend Amelia observed of me on this subject. We were teaching English at the same community college when she said this, and a colleague had brought in her brand-new baby to show off in all his baby splendor. The other teachers smiled and oohed and aahed and complimented the mother on such a beautiful child, then got back to work. I, meanwhile, completely lost my shit. "Oh my God," I said. "Amazing. Oh, oh, oh. I need one. I must have one of these. I must have one now. Give him to me." I took the baby from its slightly perturbed mother and pressed it to my chest. I announced to a roomful of coworkers that my ovaries were throbbing, that I felt as if they were about to burst.

"Sounds like endometriosis," Amelia said.

"No, you jerk. It's my biological clock."

"Oh, I see. Puke," she replied. "But thanks for clarifying."

I ignored her and began kissing my colleague's baby on its rolls and folds of puppy fat, breathing in the baby smell of its bald, baby head. "I need one of these," I repeated. "I want one."

"Oh, pull yourself together," Amelia said, taking the infant from me and passing it back to its mother. "We're practically children ourselves."

"No," I said. "I'm twenty-eight and you're thirty-two."

"Exactly," she said. "Children."

In a sense, I knew she was right. For people like us, it was weird to want a baby at our age, much less to have one. In 2008, 72 percent of college-educated women between twenty-five and twenty-nine had not yet had children. All of my closest friends were in that 72 percent. Amelia was perhaps the most adamantly in that 72 percent. At the time, she was absolutely certain that she didn't want children at all. Much later, after her marriage had ended and she'd started down the path of single-motherhood and then a healthier relationship, she'd tell me that what she really had been feeling was that she didn't want to have children with her former husband. But at the time, she'd felt sure that motherhood wasn't for her. And really, there wasn't anything unusual about it. "I have my work," she'd told me. "My students. My friends. My dogs. My adorable nieces and nephews, on whom I get to lavish attention when and only when I feel like it. What else does a person need?" It was all perfectly reasonable. I recognized that *I* was the weirdo, and yet there I was. If I'd announced to her or to any of my friends like her that I was planning to have an orgy or an open marriage or a spiritual conversion or a monthlong lemon-coconut-water-cayenne cleanse, they would have shrugged and rolled their eyes. But a baby? It was, as Amelia had put it, extremely odd.

Fortunately, when it actually happened a year later, I had Tracy, my one and only mom-to-be friend whom I could talk to and commiserate with about everything I learned and experienced and most of all worried about along the way.

"Are you taking folic acid?" I asked her not long after that first appointment with the nurse. "You have to take folic acid. And a prenatal vitamin? It's important for preventing spina bifida. Are you thinking about natural childbirth? Are you leaning toward a midwife or an obstetrician? Your chances of having an unnecessary C-section go way down with a midwife. Have you picked a hospital? Northwestern is basically a baby factory, totally impersonal. Would you ever consider a birthing center? Also, have you started looking into childcare yet? When do you think you'll go back to work? Have you heard anything about HypnoBirthing?"

And so it went. Looking back, I wish I could say I'd never been this person. I wish I could say I found the world of pregnancy vigilance and baby-planning mania pointless and bourgie and gross. I wish I could say I bristled at what seemed the widely held assumption that having a child was a fraught and perilous event that could be navigated only by those who exercised the highest level of caution, preparation, and care. I wish I could say that I didn't spend many, many hours of my life deciding which stroller I would buy, or which crib mattress, or which car seat, or which baby monitor, or which baby-wearing sling. I wish I could say I didn't spend a great deal of money on HypnoBirthing instructional DVDs that I barely watched, and on a certified doula whom I'd send home one hour into labor because, in the pain of contractions, her face and voice enraged me. I want so badly not to have been the kind of woman who tried to forge an identity—or, help me, God, a . . . brand—out of pregnancy and motherhood, an identity that other women would notice and approve of and admire. I want this so badly that I'm tempted to rewrite this story altogether, to draw myself as a caution-to-the-wind alterna-mom—the kind of pregnant woman who seems hardly to notice she's pregnant—gaining only seven pounds during her final trimester, drinking the occasional glass of wine, raving about pregnancy sex, traveling to Goa during her thirty-fourth week, going into labor at a crowded music venue. How I wish I could say that had been me.

The truth, though, is that right from the beginning I was as self-conscious and insecure and competitive about motherhood as I'd been about anything else in my life. As Adrienne Rich wrote in her memoir of motherhood, *Of Woman Born*, "I had been trying to give birth to myself; and in some grim dim way I was determined to use even pregnancy and parturition in that process." And so the unappealing truth is that I came home from my appointment with the nurse practitioner that day, made myself a pot of decaffeinated Earl Grey tea and a plate of saltines, sat down at the dining table, and read every pamphlet, every brochure, every piece of printed information she'd given me, not just the warnings and prohibitions but the footnotes too, the small print elaborating the horrible fates that might befall me and my child if I failed.

Then I went on the internet and read more. I wanted to read every horror story, every guideline, every morsel of advice. I wanted to know everything that could go wrong if proper precautions weren't taken: miscarriage, preterm labor, stillbirth, rare chromosomal syndromes, and emergencies that might leave me hemorrhaging on the kitchen floor. I read and read and read. "Terrifying," I said to myself, determined to go over the material with Pete the moment he walked in the door, and also to tell Tracy all of it, to get her up to speed as well as every other pregnant woman I encountered. I ate it up—the competitiveness, the performance, the fear. What kind of pregnancy did I want to have? The best one possible. The one that would demonstrate to the world that I'd done the homework and applied myself, given the task at hand my full and undivided attention. And what kind of parent did I want to be when the pregnancy was over? Well, the kind that viewed parenthood not simply as an event in which I was just one of many participants but as a process I carefully orchestrated—the general commanding her troops, the scientist studying the data, the director with her eye pressed to the viewfinder. The kind for whom parenthood was not a state of being, but an extended and intensive exertion of mind, body, and soul. I wanted to be an amazing mother, amazing in her own right but, also, better than everybody else.

If someone had suggested to me at the time of my first pregnancy that there might be certain drawbacks to viewing motherhood in this way—as a contest, an Olympics of sorts, an arena to prove my goodness and my worth, that perhaps viewing the parent-child dynamic as an endeavor rather than simply as a relationship might not be a recipe for well-being or even baseline sanity—I would have surely dismissed that person out of hand. In truth, I'm not even sure I would have understood what that person was talking about—the implication that there might be any other way. Even before I became a parent, my notions of what it meant *to be a parent*, that this was a fundamentally anxious endeavor that required planning and control at every level, were so deeply ingrained, so omnipresent and unexamined in those around me, I couldn't have begun to question the soundness of my own enthusiasm and competitiveness as I entered the fray. I wasn't really aware of entering anything at all—but simply thought I was moving forward to a new stage of life I'd occupy in my own way and make my own.

Other parents often describe being swept up by the intensity and relentless pace of parenthood. There's a mania about it, and a constant economizing of time and resources that, once you're in it, makes it easy to lose sight of the forest for the trees. Still, my own innocence, looking back, seems particularly extreme. I set out into the landscape of competitive, intensive, hypercontrolling parenthood with so little self-awareness, diving headfirst into the world Jennifer Senior describes so evocatively in her book, *All Joy and No Fun: The Paradox of Modern Parenthood*. Senior captures the sleepless, manic, tightly regimented lifestyle of families whose days are crowded with drop-offs and pickups, classes and playdates, birthday parties and lessons and countless other child-centered activities. She describes how together, these activities make up what sociologist Annette Lareau named "concerted cultivation."

Senior offers several theories about how this became the accepted standard for middle-class parents. She refers, for example, to a century of shifting attitudes about the role of children, one of which the sociologist Viviana Zelizer calls the "sacralization of child life," a shift in which children became "economically worthless and emotionally priceless." Senior speculates about social changes brought on by women's full-fledged entrance into the workforce over the past five decades, and how this movement has stoked fears about the quantity and quality of time parents (but especially mothers) devote to their children. As Hilary Levey Friedman explains in *Playing to Win*, a heightening sense of class anxiety permeates much of twenty-first-century American life, and a symptom of that is the fact that parents now view their children's educational achievement, prestige, and future success as "the only protection, dicey as it may be, against future family downward mobility."

Senior also details the unprecedented expansion of choice that has changed the way parents approach matters of family life large and small. "Not long ago," she suggests, "mothers and fathers did not have the luxury of deciding how large their families were or when each child arrived. Nor did they regard their children with the same reverence. . . . They had children because it was economically necessary, or because it was customary, or because it was a moral obligation to family and community." By contrast, for many parents today from the middle class and above, caring for children is not an obligation or a necessity, but a long-anticipated life decision; we take on parenthood after a level of deliberation and preparation that would have been foreign to our grandparents or even our parents. And because we have our children later, because we have fewer of them, because many of us really, really want children if and when we have them, our identification with both the parent-child relationship and the work that parenting entails takes on enormous significance.

When child-rearing is something most people do for one reason or another (economic necessity, religious obligation, creating future warriors for battling rival tribes, and so on), when birthrates are high, parenthood common, children abundant and well integrated into various aspects of communal life, a baseline level of cooperation and benefit-of-the-doubt-giving pervades. But when *being a parent* is elevated to the most important thing you will ever do, a thing *you* in particular have chosen, a special duty and responsibility that only some accept, the stakes rise. If parenthood is no longer just a relationship or a part of "ordinary life" but instead a new kind of secular religion, then true tolerance of each other's parenting differences becomes a lot more complicated and a lot less common. As Paula S. Fass writes in *The End of American Childhood*, "Once having children is defined as an individual choice, American parents often imagine that when they do not succeed or are less than completely successful . . . it is somehow their fault. Having made the choice, they are somehow obligated to do it right." But obligated to whom?

As my first pregnancy progressed, I continued to study for parenthood as though giving birth was a final exam. My belly swelled. I settled into my new job, the job of preparing to be a mother—the first job besides writing that I'd ever really cared about. I complained incessantly about every minor pain and inconvenience of pregnancy, because when you are pregnant you get to complain; you have complaining carte blanche. I let myself gain thirty pounds. At my favorite Mexican restaurant, I couldn't drink beer, so instead, I ate buckets of guacamole. I ate it with a spoon. My hair turned shiny and my fingernails grew. All the complaining was pure performance; pregnancy agreed with me.

Early in my first trimester, I'd withdrawn from the second graduate program I'd just begun—the course work was intensive and inflexible, and I didn't see how I could manage it with a newborn—and found a job as an assistant at a law firm in the West Loop that mainly conducted class action lawsuits involving overexposure to asbestos. The plan was simple. I'd work until a few weeks before my due date, and then I'd quit, have the baby, stay at home to take care of it, writing when I could. I aimed to write a novel while the baby napped, because babies, I'd been told, napped constantly. Babies loved to nap.

In this manner, without ever formally deciding, I became a stay-at-home mother, a demographic that rose from 23 percent in 1999 to 29 percent in 2012. As is the case with so many aspects of parenthood, a woman's staying home is often talked about as a deliberate choice, an issue that's black and white, either/or. The choice is assumed to tell the world something about who we are and what we value: A partnered, working mother might love her children, but not quite enough to prioritize them above her career. A stay-at-home mother might be intelligent and educated and capable, but not quite enough to go out and hack it in the world beyond the nursery. The reality for me was that my balance of work and parenthood was always more improvised than decided, always more a response to circumstance and lack of alternatives than dogma. If I'd been a citizen of one of the forty-one industrialized nations that offer parents paid maternity leave—to say nothing of subsidized childcare, quality early childhood education, or a host of other family supports—I might have made a different choice. But I lived in America, and so the calculation was simple.

At the time I became pregnant, I had a BA in English, an MFA in fiction writing, and three years' worth of assorted freelance work, fellowship-facilitated writing projects, and various stints as an adjunct professor. My income from these pursuits added up to $15,000–$20,000 per year, enough to live on when combined with my husband's income, but hardly enough to justify, in my mind, placing my soon-to-be baby in the care of strangers, a prospect that, in Chicago, would devour most, if not all, of the money I brought in. And yet, as simple as it seemed, the prospect of not working at all for three, four, or five years still worried me. I feared total financial dependence. I liked working, being surrounded by people with different ideas and talents, feeling a part of the goings-on of the world. I liked babies and kids as well. But I *really* liked adults. I liked thinking, solving problems, talking to people, accomplishing things, working toward tangible results. I began to worry that maybe spending my days in an apartment with a baby wasn't the best plan after all. When I mentioned my concern to Tracy, she said that she understood my fears, and that though she thought it was awesome that I was going to have so much time with the baby (she was going to have only six weeks of leave before returning to work full-time), she also thought that if she had to do what I was doing she'd probably go insane.

A few days after talking to Tracy, I went to look at day cares that offered part-time enrollment. The first one fronted a busy, commercial street. Large rolls of brown paper had been secured with masking tape to the windows to shield the children from the view of those passing by. I walked inside and introduced myself to a woman sitting in a hard, plastic chair with two babies on her lap. The two babies were smiling and drooling, while all the others in the nursery screamed. They were screaming from their cots and crying from their cribs and whimpering from the play mats and mountains of plastic toys around the floor. The room itself seemed to howl, to vibrate with their collective baby misery. The lighting was fluorescent. The walls, cinder block. The construction paper drawings taped to the furniture to help brighten the space only made it seem drabber. The air was stale. Nearly every nose in the room was running. "Come in," said the woman. "You're here to look around?" I nodded, attempted to return her smile. Then I told her that I'd forgotten to pay the parking meter, hurried back to my car, and never returned.

The second day care I visited was clean, quiet, sunny, and peaceful. The staff seemed professional and engaged, the children well cared for and content. There was soft light. Music playing. Aesthetically pleasing wooden toys. Sanitary wipes everywhere and one caregiver for every three children. *This isn't so bad*, I thought. After my tour, I asked the director how I might go about applying to enroll my baby in a day or two of care. She explained that I'd need to fill out an application and then pay a deposit to secure my spot on their wait list.

"How long is the wait list?" I asked.

"Three to four years," she said.

"You mean three to four months?" I asked.

"No," she said. "Three to four years."

All the way home, I told myself how wonderful and selfless it was that I had decided to stay home full-time with my baby, that I didn't have to dump him in some soulless center or hire a stranger to raise him. Whenever friends or family members or people I met would ask me how I'd come to this decision, I didn't say, "I'd never get a job that would pay me enough to afford decent childcare." And I didn't say, "I'm afraid that any job I'd find wouldn't offer me the flexibility to give a baby the attention and care it needs to thrive." And I didn't say, "I have no family nearby who are willing to help with regular childcare." And I didn't say, "I live in a society whose policies reflect the fact that it is still deeply ambivalent about mothers working." Instead, I'd say, "I just know that it's the best thing for us."

In a piece in *Elle* called "Having a Child Will Bankrupt You,"

Bryce Covert writes about the many and varied challenges parents face in finding affordable, quality childcare in this country. She cites a 2016 poll from Harvard's School of Public Health that shows that the most common challenge parents said they face when trying to get childcare is the cost. She also cites another report, which finds that in some states the average price of day care for an infant reaches as much as $17,000 a year in 2015; it's nearly $13,000 for a four-year-old. Putting two kids in a center costs families more than what they typically spend on food and, in much of the country, on housing. "In 28 states and Washington, D.C., sending an infant to daycare costs more [per year] than sending an 18-year-old to public college. The price tag has been climbing at an extraordinary rate: The cost for families with a working mother rose 70 percent between 1985 and 2012."

Covert goes on to highlight a recent paper showing that the increase in the price of day care between 1990 and 2010 resulted in a 5 percent decline in the overall employment of women. According to Covert, "Even families who can afford childcare might not be able to get it . . . Many centers are simply full; in other places, they don't exist. In a study of eight states, the Center for American Progress found that more than 40 percent of children live in what it calls 'child care deserts,' or zip codes where there are either no day care centers or more than three times as many children under the age of five as there are available spots."

It's undeniable that I enjoyed a level of privilege when it came to work-life balance that is out of reach for many women. I did not live in a childcare desert, even if wait lists were long and affordable options few. I had a supportive partner who was able to provide us with enough income to live on and a source of health insurance. I enjoyed the luxury of having any choice at all about whether and how much to work outside the house. And yet, the choice I faced was not really a choice in the way I'd always assumed mothers chose to work or stay home. It was more of a settling, a resigned acceptance of the idea that for a mother, the ability to work is a privilege and not a right. That's a hard thing to accept. Easier to tell yourself you must be doing what you've wanted all along, that you're making a noble sacrifice for your family.

Years later, a friend with a successful career in law told me how all through her first pregnancy and maternity leave, her best friend ended every conversation by saying, "Oh, how can you leave the baby so soon? I can't believe you're going to leave him." I don't think I ever said that to my working-mother friends. I hope I didn't. But the fact remains, I certainly thought something similar, silently putting other mothers down to lift myself up, disparaging their "choices" to feel better about my own. And many of them would later tell me that at one point or another, they had done the same.

Rather than questioning the system and the culture and the lack of support that makes it so hard for all of us, we turn against one another, take pride in our differences, flaunting and justifying whatever path we've chosen, as though any new mother would "choose" to leave her child forty hours per week, fifty weeks per year, if there were more flexible options—as though any new mother would "choose" to give up her work entirely, her financial independence, her career, her education, a chance at a stimulating and productive life among other adults if there were better possibilities or compromises. In trying to promote a spirit of acceptance, it has become common to say things like, "Every mom makes the best choice for *her* family." Maybe. Another way to look at it is that we each get to choose from a handful of lousy options, then we try to make the choice go down easier by telling ourselves that what we chose makes us unique and special, better than those who chose a different way.

For my first years as a parent, whether the issue was childbirth or childcare, parenting style or safety protocols, I remained fixated on making the right choice for my children. It was only much later that I began to see how profoundly the choosing itself—the false sense of control and entitlement that choosing entails—had affected my experience as a mother. It created an extra layer of anxiety to a parenting culture that even under the best of circumstances can erode a woman's self-confidence, her very sense of self. Jennifer Senior describes the impact this parenting culture has on our sense of autonomy, our marriages, and our free time. Julie Lythcott-Haims describes the toll it takes on our children as they grow into young adults. And in *Excellent Sheep*, a powerful critique of elite institutions of higher education, the social critic William Deresiewicz describes the toll it takes on higher education itself, as students are increasingly unable to take risks and think independently. But far less attention, it seems to me, has been given to how these changes in parenting culture, the convergence of parenthood with a capitalist ethos, have produced a kind of conspicuous child-rearing—a style of child-rearing in which every parenting choice is not only a choice but a statement—and how that conspicuous child-rearing impacts adults' relationships with one another.

I recently spoke with a woman named Marissa whose experience in a moms' group illustrated for me how poisonous our culture of parenting can be when it comes to such relationships. When Marissa's daughter, now two, was an infant, Marissa found herself feeling lonely and isolated. She was told, as I had been told by friends and family, that the best way to feel better was to find a good moms' group. She did, and at first, it worked. There were about fifteen other mothers in the group, and she liked many of them, found them smart and engaging. She told me how her first impression was that "this mom-friend thing is a thing. I get it. You have to have mom friends." And yet, she wasn't in the group very long before she started to notice something else, a strain of competitiveness that seemed to emerge whenever the women were together.

"I had wanted to have a home birth," she told me. "It was something I really wanted. And of course, there were plenty of people who thought I was crazy for that, but I decided to go for it anyway." Marissa labored at home with a midwife for thirty-six hours, but the delivery didn't progress as she'd hoped. The midwife spotted meconium, and there were signs that the baby might be in distress, so after nearly two days, they checked into a nearby hospital where Marissa eventually delivered by emergency C-section. The baby was healthy. Marissa recovered well from the surgery. But when she told her new mom friends, many of them strong proponents of natural childbirth, she noticed something unpleasant: "I didn't expect it," she told me. "Because, I mean, how can you compete at childbirth? But I noticed there were some people who just couldn't help themselves . . . there were women who, it was like they didn't know what to say when I told them I'd had a C-section, and so they'd say something like 'Oh, did you try laboring in a tub? Did you try perineal massage? Did you try hypnosis, or this or that?' And I was like, 'Oh, thanks for your advice. Obviously, I should have had a tub.' "

I asked her why she thought these other mothers were so quick to question her in this way, and she told me she'd asked herself the same question. "I don't think it's intentional meanness," she said. "I think many people don't know how to respond to someone else's disappointment, to someone else's emotions. Like they don't know how to just be empathic. To say, 'Oh, wow, that sucks that it didn't go the way you'd hoped. I'm so sorry. But you obviously did the best you could, and I'm glad you came through it. I hope you have a better experience next time.' They can't say that, because if your C-section happened because you did something wrong, then that means they can make sure it won't happen to them. Or it means that their successful, natural birth happened because they did everything right. They can take credit for it.

"I felt like I just couldn't win. I'm sure because where I live in

San Francisco, there's a lot of sancti-mommy stuff around natural everything. Some people judged me for wanting a home birth, but then there definitely was all this judgment about me having a C-section. They wouldn't say it, but you could tell they were thinking it. Most people would look at me with pity. Like I had been too stupid or hadn't been able to stand up for myself or had been a victim of excessive interventions. People close to me tried to focus on the positives. But people I met in these mom groups, there was judgment on both sides."

I asked Marissa if she experienced this same tension with issues other than childbirth, and without taking a breath, she began listing them: sleep, feeding, screen time, every developmental milestone. "Our daughter," she tells me, "was kind of a magical sleeper. At twelve weeks, she started sleeping a solid six-hour stretch. It was a blessing. I knew it was a huge blessing. But I would never talk about it, because I didn't want anyone to feel competitive with me. And once we started getting past four months, we were in that phase where there's all of these developmental milestones and these arbitrary windows. As a first-time parent, you want to know what's normal. But I have friends whose kids didn't walk until eighteen months and ones whose kids walked at one year. And you can tell everyone's watching and sizing each other up. I just think it's weird that that's how we relate to each other. I mean, it makes it so hard to have an authentic conversation with someone, because you're worried about saying something that sets them off and makes them feel bad. You don't know what's going on in their family. And so everything is tense and fraught. If there's a preexisting friendship and it's someone you trust, that's one thing. But otherwise, the competitiveness can make it hard to connect."

My friend Tiff describes a similar experience surrounding after-school activities. "The kids are so scheduled," she says. "They're in school longer than we were. And the parents talk to other parents in a passive, though very competitive way. It starts at pickup at the school when a mom will say, 'Oh, hey, it's great to see you. . . . So, what activities is Ella doing after school?' And it feels like a loaded question. Like the parent wants to see if they're measuring up to you in terms of what kinds of extracurricular activities they're exposed to. My kids are in fewer activities than many of their peers. My kids like to go home and watch TV. That's not a choice that's widely celebrated or even talked about in my parenting circles. And if I say something like that, I feel embarrassed. But a part of me also feels happy that they can relax after school."

Tiff's allowing her kids the luxury of watching television brought to mind a dinner Pete, the kids, and I went to with a few other couples and their kids. We were at a restaurant where the service was friendly but slow, and after five minutes, all of our kids were growing restless. My husband and I reached for our iPhones, because years earlier we'd decided (or at least accepted) that we'd let our children play on screens while they waited for food in restaurants. Another couple, for reasons of civility or table manners or brain development, had a no-screens-at-the-table policy in effect, so instead they reached for the piles of toys they'd carried with them, in big tote bags brimming with markers and Play-Doh and Disney figurines. They poured these nondigital diversions onto the table, turning the place settings into an elevated rec room. Another couple at the table disapproved of both of these choices. They wanted their children to sit nicely and participate in the conversation. Mostly this meant their kids flopped around and played with the saltshakers and kicked each other's knees. The one childless couple at the table grimaced at all of us. I could see them silently interrogating each other, trying to understand how it was possible that all six of their friends were such ineffectual parents. Everyone was tense and unhappy. Everyone felt watched and judged. Everyone was wondering who was doing it the right way. But worst of all, worse than the atmosphere of guardedness and anxiety, was the fact that no one was acknowledging any of it.

This, it turns out, is the most important rule of parenting as a competitive sport: Nobody ever, no matter what, admits to competing. We smile and nod and hold our judgments until we get home from the restaurant. We say things like, "There's no single right way." We say these things as we sip our drinks, and only when we get home do we say to our partner or the nearest person who will listen, "What the fuck are they doing with those kids?" Nothing is acknowledged. Nothing is discussed. And on and on the parenting game goes; it's hard to win while pretending not to play.

That morning in Chicago, the day after we returned from Virginia, when my father told me to give my mother a couple of days to settle down, I understood his rationale. My mom was upset not because she had been caught doing anything wrong, but because *I* had been. Do we ever really know where we stand if not in relation to those around us?

Once, when I was in my early twenties, I was riding a bus in San Francisco. Across the aisle from me sat a woman with twin toddlers. I don't remember the woman's face or anything about her, because my eyes were on the children. They were playing, and then they were fighting. They were being difficult—bickering, hitting, whining. I was watching them, wondering why the mother didn't do something, and then suddenly, as the bus slowed and then stopped, she rose, pushed the children aside, and yelled, "*Get the fuck away from me!*" Then she pushed past them, got off the bus as though she were abandoning them. They both cried and howled and lurched after her. "Mama, Mama!" they screamed, tripping down the stairs of the bus as she pretended not to hear them. *That is a horrible mother*, I thought. *I will never be that kind of mother.*

Or another memory: Growing up, I was friends with a girl who lived in a house at the top of a grassy hill beside a lake. She was my best friend, and I loved her. We played for hours, singing, dancing, chasing the geese into the water. Her mother was always kind and gentle and loving. When I was there, she called us "my girls" and treated me as if I were her own. Whenever we wanted to watch a movie, she would make us an enormous bowl of popcorn and sit on the floor with us while we watched *The Goonies* or *Back to the Future.* She didn't just turn it on but watched it with us, laughed when we laughed. Sometimes we'd lean against her and she'd put her arms around us, bowl of popcorn on her lap, and she would pick up the popcorn with the tip of her tongue, piece by piece, which delighted me. When I grew older, after they moved away, I'd remember her and think, *She was a very good mother, the best kind of mother, the opposite of the woman on the bus in San Francisco.* My mother, with her temper and impulsivity and anxious love, was somewhere in between, impossible for me to idealize or dismiss. These were all faint memories by the time I had kids, but it didn't matter, because after I became pregnant, almost no day went by without my evaluating someone's mothering in present time, forming these categories, erecting these columns.

In some ways, I suppose, this is inevitable. We are social animals. We thrive together and falter alone, vying for status, guarded against others' attempts to knock us down. We learn things by watching others do them and seem programmed to share what we know. It's hard to imagine any moment in history when women didn't look to one another for models or guidance. When one reads of the way the Puritans parented, or the Victorians, or the ancient Babylonians, or the early cave dwellers, one reads about *their* customs and practices and values regarding children. *Their* as in *they.* A plural unit.

And yet that day when the nurse at the clinic asked me what kind of pregnancy I wanted, she was inducting me into our current culture of parenthood as an expression of individualism. The way we parent today is molded by our particular class affiliation, political orientation, aesthetic preferences, and personal convictions and beliefs. Attachment parenting, helicopter parenting, free-range parenting, permissive parenting: There are as many brands of parenting as there are of breakfast cereal, and every decision we make about raising our children enhances or detracts from our chosen brand. In a country and culture where so much of our life is commodified and monetized, this shouldn't be surprising—and yet surprising or no, it creates a particular and peculiar tension, a space between us and our fellow parents that can be difficult to bridge.

About a month after I returned to Chicago, on a windy afternoon in April, I finally broke down and decided to confide to a non–family member about what had happened. Well, *decided* isn't exactly the right word—*confessed* seems closer to the truth. I opened my mouth and found myself describing what had happened—or what was happening. I hadn't heard back from my attorney and didn't know how the case would proceed. The person I decided to tell was Tracy.

She was still one of my closest friends in the city, though in the years that had passed since our pregnant days of frequent lunches and drooling over stroller porn, our friendship had changed, atrophied in the way so many of my friendships did during those first few years of parenthood. Spontaneous lunches or evenings out had become impossible. Get-togethers were now scheduled weeks or even months in advance. And whenever we finally did manage to hang out, there was now only one topic of conversation, our children, which in some ways was fine; I appreciated the chance to talk about parenthood, to have someone who was in the same place. And yet as we talked about whose kids were doing what, who was struggling more with sleeping or nursing or preschool admissions, there was also a part of me that thought, *Wait . . . Is this all that we are now? Didn't there used to be something else?*

Our lunch that day went well at first. A warm morning. The thawing snowbanks glistened. The sun shone lavishly across the sidewalks, the pools of melted slush, reflecting off the lake, scattered bits and shards of light across the Loop's glass towers. We decided it was just warm enough to eat outside, so we snagged a table at a French bistro off Michigan Avenue. There was sliced baguette, salades Niçoises, and coffee, the usual declarations of how it had been too long, the usual inquiries into how the kids were doing, the husbands and parents and work. And then, at some point in the conversation, I grew quiet, began to speak, stopped myself. I confided that I'd been dealing with something difficult, the aftermath of something really scary.

I told her what had happened the day I left my son in the car. I told her I still didn't know what would come of it, if I'd face criminal charges, if there would be an investigation from Child Protective Services. I was shocked by it all, lost and afraid, and I still couldn't get my head around the fact that it was really happening, that what I'd done was wrong, that we lived in a culture where letting a kid wait in a car for five minutes was a criminal offense.

As I finished talking, the busboy came to refill our glasses. I took a sip of water, fiddled with my napkin, waiting to see how she'd react. What was I expecting? I suppose I was expecting her to be as stunned by it as I had been, to say, "Are you kidding me?" Or maybe that wasn't what I was expecting. Maybe there was doubt beneath the expectation, a flaw beneath the surface of our friendship that I wanted to test with the weight of this confession to see if it would crack.

"So now I'm just waiting," I repeated. "I'm sort of a mess."

She said nothing. She was looking down at the food on her plate, moving it around here and there without eating. Then she was nodding, nodding vigorously as though to wrap up the conversation. If people still wore watches, she would have looked at hers. She would have said, "Look at the time."

"Tracy," I said.

She was trying to smile and not quite making it. She took a sip of her coffee, then put down the cup. Then she took another sip. A gust of wind blew in off the lake and we clung to our napkins. She was sinking into her sweater, squinting a little, the sun and shadow moving across her forehead. I closed my eyes for a moment against the brightness and then opened them.

"I don't know," she said at last. "I don't know what to say. The whole thing. It's intense."

"Intense? Do you mean ridiculous? Absurd?"

She didn't answer. She looked off in the distance.

"I don't know," she said. "I mean, I wouldn't do it. I just wouldn't. The world is crazy. You never know who's around. But I obviously don't think you're a bad mom . . ." She seemed to be searching for the words. "I think you made a bad choice."

I started to defend myself, to spew off some of what I'd learned over the past weeks of late-night Google searches. I'd read about the statistical near impossibility of child abductions, the fallacy of stranger danger. I started to explain, then I stopped. I realized that nothing I said would change her opinion on the matter. We'd entered the realm of religious devotion and vaccination debates, a realm where facts were useless. I went to pick up my glass and found I was shaking.

"Well," I said. "I guess we see things differently."

"I mean," she went on, "I *know* you're a good mom. We all make mistakes."

"Thanks. That's nice of you to say. Now I know who to turn to if the judge wants a character reference."

"I'm sorry this is happening. It'll be okay," she managed. "It will probably be okay, right?" She was wincing as she spoke, holding back.

There was something off about the pitch of her voice. It was too high, too effortful.

I felt nauseated and gestured for the bill. I remember the effort it took to pretend to eat my salad while we waited. One olive. One green bean. "Well, then," I said. That was the best defense I could muster. "Well." It was like someone had tugged a loose string on a sweater and our years of friendship were unraveling in my hands. I wanted to cry. I wanted to run away. And at the exact same time, I wanted to tell her to go fuck herself. I wanted to say something hurtful like, "I might leave my kid in a car for a few minutes, but at least I don't leave him to stare at a wall at some shitty day care five days a week." I'd never felt more hurt, more defensive.

I'd like to say this story has a happy ending, that that night one of us called the other and both of us apologized, her for not being more empathic, me for being so defensive. I wish I could say that we put the whole thing behind us and brought the bad feelings out into the open and became better friends in the end. I'd like to, but that's not what happened. We didn't talk for a long time, and when we finally did, something had changed between us. It was never quite the same. The element of competitiveness and insecurity that had been submerged was now unearthed, impossible to ignore. And as tempting as it might be to blame it all on that one lunch, looking back, I can understand how satisfying it must have been for her in that moment, how irresistible after years of listening to my unsolicited parenting advice, all those tips and friendly suggestions and mentions of helpful resources from the mom who knew everything, the mom who told you when you'd improperly installed your car seat or were using non-BPA-free bottles, finally to be the one who knew better, who hadn't been caught in the wrong. I see that lunch now as the final scene in a subtle drama of insecurity and competition I'd been enacting for four years, a drama that made genuine friendship impossible.

Of course, I didn't know any of that then.

I knew nothing other than my feelings—anger, hurt, fear. I cut my boiled potato with my fork. I blinked back tears and tried to swallow and kept checking the time on my phone. Finally, I looked around more urgently for the waiter, reached for my wallet. "I really have to get going," I said.

Even now, years later, I can remember the details of that lunch because it signaled the beginning of a shift for me. Until that day, beginning with the moment that nurse gave me all those brochures about pregnancy, I'd been an uncritical consumer of anxiety. I'd been dangerously incurious about the cultural forces informing my thoughts and deeds. Or perhaps I simply didn't have time to be curious or to formulate good questions. My days and nights were taken up with protecting my little ones from the realities of modern life: its cars; its germs; its hordes of nameless strangers; its overcrowded, impersonal public schools; its processed, sugary foods; its sharp or electrical objects and addictive, digital screens. This parade of worries didn't abate after that day in Virginia, even as I began to see it for what it was, a socially contagious stream of general anxiety that attached itself to one threat, then another, then a different one after that, morphing and evolving but ultimately inextinguishable. If anything, after returning from Virginia, my anxiety intensified. Suddenly I had more to worry about: the stranger in the crowd, the anonymous Good Samaritan deputized by the camera on her phone, ready and waiting to record every misstep. How would my mothering look to a tired caseworker from Child Protective Services? Was the oven clean? Were the beds made? Was I nurturing enough, attentive enough, cautious enough? And when had I last trimmed Felix's fingernails, which grew so fast, or changed the batteries on Violet's electric toothbrush? Were their bodies healthy enough, their minds well nourished, their bedrooms tidy and inviting? Was I cautious enough, protective enough, doing everything in my power to keep them safe? How good a mother was I really? And did others see me as I saw myself?

The hoary, cobwebbed old wisdom is that parenthood is supposed to make you a better person. In some ways, this is true. Parenthood offers the opportunity to engage in a deeply intimate relationship with a human who is dependent on you for all of his physical, emotional, and psychological needs. It demands patience, sacrifice, compassion, and humility. It stretches us in ways not many experiences can. But at the same time, I began to realize, there was something about it that made people worse or, at least, worse to each other—worse neighbors, worse citizens, worse friends. That something, I'd come to see, was not parenthood itself but the anxiety that so often surrounds it. Parenthood and fear: Somehow, somewhere along the line, the two had become synonymous. I began to feel it that day, leaving the restaurant. But I didn't yet understand it. And so over the next two years, as I navigated my way through the consequences of what had happened in Virginia, I read and researched and began to challenge notions about parenthood I'd never before questioned. Where did parental fear come from, and what were the forces that sustained it? How had a biological imperative become a labyrinth of societal anxieties? How had we managed to take this thing—raising a child—that's already next to impossible, and make it even fucking harder?

3

THE FABRICATION OF FEAR

"I suppose," I said to my friend Claire, "that I'll get a lot of writing done if I go to jail. Maybe I'll even finish my novel. Will you smuggle me in paper so I don't have to write on my bedsheets?"

"Of course I will," she said. "But also, stop."

Four months had passed since the incident in Virginia. We were sitting on her porch, watching our kids chase each other with bubble makers through the yard. Violet hadn't figured out how to blow bubbles yet, but she seemed to be enjoying squirting the soapy liquid at the plants, the dog, her friends. It was a lovely summer evening in the suburbs. Fireflies blinking, the smell of cut grass, a cool breeze coming in off the lake. For the first time, I felt calm enough to joke about the situation, even if my family couldn't appreciate the humor.

"This whole thing is insane," Claire said. "I still can't believe it."

Coming from a mere acquaintance, this would have been reassuring, but from Claire, it was more than that; it felt like a pardon.

Claire had always seemed to me the sort of mother to whom I could never measure up. When she adopted her first daughter, ten years earlier, she decided to leave behind a career in advertising because she wanted to pursue work that was more compatible with family life and wouldn't require long hours and travel. She stayed home with her daughter, had two more kids, started a blog about her experiences as a mother. The blog led her to other forms of advocacy, writing, and consulting. She launched a second career related to this work, and amid all this she kept a clean house and tight schedule. She was the sort of mother who folded the fitted bedsheets, drove multiple carpools, and volunteered for everything. Her children's birthday cakes were home-baked and sometimes gluten-free. She wrote personal thank-you notes promptly, kept photo logs of all of her children's accomplishments, and scoured her kitchen until it smelled like lemons. If anyone were in a position to judge me for what had happened, it seemed to me it would have been her. Instead, she was indignant on my behalf.

"Who in the world hasn't left their kid in the car for a minute while they run a quick errand? I've done it! How could anyone not do it occasionally? Every time my one daughter falls asleep in the car on my way to dropping off my other daughter, I pull up and leave her there while I run her in. What, I'm supposed to wake her up, drag her screaming across an icy sidewalk? I just can't believe what you did was against the law." Claire grew quiet for a moment, and I thought maybe she was reconsidering, letting her mind run through all the unlikely disasters that might happen in those few minutes of school drop-off. But when she spoke again, it was to say, "You know who you need to talk to about this? There's this woman . . . this parenting author I interviewed once for my blog."

I was skeptical, to say the least. A parenting expert was the last person I wanted to talk to; how could a self-proclaimed expert make me feel anything but more shitty about my lack of expertise? But Claire assured me this woman was different, not the usual sanctimony and smugness that came off the pages of those books. Indeed, the more I got to know this expert in the years that followed, the more I began to see she wasn't really that interested in parenthood at all, but in society, superstition, and fear. Her name is Lenore Skenazy, and she founded a blog, a book, and a movement called *Free-Range Kids*.

I reached out to Lenore in a Facebook message a few days later. I described my situation and asked if she might have time to chat. I hardly expected her to reply, so it came as a surprise when she responded right away.

"Would be happy to talk. When's good? After dinner and before kids' bedtime?"

Skenazy founded *Free-Range Kids* in 2008 after writing a column for the *New York Sun* about her decision to allow her nine-year-old son to take the subway by himself. The column resulted in a flood of both support and outrage. Supporters pointed out that parents had been giving their kids this kind of opportunity for independence for generations, that this notion of child imperilment in public spaces was in many ways a new and arbitrary construct. Critics dubbed her the worst mom in America, a criminal child neglecter, a woman who didn't deserve to be a mother. To these charges, Skenazy fought back, arguing that allowing children freedom and a reasonable amount of independence was not incompatible with (and was even indicative of) good parenting. On her website, she devotes the movement to "fighting the belief that our kids are in constant danger." I wasn't sure what to expect of her, much less how she might help me. I had little interest in talking to a fringe expert who would tell me to forgo seat belts and bike helmets to help my kids toughen up. But I was also desperate for advice and emotional support from anyone who had been through anything similar.

I called her one evening while hauling the garbage down to the end of our alley. Pete was giving the kids their evening baths. I had about twenty minutes to talk, and was relieved when she answered on the second ring and called me by my first name.

"Kim?" she said, as though we were picking up a thread we'd left dangling in some earlier conversation. "What's going on now, Kim? How are you? Sounds like you've had a rough few months."

I balanced the phone against my shoulder and swung the trash bag into the bin. "It's true," I said, walking back down the alley. We lived in an end unit on the street-facing side of a double row of town houses. Each unit in each row had a small garage that opened onto the alley. On summer evenings, the dozen or so kids of the complex would play in the alley while their parents stood in the open garages, talking, and drinking beer, and watching. A few of the parents were out now, including the blondest of the two blond moms who were always smiling.

A different, more glass-is-half-full kind of person, would have looked at this arrangement—kids playing in alley, parents socializing and looking on—as a picturesque vision of American middle-class life. Family! Neighbors! How wonderful and warming it would have seemed to this other, more positive person. But for me, in the three years we'd been living there, I'd come to dread these moments of communal parenting, these forced encounters where I could stand beside these totally nice and perfectly normal and pretty much pleasant humans with whom I shared living space, while their kids did their thing and my kids did some other thing and we all looked on, watching and waiting to make sure no one hit anyone else or hogged the toys or said anything unkind. A different sort of person would have enjoyed standing and chatting about who was going to which camp this summer and who to which school in the fall; about who had learned to ride a bike and who was taking swim lessons and who had given up a nap and a hundred other small matters about which I could not have cared less.

I say that *I* had come to dread these evenings and not *we* had come to dread these evenings because my kids seemed to rather like these evenings and because Pete categorically refused to participate in these evenings. *Hell no*, was how he put it when I asked if he'd come down and stand there. *Why would I stand down there with those people? I have nothing to say to them.*

"Maybe because your kids want to play outside like the other normal children and someone has to watch them and I'm tired of doing it by myself, and also, they're our neighbors. They don't have to be our best friends, but they're our neighbors."

"Neighbors are overrated," he said. "Anyway, aren't there like ten adults down there? Why does there have to be a one-to-one ratio? Something's going to happen that requires the intervention of ten adults? Are we expecting an armed insurgency? A tsunami off Lake Michigan?"

I don't remember how I responded to Pete's objection on any of the many occasions we had this conversation, but I doubt it was with kindness. It was a familiar dynamic between the two of us, a dynamic that had probably always been present in our relationship but that parenthood had exacerbated and intensified a hundredfold: my caring about a thing, an issue, an obligation or need of our shared family life—my caring what other people thought about us as a family—and his caring less, then my caring about his lack of caring and then his frustration at my agitation about this discrepancy in our caring because really, why did we have to care so much about every small detail?

As I walked back toward my garage that evening while talking to Lenore, past the kids on their pogo sticks and trikes, it occurred to me for the first time that maybe Pete had been right. How much could be gained by giving up our evenings to stand beside these people with whom we shared nothing other than property taxes and shoddy plumbing? The blond women spoke to each other softly and sipped their plastic cups of white wine. I imagined one saying, "She always has seemed a little off," to an officer, a social worker, a social service caseworker, any state-sanctioned policer of bad parents. I hurried from the alley, fled their gaze, went around to the front porch, and sat on the stoop, where the only people who would see me were the ones passing by on their way home from the train, or the nice childless gay couple who lived across from us, the only neighbors whose company I truly enjoyed. "Lenore," I said into the phone. "Thank you so much for talking to me. I'm a little shaken up. I know I summarized the problem in my message, but should I tell you the longer version of what happened?"

"Ha," she said. "Don't bother. I bet *I* can tell *you* what happened." Apparently, she knew this sort of story by heart. "Just let me close the office door first, because my husband's heard this spiel a million times. I've talked to so many people in your shoes. He's supportive, of course, but you know, how many times can he listen to the same conversation? Okay, so, here's my guess. You were running errands with your kid when you decided to leave him in the car for a couple minutes while you ran into a store. The conditions were perfectly safe—mild weather, good neighborhood—but when you came out, you found yourself blocked in by a cop car, being yelled at by an angry onlooker, pitchforks out, strangers accusing you of child neglect or endangering your child. Is that about right?"

"Close enough. How did you know?"

"I know because I've heard it all before."

I could hardly believe what she was saying. I sat there on the stoop, and we talked about the many cases she had heard since she'd become known as a parenting-rights advocate; and what stuck with me most about this first conversation was not her sympathy for my particular case, but her certainty about the factors that had caused it to occur.

"Listen," she said at one point. "Let's put aside for the moment that by far, the most dangerous thing you did to your child that day was put him in a car and drive someplace with him. In 2015, on average, 487 kids were injured in traffic accidents every day—and about 3 died. Not every year, mind you. Every day! Now that's a real risk. So if you truly wanted to protect your kid, you'd never drive anywhere with him. Or you'd drive as little as possible—the less the better. But let's put that aside for the moment. So you take him, and you drive, and you get to the store where you need to run in for a minute, and you're faced with a decision. Now, people will say you committed a crime because you put your kid 'at risk.' But the truth is, there's some risk to either decision you make." She stopped at this point to emphasize, as she does in much of her analysis, how shockingly rare the abduction or injury of children in nonmoving vehicles really is. For example, she points out that statistically speaking, it would likely take 750,000 years for a child left alone in a public space to be snatched by a stranger. "So there is some risk to leaving your kid in a car," she argues. "It might not be statistically meaningful, but it's not nonexistent. The problem is, there's *some* risk to every choice you make. There is always *some* risk. So, say you take the kid inside with you. There's *some* risk you'll both be hit by a bad driver in the parking lot. How many times have you almost been mowed down by someone futzing on their phone as they leave Trader Joe's? There's *some* risk someone in the store will go on a shooting spree and shoot your kid. There's *some* risk he'll slip on the ice on the sidewalk outside the store and fracture his skull. There's *some* risk no matter what you do. This is just part of being alive, whether you're six or sixty. So here's the question I'm interested in: If every choice has a risk, why is one choice grounds to punish and shame you, and one is okay? Could it be because the one choice inconveniences you, makes your life as a mother a little harder, makes parenting a little harder, gives you as a busy, working mother a little less time or energy than you would have otherwise had, makes you wonder if you really are trying to do too much?"

"You think this is directed at women?"

She hesitated.

"What I can say is that most of the people who contact me about experiences like yours are women. Occasionally there is a man, but usually, it's women. Now, maybe that's coincidental. I can't prove it's not. But I do often ask myself: If men were the ones doing the majority of schlepping the kids around on errands, if men were the ones who were more often dragging the kids all over town to get groceries or dry cleaning or whatever, would I get fewer of these calls? I can't prove it, but it wouldn't surprise me."

Skenazy told me about other cases she knew of or had dealt with directly over the years, other parents who'd had to go to court, who'd been investigated by Child Protective Services, who'd been placed on a registry of child neglecters, all for allowing their kids to do things they'd done hundreds of times themselves as children.

She told me all this, and I found myself wanting to slow her down, to argue the other side. *There's always another side*, I think, and so I said to her something I was sure she'd heard before. "Of course," I said, "things are different now than they were when we grew up."

"They sure are," she said. "The world we live in today, for people like you and me, anyway, is a much safer place. Crime is down. Murders are down. But that's not the biggest difference. The biggest difference, the thing people are really referring to when they say, 'Well, times have changed,' is that there's been this huge cultural shift in how we view children, in how we view parenting, in how we view the ability of children to move through the world."

"You're talking about safety? About risk prevention?"

"No," she said flatly. "Safety and risk prevention are rational processes. I'm all for safety. I'm pro–seat belt, pro–bike helmet, pro–annual checkup. What reasonable person could be otherwise? No, I'm talking about something else—the fact that we now live in a society where most people believe a child cannot be out of an adult's sight for one second, where people think children need constant, total adult supervision, where we believe that predators are lurking on every corner, waiting to steal or sodomize or kill our children."

I remembered how about a month before my trip to Virginia, Felix and I were having lunch with Tracy and her son. While we waited for our table, the boys sat down and began playing Battleship. Our name was called. Our table was ready, but the boys asked if they could finish their game while my friend and I went to the table and ordered. She and I looked at each other. *Why not?* I thought. But before I could say so, the hostess interrupted. "I don't feel comfortable with that," she said. "Someone needs to be watching them."

"I was just about to say the same thing," my friend said.

"Me too," I added.

It had felt obvious. Of course they needed eyes on them at every moment. Of course they couldn't sit ten feet away from us playing Battleship. What if they choked on something? What if they both lost their minds and ran outside into traffic? What if a pedophile came into the restaurant and grabbed them both and dragged them kicking and screaming into a white van parked outside, all while we were browsing our menus, trying to decide between the eggs Benedict or the spinach-and-goat-cheese omelet? It could happen. It had probably happened at some point, somewhere. Hadn't I seen something like it in a movie?

"Come on, boys," I had said. "You can finish the game later." This was the reality of parenthood. This was a way of being we'd all accepted.

"Are you there, Kim?" Lenore asked.

"Sorry, I'm here."

"I have to run in a minute," she said. "But I want you to listen carefully to what I'm about to say and to think about it too, and then we'll talk again soon."

"I'm listening," I told her.

"This shift that's taken place, this idea that it is not safe for children to be out of our sight at any moment, this idea that a good parent is a parent who watches and manages and meddles and observes ceaselessly. This is not insignificant. This has profound consequences in the lives of parents and children. And most importantly, Kim, this is a shift that is not rooted in fact. It's not rooted in any true change or any real danger. This shift is imaginary. It's make-believe. It's rooted in irrational fear."

I told her that I didn't understand, that people don't just change the way they live their lives for no reason. There has to be something behind it. Some reason or cause.

"Maybe," she said. "If you figure out what it is, you'll have to let me know. In the meantime, do you have a lawyer?"

After we said goodbye, I went back inside, went into the kitchen. I could hear Pete and the kids upstairs. There were dishes to be done, crumbs to be wiped, but I found myself walking not to the sink but to the window that looked down onto the alley. The children were still playing. They pedaled their bikes in narrow circles, wove their scooters in lopsided figure eights. Some shot foam bows and arrows up into the air, then retrieved them, then shot them up again. The children played while on both sides of the alley the parents stood and made small talk and sipped their beers and watched. They were socializing. But they were also watching. Observing. Just in case. Pete came up beside me, and I nearly jumped. "Didn't you hear me calling?" he asked. "What are you doing?"

"Thinking," I said. "I was thinking."

"Can you do that later?" he asked. "After the children are in bed?"

. . .

"Are you going to go to jail?" Felix asked me one morning, a few weeks after my phone call with Skenazy. As every parent knows, children hear everything we say, but particularly the things we really don't want them to hear. Pete and I had been careful to discuss my legal issue only when we were certain our son was sleeping, or at least out of earshot, but clearly we hadn't been careful enough. He was almost five, approaching what I imagine must be a terrifying age for children—the age when they begin to appreciate how far the world extends beyond the people who love and care for them, and worse still, that those who love and care for them do not have dominion over this world. The moment I realized this occurred was when I was about Felix's age, five or six. On the way to see a movie one snowy day in December, my mother lost control of our station wagon and skidded across a highway into a gully with me and my sister in the back seat. No one was injured, but I remember it clearly, because it was the first time it occurred to me that things could happen, bad things, that my mother could not prevent or control. The car was spinning and she couldn't right it. We were screaming and she couldn't comfort us. It was the moment she stopped being God and started being Mom. Now I was watching Felix make the same discovery, only at a much slower, much less jarring, but somehow equally terrifying pace.

When he asked the question, he was eating breakfast as I was running around our town house, gathering items into his backpack, gathering Violet's curls into a ponytail, gathering dishes into the sink to be dealt with later, and searching for the cup of coffee I'd put in the microwave to reheat a few minutes before. Beneath the table, Violet was now crawling around, trying to make our dog kiss her on the face. "Oh, you a good girl, Liza. I love you, Liza. Kiss my mouth. Kiss my mouth, Liza."

"Liza's mouth is dirty, Violet. Don't make her kiss you."

"Kissy, kissy, kissy," my daughter called in her little-girl voice.

Liza began to shake. For a moment, I wondered what would happen if the normally docile terrier nipped my daughter on the nose. Didn't emergency rooms have to report dog bites to Child Protective Services?

"Let's put Liza in her crate for a while," I said, scooping her up.

When I returned to the kitchen, Felix repeated his question. "Why do they want you to go to jail?" He was eating half a bagel and a bowl of raspberries, his lips pink, cheeks smeared with butter and crumbs. I watched him eating his grown-up breakfast and, for a moment, felt the short time span of his little life blur around me. He was a full-on little boy. A person. He had preferences and opinions. A buttered bagel was superior to one with cream cheese. Daddy was the most fun at horseplay. Trains and buses and planes and cars and all things that sped were better than the world's stationary wonders.

"Felix," I said, "I'm not going to go to jail." As strange as this seems to me now, I hadn't talked to him at this point about what was happening. He hadn't mentioned seeing anyone record him that day, and because we assumed he wasn't aware of what had taken place, Pete and I thought it best not to broach the subject. Besides, this was a weird, legally ambiguous, socially fraught mess. I put my hands on his shoulders. I needed to know what he knew. "Why do you think Mommy's going to jail?" I asked him.

"Because you let me wait in the car that day."

"Do you remember that day?" I asked him.

His eyes were wide open and earnest as he nodded. "Some people saw you leave me in the car and recorded me on their phone. Now they want you to go to jail. It's my fault."

"No," I said. "It's not your fault. And Mommy's not going to jail." I summoned every ounce of certainty and calm I could muster. "Listen," I told him. "Mommy let you wait in the car that time, and I wasn't supposed to. It was a mistake. But it's going to be okay. We just have to explain to some people what happened."

"Why did you let me wait if you weren't supposed to?"

"Because I didn't know. I made a mistake. Mommies make mistakes sometimes. But I'm not going to jail. You don't have to worry about that, okay? And remember, none of this is your fault."

"I know," he said, then asked, "Whose fault is it?"

"Nobody's," I said. "Sometimes bad things happen and it isn't anyone's fault. They just happen for no good reason and we have to deal with it." How could I have expected him to grasp this, a concept many adults fight against all their lives, a concept I myself struggle against?

"I think it's your fault, Mommy," he said, impaling a raspberry on his little finger, then popping it into his mouth. "I think it's Mommy's fault."

"Yeah?" I said. "Join the club."

Of course, he was right. What was happening *was* my fault; or, at least, there was a clear relationship between action and fallout. Let kid wait in car, get in trouble. There was a simple cause-and-effect sequence no one could deny. In a strange way, I appreciated the clarity of it. By that stage in the parenting game, I'd come to understand that any mistake or miscalculation I made could and probably would have grave consequences. If I didn't breast-feed long enough, I'd be robbing my children of top-notch immune systems. If I let them have too much screen time, I'd inhibit their social-emotional development. I'd accepted the idea that actions and choices that didn't even seem like mistakes at the time could prove themselves to be mistakes days or weeks or even years later. In this way, I began to see how a good parent served as a kind of oracle, sensing and anticipating dangers long before anyone else could perceive them.

I first came to appreciate how important this skill was midway through my pregnancy, when I suggested to Pete that perhaps we should take a childbirth and parenting class, considering how little we knew about, well, parenting.

"A class?" he said. "Like something that will cost money?"

"No, let's just find a stranger on the street who will give us advice for free. Yes, something that will cost money."

He reminded me of how little of that we had.

I told him I understood, but that this wasn't like the usual things I wasted money on; this was the well-being of our child. "Plus," I said, "don't you think it would be nice to meet some other soon-to-be parents?" I had only to glance at his face to know the answer, but I didn't relent.

The next Tuesday, we began attending a class for pregnant couples at a yoga studio that specialized in family health and wellness. We shelled out a month's worth of grocery money to sit on loom-woven floor cushions once a week with eight other couples while a doula not much older than myself, a woman with indigo tattoos on her wrists, a nose ring, and a perfectly tousled side braid, lectured us on the many ways that childbirth, an experience with the potential to be beautiful, transcendent, profound, even orgasmic, might quickly turn into a hellish cascade of unnecessary medical interventions if approached incorrectly. When I remember this woman now, she seems common enough. I feel like I've seen her a hundred times in the nutritional supplement aisle of Whole Foods, and yet at the time, there was something about her calm, self-assured, authoritative manner that I found seductive. If she'd ever experienced any of the anxieties I was feeling about motherhood, she'd found a way to push them deep into her being or encase them in steel. I could surely learn a thing or two from a woman like this, so I forced myself to consider every word of warning she offered.

Mostly, these warnings related to the sacred but surprisingly vulnerable process of mother-child bonding, a process that, as she described it, was under constant threat by interlopers eager to interfere with what should be a natural and immediate union. For the next month, examples of such interference emerged as the main theme of the course. Medical professionals could interfere by imposing unnecessary and even dangerous procedures. Pediatricians could interfere by being insufficiently supportive of nursing or by creating anxiety about baby's weight gain or feeding schedules. Even one's own family members could interfere with bonding by imposing their own ideas onto impressionable new parents who lacked the confidence to erect a clear boundary around themselves and their child. To illustrate her points, she showed the class a video produced some years ago in Scandinavia of a baby who, immediately after being delivered (naturally, natch), was simply deposited on the mother's belly. Not given an Apgar test or azithromycin drops in the eyes. Just placed on Mama's still-heaving belly. This little thing, almost more rodent than human, after an hour or so, scaled its mother's frame without any assistance (though would a little assistance have killed it?), found her breast (this is why areolae grow darker during pregnancy), and started, no doubt to its infinite relief, to chow down.

You see, the teacher and the video said, nature knows what she's doing. People have been having babies far longer than they've been having interventions. This is how much a newborn can do *on its own*. Now just imagine what it can do with just your love and care.

Each week, I was drawn back to the studio, where I found myself listening attentively to this woman, nodding at everything she said. Gradually, each warning, each caution, seemed increasingly plausible. I felt a new strain of anxiety passing between me and teacher—anxiety not about the health or safety of the child I was carrying, but about the distance that would materialize between us when I gave birth, the need that would suddenly emerge for me to manage and minimize this distance, to keep others out. I didn't recognize it at the time, but this was the first iteration of stranger danger, a theme that would re-emerge again and again in the years that followed.

. . .

A while back, an acquaintance of mine, not a parent herself, was telling her mother how many of her closest friends seemed to lose their minds after having babies. It wasn't just that they were exhausted or overstretched or even a bit depressed, which would all have made sense. It was more that they seemed to be freaking out about everything. Rational, levelheaded women, who had a decade or more of adulthood under their belts and had always seemed adept at managing and tempering their emotions, suddenly were convinced that every single infinitesimal decision they made regarding their babies would determine whether it became secretary of state or a toothless meth head. My friend's mother listened as my friend offered various examples of this behavior, and then said, quite matter-of-factly, "I think you've all lost your minds." She went on to explain that when she had been a young mother in the seventies, it wasn't easy, but everyone just did the best they could, helped each other out when possible, and didn't worry about the rest. "The way you talk," she said to her daughter, "I can't tell if these women are having babies or running corporations."

Nostalgia, of course, is an easy trap. The women of our mothers' generation might not have had our problems, but they surely had other problems all their own. That said, for anyone observing the arc of parenting norms from World War II to the present, it's impossible not to notice two distinct, parallel waves of anxiety, both of which seem to have reached peak madness over the past ten years. The fear emerges from a particular set of historical and cultural changes, each impacting the lives of families in unique but often mutually reinforcing ways.

I've come to think of one strain of this fear as *motivating fear*, and it is a form of anxiety that was intensely familiar to me from the moment I learned I was pregnant. Motivating fear is fear that compels a parent to do something for or with or on behalf of her child. The inner dialogue of motivating fear goes something like this: *If I don't enroll in an expensive pregnancy and infant-care class, I might end up delivering prematurely by Cesarean section, with all the neonatal health problems that entails.*

Or:

If I don't breast-feed enough, my baby will lack important antibodies and healthy attachment skills and maybe even IQ points.

Or:

If I don't play with my baby enough or give it the right amount of stimulation or do the right kind of sleep training or feed it the right type of food or enroll him in the right kind of pre-school or offer him the right sort of enrichment or buy him the right kind of toys or give him the right kind of attention or provide the right sort of discipline or sign him up for the right amount of sports or extracurricular activities, then surely there is a moderate to very good chance that my child will end up__________.

I offer only a blank here, because the second conditional clause seems to go on without end. In his book *Paranoid Parenting*, the sociologist Frank Furedi argues, accordingly, that "today, parenting has been transformed into an all-purpose independent variable that seems to explain everything about an infant's development." He goes on to chronicle specific examples in which parenting decisions are put forth as a primary cause of a growing number of undesirable outcomes: the terrible twos, failure to bond, failure to thrive, development of speech impediments, development of orthodontic problems, dyslexia, student anxiety, failure in school, depression, low IQs, violent behavior, eating disorders, and overall psychological damage. He describes the various manifestations as a kind of "parental determinism" that begins at conception and extends into adulthood. This determinism leads parents to take on the job not just of loving, feeding, and teaching their children, but of providing them with endless opportunities for adult-directed play, entertainment, and enrichment. As Furedi explains it, in the modern American family, parents dissect almost every parenting act, even the most routine, analyzing it in minute detail, correlating it with a negative or a positive outcome, and endowing it with far-reaching implications for child development. "It is not surprising," he writes, "that parents who are told that they possess this enormous power to do good and to do harm feel anxious and overwhelmed."

The historian Peter N. Stearns analyzes the historical and societal changes in the post–World War II years that set in motion this brand of determinism. In the 1940s and 1950s, the expansion of child-focused consumerism and commercialism introduced parents to the idea that they could impact their children's happiness and growth not only by what they did for them or said to them, but by what they bought for them. Growing commercialism—the suburbanization that made spontaneous play and independent movement more challenging—became "symbiotically intertwined" with an emerging belief that parents had a responsibility to keep children entertained. "Parents," Stearns writes, "were increasingly rated not for their ability to discipline or promote morality, but for their good humor and willingness to keep children amused."

At this same time, education shifted away from rote academics toward the skills of socialization needed in corporate management and a social economy. Academic performance came to be measured in softer ways—more emphasis was placed on group projects and classroom participation over strict skill mastery—and achievement in such categories came to be seen as essential for overall, future success, offering parents new motivation to ensure and facilitate their children's future. Alongside these changes arose what the sociologist Martha Wolfenstein called "a new fun morality," in which the idea of entertaining children and preventing child boredom became a new parental responsibility. Paradoxically, the rise of fun morality occurred simultaneously with the spread of suburbanization and the rise of car culture. Just as experts were warning parents of the dangers of child boredom and lack of attention, many families were moving to suburban homes, where "yards were often isolated, limiting the capacity of children to join in the kind of spontaneous cohorts that had earlier formed in small-town America." The result of this was a parenting culture and experience more demanding than ever before.

These pressures continued to build well into the seventies and eighties, when what psychotherapist Nathaniel Branden referred to as "the psychology of self-esteem" infiltrated most areas of middle-class parenting culture, informing parents of the importance of doing whatever was necessary to instill in their children a fundamental sense of confidence and self-worth. From here, the trends continue, and it's not difficult to draw a line to the kinds of hyper-organized, over-scheduled, micromanaged childhoods that have become so common. When my friend's mother observed that it seemed as though our generation had lost its mind over kids, what she really should have said was that the boomer generation, dazed by a postwar economic surplus from 1947 to 1949, and shaken by vast social changes, such as divorce, women's en masse entrance into the workforce, white flight, and suburbanization, began the process of losing its mind, and we, a generation or two later, were finishing the job.

I myself had certainly played an active role in the mania of motivating fear. As my own mother recounted to her friends that afternoon in Virginia, "There's the baby sign language, the breast-feeding on demand, the co-sleeping, the mommy-and-me classes . . ." There was baby language immersion and baby yoga, an endless expanse of services and products for a concerned parent to buy. But strangely, the more I bought, the more I did, the more there was, it seemed, to buy or do; perhaps because fear tends to feed on itself, drawing parents into an ever-accelerating arms race of devotion. When it seems everyone is shelling out for lessons, tutors, high-end birthday parties, and educational consultants, who wants to be the parents who tell their kid to go entertain himself or to figure it out? As William Deresiewicz says of the scramble that comes later in that final, all-important parenting step of securing a desirable college placement, there comes a point when "the main thing that's driving the madness is simply the madness itself."

I participated in this madness. From the moment I stepped into that nurse's office to the moment I returned home from Virginia, I was fully on board, a full adherent of the extravagant anxiety of modern American parents. What I didn't know, though, what I didn't realize, was that there was an additional realm of parental fear with which I had scant experience, a wave of fear that had started later, not long after I was born, in the early 1980s; a kind of fear that was still evolving, but that had already proved equally transformative for American parents and American children.

So much has changed in a single generation when it comes to the raising of children, and most of us have a favorite memory that illustrates the distance we've traveled. My father, who grew up in Utica, New York, during the fifties and sixties, recalls his mother sending him to the store on a regular basis at the age of eight or nine. "A loaf of bread, a pint of milk, and a pack of Pall Malls." These are fond memories, he tells me. He was proud that his mother trusted him to bring back such necessities. He felt a sense of accomplishment when he returned with correct change and a bag of what was needed. Other friends of my generation might not have been sent to the store for parents' smokes, but we remember walking to school, to swim or soccer practice, riding bikes to the houses of friends, trick-or-treating on our own, playing on our own. Waiting in cars while our parents ran errands. My friend Megan remembers how, as a girl of twelve, she and her friends would play a game in which they'd walk to the main road and pretend to be hitchhikers, then run away laughing if a car ever slowed down. Friends who grew up in cities remember riding buses and subways on their own. Those who lived in the country or suburbs recall long walks through the woods, secret clubs, afternoons spent building and scaling constructionally unsound forts made out of whatever they could find in their parents' garages.

Similarly, the novelist Mona Simpson writes, "I wish I could give my son the freedom I had as a child, though even now, I'm not sure of what that consisted. Perhaps it was the land, the sheer size and range of it, the way we could run until we dropped down with our hearts knocking like bells in our chests and the sky carousing above us. There were few boundaries. I don't remember ever being told we couldn't cross the highway or the railroad tracks. But perhaps it had nothing to do with the outdoors. Perhaps it was the luxury of being unnoticed, of being left alone." And in an article in *The Atlantic* titled "The Overprotected Kid," the journalist Hanna Rosin writes, "Like most parents my age, I have memories of childhood so different from the way my children are growing up that sometimes I think I might be making them up, or at least exaggerating them." Rosin, like me, was born between 1970 and 1980, the last decade before a radically new construct of vulnerable childhood began to take hold.

The world is supposed to make sense. We want and need the things that happen to us and to those around us to adhere to laws of order and justice and reason. We want to believe that if we live wisely and follow the rules, things will work out, more or less, for us and for those we love. Psychologists refer to this as the Just World Hypothesis, a theory first developed by the social psychologist Melvin Lerner. Lerner postulated that people have a powerful intuition that individuals get what they deserve. This intuition influences how we judge those who suffer. When a person is harmed, we instinctually look for a reason or a justification. Unfortunately, this instinct leads to victim-blaming. As Oliver Burkeman writes in *The Guardian*, "Faced with evidence of injustice, we'll certainly try to alleviate it if we can—but, if we feel powerless to make things right, we'll do the next best thing, psychologically speaking: we'll convince ourselves that the world isn't so unjust after all." Burkeman cites as evidence a 2009 study finding that Holocaust memorials can increase anti-Semitism: "Confronted with an atrocity they otherwise can't explain, people become slightly more likely, on average, to believe that the victims must have brought it on themselves."

So what happens when the victim is a child, a little boy walking to school, a little girl riding her bike, a baby in a car, victims impossible to blame? Whom can we hold accountable when a child is killed or injured or abused or forgotten? How can one take in this information, the horror of it, and keep on believing the world is just?

In his history of childhood in America, the historian Steven Mintz defines a "moral panic" as the term used by sociologists to describe "the highly exaggerated and misplaced public fears that periodically arise within a society." Mintz suggests that "eras of ethical conflict and confusion are especially prone to outbreaks of moral panic as particular incidents crystallize generalized anxieties and provoke moral crusades." The late 1970s through the early 1990s was a period in American history rife with sources of ethical conflict and confusion.

Mintz describes how worldwide recessions and the Great Inflation produced anxieties that the United States was in economic decline. In the span of a few years, just as the echoes of the Vietnam War were beginning to recede, America was confronted with crack cocaine and AIDS—and the general response to both demonstrated a profound, practically homicidal ignorance of how to address these issues. Environmentalists publicized the potential destruction of population growth, pollution, and resource depletion, and looming above all this was the omnipresent threat of the Cold War's turning hot. Unfortunately, just as there is little individual Americans feel that they can do today about the threats of climate change, rising income inequality, and the dehumanizing effects of automation and globalization, people in the 1970s and 1980s felt they could do little to protect themselves from what seemed to be the encroaching disasters of the day. "Focusing concern on threats to children," Mintz suggests, "may have provided a solution to this psychological dilemma. Anxiety about the future could be expressed in terms of concerns for children's safety," which, after all, feels more manageable.

Accordingly, the America of the late 1970s and early 1980s saw a surge in expressions of fear-based child-safety measures. It was no longer acceptable to let kids walk to the store, play unattended, or ride their bikes around the neighborhood. The distance children were allowed to roam contracted, and eventually disappeared; unsupervised children were now unsafe children. Concern can take many forms. One can imagine an alternate history where, against this backdrop of general cultural anxiety, parents project their unease onto issues of children's health or education or social supports. But this is not what happened, because unlike more gradually intensifying fixations, moral panics such as the one surrounding child safety need catalysts. Incidents to launch them into public consciousness. One can see how events such as the 1979 kidnapping and killing of Etan Patz, the 1981 abduction and decapitation of Adam Walsh, or the 1983 child-abuse accusation scandal that began when the mother of a preschooler in Manhattan Beach, California, later diagnosed as mentally ill, went to the police claiming that her son was being sexually abused by the childcare workers at McMartin Preschool instigate the type of moral panic Mintz describes. In the preschool child abuse case, the charges were eventually dropped because of lack of evidence, but not before precipitating the longest and costliest legal case in American history, setting off a nationwide witch hunt, and resulting in the wrongful conviction of dozens of childcare workers charged in similar cases, all of which were eventually overturned.

These events conspired to unleash in the American imagination an image of the vulnerable or threatened child, the child who, at any moment a parent is not looking, might be abducted, raped, tortured, and murdered. Not only was coverage of these events televised and sensationalized; it was also long-lasting. Popular magazines from mid-September 1986 to mid-February 1987 published an average of one story per week about child abuse, child molestation, or missing children. The networks aired multiple made-for-TV movies and docudramas on the subject. In 1986, NBC aired *Adam: His Song Continues*, a docudrama about Adam Walsh, which ended in a roll call of 55 missing children. (His father, John Walsh, would extend entertainment vigilantism to its logical conclusion by creating *America's Most Wanted* in 1988.) And Americans who might not have tuned in could receive the message in other ways. As the sociologist and criminologist Joel Best tells us, Americans during this period "saw photographs of missing children on milk cartons, grocery bags, billboards and televised public service messages. Toy stores and fast-food restaurants distributed abduction-prevention tips for both parents and children. Parents could have their children fingerprinted or videotaped to make identification easier." And none of these frequent reminders bothered to distinguish between custodial disputes and runaways, which accounted for the vast majority of missing children cases, and the much less common occurrence of stranger abduction, which account for just 3 percent of all cases. None of these reminders came with an asterisk that a child was more likely to die from choking, not just on food but on anything a small person might happen to introduce into his or her windpipe, than at the hands of a stranger. Instead of facts, we set our imaginations on the stricken faces and broken lives of people like the parents of Adam Walsh and Etan Patz.

Psychologists often refer to a phenomenon called the availability heuristic. In its simplest terms, the availability heuristic tells us that people judge the likelihood of something happening not by facts or statistics or rational thought, but by the ease with which we can recall an example of its happening. This made perfect sense for our hunter-gatherer forebears, or maybe for anyone without access to a television or an internet connection. But for people raising children in the age of mass media, the psychology fails us. No parent could forget the faces or anguished stories of parents whose child has gone missing. How easy it is to recall these examples, regardless of how rare they might be. A 1986 national survey of youth found that kidnapping of children and teenagers ranked highest in a set of national concerns, higher than the possibility of nuclear war and the spread of AIDS, which tied for second.

The kidnapping panic of the 1980s was certainly not the only event of recent decades to transform norms of parental supervision and childhood independence. Later, as the missing-children movement grew, other parallel movements arose to combat child abuse, crack cocaine, teen pregnancy, pedophilia, drunk driving, playground safety, sexual exploitation, and so on. In the early 1990s, fears spread over a surge of youth gang violence, and five years later, another panic arose over claims that bands of youthful "super-predators" were killing and assaulting without remorse. "These panics," Mintz explains, "arose from legitimate worries for the safety of the young . . . but they were also fueled by interest groups that exploit parental fears, well-meaning social service providers, child advocacy groups, national commissions, and government agencies desperate to sustain funding and influence. If panics arise out of a genuine desire to arouse an apathetic public to serious problems, the effect of scare stories is not benign. They frighten parents, intensify generational estrangement, and encourage schools and legislatures to impose regulations to protect young people from themselves." And if the kidnapping panic of the 1980s changed the way we perceive the risk of allowing children to be unsupervised in public places, we can see a parallel process play out with children and cars in more recent years.

In March of 2009, almost exactly two years before I let my son wait in the car, the journalist Gene Weingarten published a Pulitzer Prize–winning article in the *Washington Post Magazine* titled "Fatal Distraction: Forgetting a Child in the Backseat of a Car Is a Horrifying Mistake. Is It a Crime?" The answer that emerges in his reporting, reporting that is difficult to read for the magnitude of the human suffering it describes, suggests it isn't. While many parents who lose children in this way are charged with manslaughter, and some are convicted, Weingarten details the reality that nearly all of them are good, loving, attentive parents, who "one day [get] busy, or distracted, or upset, or confused by a change in his or her daily routine, and just . . . [forget] a child is in the car." Weingarten goes on to describe the unimaginable, how approximately fifteen to twenty-five times per year in this country, regular, well-meaning parents "accidentally kill their babies in the identical, incomprehensible, modern way." "Fatal Distraction" illustrates the correlation between air-bag-safety campaigns (which advocate putting children in the rear-facing car seats in the back seats) and hot-car deaths, and humanizes the parents in these cases, revealing the cruelty of their criminalization. It would be hard to find fault with Weingarten for writing his piece. And yet the purest of motives can have unanticipated consequences for children, parents, communal life, and public policy. The murders of Etan Patz and Adam Walsh were covered so extensively, we remember them as though they happened to children we know. We know their names, recall their faces and their parents' pleas. We remember Weingarten's description of the hyperthermic victim, the small corpse, the bloated green abdomen, and we imagine for the slightest second what it would be like to be that child, that parent, to occupy that pain or grief.

There are twenty million children in America under the age of five. Thirty-seven on average die in hot cars. Thirty-seven out of twenty million is not a lot, but it is not nothing. For us to live in a just world, surely the risk of such things happening must be zero. No child should ever be abducted or raped or murdered. No child should ever be forgotten for hours in a broiling car. We say to ourselves that we do not want to live in a world where such things happen. And so now children do not walk to school on their own as Etan Patz did that morning in May 1979. They do not wait in cars, even for a few minutes, even on a cool day in front of a busy store. And we arrest parents who let their children wait in cars for five minutes, parents who let their children play alone in a park. We do this as though it could revive those children we lost, as though in doing it we can make the world right. And so children do not go to the store to buy bread and milk for their parents. They do not play pretend-hitchhiking with their friends along a road. They do not take long walks through the woods, or ride bikes along paths, or build secret tree houses or forts while we are inside working or cooking or talking to other adults or leading our lives. They are no longer afforded, as Mona Simpson writes, "the luxury of being unnoticed, of being left alone." Whatever we have to do to feel safe from such horrors, no matter how rare they might be, we vow to do it, to pay whatever price is set for a feeling of safety, a feeling of control.

My father is not old enough to remember the fear that swept through American communities during the polio outbreaks of the forties and fifties. He doesn't remember being kept home on summer days, being warned that an afternoon at the swimming pool or movie theater might bring death. The vaccine was introduced in 1955, five years after he was born, and by the time he was older, the epidemic of fear had been eliminated ahead of the disease. But he and my mother both remember other expressions of national terror. My father remembers the A-bomb drills in middle school, as frequent as fire drills (and active-shooter drills) today. "Sometimes, we'd be told to crouch under our desks when the siren went off, hands over our head. Sometimes we'd go into the hallways and ball up in lines against the wall." A little smile plays on his mouth when he recalls these precautions. "All this would have been very helpful in the event of thermonuclear holocaust," he says sarcastically. "By the early sixties, there was a large enough arsenal to turn New York State into a sheet of glass. But . . . I suppose it was something to do."

Near the end of the Cold War, when my sister and I came along, parents still worried about what the arms race meant for their children's future. But now they had other concerns. At this time, popular magazines published stories with titles such as "How to Protect Your Children from People They Trust," "The Mind of the Molester," and "Our Daughter Was Sexually Abused." I doubt my parents read any of these features, but the tenor of anxiety they created surely permeated the circles in which my parents moved. From my three years of middle school, I really remember only two instructional moments: There was the day my eighth-grade life science teacher brought in a cooler full of thawed supermarket squid for us to dissect. We were then allowed to remove the ink gland and write our names on our lab with it. And there was the day we were all herded into the auditorium for an educational play about sex abuse. At the end of the production, the cast came onstage, all enthusiasm and smiles, and shouted to the kids in the audience, "What do you do if someone touches you in your private places?"

"Tell someone!" we shouted back.

"And what if they don't believe you?" the actor asked.

"Keep on telling!" we responded.

Twenty years earlier, this sort of lurid pageant would have seemed an inexplicable exercise in paranoia; it would have made my father's nuclear-fallout drills look as quaint as ring-around-the-rosy. But the world changes, and in scrambling to absorb these changes, we fabricate new fears, fears that propel us forward (or backward). Fear is both a feeling and a force.

When I reached out to the sociologist Joel Best, to ask him how this happened—how, around the time I was born and in the decades that followed, threats to children became the number-one issue for Americans—he tried to help me see it in a larger social and historical context, explaining that people who aren't sociologists think of history as events. One event followed by another and then another. It is an extremely human trait to narrativize everything. But many sociologists don't act this way. They look at the same events, the same concerns, the same legal precedents and pieces of legislation and media relics and see, instead of discrete events, waves of social movement. Best holds that "there was a big wave before the Civil War that brought abolition. And then there was another wave from 1880 through the First World War that brought Prohibition, and the anti-immigration movement. Then . . . another movement that started in the sixties. That movement rested on the premise that children are threatened; they're at risk in the modern world and they need to be protected. And it seems that movement just continues through to today."

In his book on the subject, *Threatened Children: Rhetoric and Concern about Child-Victims*, Best describes the two common but contradictory explanations people tend to use to justify our cultural obsession with child abduction and other similar threats. He refers to these as the explanation of social decline and the explanation of recent enlightenment. The explanation of social decline should be familiar to anyone who has ever listened to a grandparent or parent reminisce about the good old days. Once upon a time, it goes, everything was better—streets were cleaner, people were honest, schools were better, neighborhoods safer; everything was bright and shining and hopeful. We believe that now everything in the world has gone to shit. Maybe it was okay for me or for my parents to wait in a car as kids, or go to the park on our own, or run wild with little supervision or monitoring, but times have changed. What once was safe now is reckless. The problem with this way of thinking, Best explains, is that "social collapse is easy to assert but difficult to prove." What looks like a wave of new problems may simply be a matter of increased awareness, better record-keeping. "We think of nostalgia as a phenomenon of individual experience, but its force on groups and cultures can be just as profound."

The second explanation offers exactly the opposite assertion about the movement of humanity. According to Best, "It argues that we have become more sophisticated; we now realize that threats to children exist; we appreciate their seriousness, and we can recognize and do something about them. Once naive, we have become knowledgeable. It doesn't matter if threats to children are increasing or decreasing. What matters is that we now understand the problem." We used to let children out of our sight, but now we know to keep close watch. We used to put them to sleep on their stomachs; now we know the risk. We used to let them spend their summers bored and aimless; now we know the importance of extracurricular activities and structure and enrichment. The list could go on. But as Best points out, the difficulty with this second way of thinking comes when we take for granted the correctness of our current interpretations of social problems—when we assume that we, unlike them, those well-meaning idiots from the past, are the ones who are truly in the know. "No doubt," he writes, "the people in every era make the same assumption, that they correctly understand the nature of their society's problems. Salem's congregations believed they had discovered demonic forces at work, and the Progressives congratulated one another for recognizing the threat posed by white slavers."

When it comes to our current fears regarding unsupervised children, we see both versions of folk wisdom at work. In the sixties or seventies, a child could walk to school or wait in a car because people were better, the world less violent, we say. But also, parents were dumber. They simply didn't know. Sure, parents used to leave kids on their own, but they also let them drink Kool-Aid by the vat and play with toy weapons the NRA might find a touch aggro. They let them build forts in the trunks of station wagons careening down the freeway or swim without sunscreen until their skin blistered. Parents let kids wait in cars because they were idiots. But also, on average, because it was safer, because people were better then, gentler, less monstrous. It sounds so nice and pleasant, this safer, simpler past. It sounds almost too good to be true.

But that is the rational, critical part of my brain at work, not the fearful, superstitious parent part. Would it ever be possible to merge the two, to impose what I learned from sociologists on my day-to-day mom life? And even if I could, how feasible would it be if I was the only one doing it and the other parents and teachers and neighbors I encountered every day were perfectly satisfied with their unsupported conclusions and inherited folk wisdom? It's one thing to notice the emperor has no clothes. It's an entirely different thing to be the only one to say so.

And so all fall and through the winter, I did what I was supposed to do. I took care of my kids. I stayed out of trouble, didn't speed, didn't even let my kids wait in the car while I fed the parking meter or walked the grocery cart back to the corral.

Then one unseasonably warm February afternoon, Felix wanted to set up a cookie stand in our front yard.

"What's a cookie stand?" I asked.

"Like a lemonade stand," he explained. "But with cookies."

It seemed like a cute idea. We lived two blocks from a train station, and our condo fronted a well-trod street, lots of downtown commuters passing by. We baked the cookies, set up the stand, scrounged up as much change as we could from beneath the couch cushions. Felix wanted to charge two dollars per cookie, and I told him that was out of the question.

"That's what Starbucks charges," he pointed out.

"We're not Starbucks," I replied.

After a bit more back-and-forth, he hung his cardboard sign around our fence and opened shop. Business was bustling. I went inside to dig up some more change, stopped for a minute to wash a few dishes. There was a window above our kitchen sink from which I could see the yard, the little table, the back of Felix's head. I grew bold. I'd washed the dishes and I went on to dry them. And then I saw two men in police uniforms approach the yard. I dropped the dishes. I ran down the stairs, flew out the door, practically screaming. "I'm here, I'm here, I'm here. I was watching him from the kitchen. I could see him from the kitchen."

The officer, very tall and handsome, furrowed his brow. He was holding a chocolate chip cookie in one hand, a dollar in the other. "Does he have a license for this business?"

I stood without speaking.

Then he smiled, took a bite of cookie. "You two have a good day."

Fear is a feeling, but it takes up space. We invent it, and it becomes an artifact of our penchant for telling stories about the future, stories that help us order a chaotic and unpredictable world. Because we inhabit the world with other people, fears do not exist in a bubble. Often, they are communal, passed along airwaves and the internet and overheard in bits of conversation. But do we choose our fears, or are we as individuals less implicated than that; are we mere particles of dust, moved this way and that way by currents of anxiety?

I have to believe that parents have always worried about their children—sociologists and anthropologists and historians write about the many and varied manifestations of this worry. To feel and express and act upon concern for one's offspring seems as integral a part of what it means to be human as to live in groups or to look for food and shelter. I find it easier to imagine being a mollusk at the bottom of the ocean, waiting for nourishment to fall into my shell, than to imagine what life would be like as a species that does not concern itself with the well-being of its young. And yet, the objects of our worry, the unique frequency and pitch and intensity of our fears, vary across time and culture as much as the food we eat or the clothes we wear. Focusing on the history of parents in America gives a glimpse of the scope of parental anxiety. And one doesn't have to look hard or long to see that parental fears do not always correspond to the most apparent and pressing dangers children face.

Over the course of a few hundred years, American children have been exposed to the stresses of child labor, neglect, malnutrition, deadly communicable diseases, indentured servitude, and slavery. In New England's healthiest communities in the seventeenth century, around 10 percent of children died during their first year of life, and three of every nine children died before reaching their twenty-first birthdays. Puritan children regularly perished by smallpox, measles, mumps, diphtheria, scarlet fever, and whooping cough. Yet many child-rearing tracts written during that time show their parents to be more preoccupied with the perils of moral corruption, schooling, and spiritual well-being, than with physical health. Older children regularly suffered burns from candles or open hearths. They fell into rivers and wells, ingested poisons, broke bones, swallowed pins, and stuffed nutshells up their noses (that last one they still do). And yet Puritan parents did not ruminate on such dangers or babyproof their homes. They worried instead about the sinfulness of play and children's lack of internal restraints. They worried that allowing small children to crawl would indulge their animal nature, and they dressed their children in clothing to restrict such movement. They worried about instilling in children an awareness of sin and divine judgment more than about protecting or sheltering them from the horrors of death, violence, and disease.

Puritan parents' fearfulness about their children's spiritual well-being led them to child-rearing so restrictive and so punishing that often children stolen during battles with Native American tribes, once inculcated into that freer, more indulgent style of rearing, would run into the bosom of their captors when rescue was attempted. Apparently, life among the "savages" was preferable to the fear and shame that characterized the upbringing of the average colonial child.

In the centuries that followed, American children saw little improvement in their quality of life. During the Civil War, children near the battlefront regularly witnessed the destruction of towns and villages, exploding shells, burning cities, mangled corpses, and stacks of human limbs. By the end of the nineteenth century, 20–30 percent of children lost a parent by the age of fifteen, and in the first decades of the twentieth century, more than 100,000 children resided in 1,200 orphanages throughout the United States. And yet, amid this cornucopia of childhood terror, terrors from which a modern, middle-class parent's sensibility recoils, child-rearing manuals and parents' writings from these times suggest that parents often turned their anxious gaze elsewhere, toward dangers that seem to us far less pressing. They worried over the development of psychological traits such as shyness, timidity, and bravado. They worried about how the comforts of urban life might render boys soft and effeminate. As American families experienced the most rapid period of social and technological change in the history of human civilization, parental anxiety attached not onto the profound effects these transformations were having on children and family life, but on issues such as posture, hygiene, neurasthenia, masturbation, sleeping arrangements of children, sibling rivalry, the corrupting effects of radio, the popularity of comic books, the depiction of violence in television and film, the threat of kidnapping, the problems of juvenile delinquency, ritual sadism, boredom, poor self-esteem, crib death, and bullying.

With each of these parental fixations, the object of fear correlates less to the level of risk than to parents' ability (or perceived ability) to exert control over the outcome. If you are a Puritan parent, why fret over the very significant possibility that your children will perish by contagion when you lack any knowledge or medicine to manage this risk? Better to worry about moral corruption and spiritual goodness, outcomes one might hope to influence—it's the college admissions thing with the hereafter in place of Stanford. Likewise, today's parents and parenting experts tend not to focus on many of the very daunting problems facing our children when those problems are beyond the scope of an individual's influence.

Every day it seems there is less we can control about our kids' future. The schools are failing, the middle class is vanishing, superbugs grow stronger, and health care is more expensive. The political landscape is unstable. The seasons are slipping, and we might not recognize the climate of the planet our kids will inherit. College education floats further out of reach. Guns are everywhere. People are often angry, suspicious, and judgmental. Americans turn on each other and search for scapegoats to punish and blame. Our food makes us fat and sick. As William Deresiewicz writes in *Excellent Sheep*, "Families are scared, and for good reason. Social mobility has stalled. The global playing field is getting ever more competitive. . . . The future since 2008, has looked more daunting, especially for young people, than at any other time in memory." And yet, it feels as though nothing I do as an individual is going to have much of an impact on increasing class stratification or the melting ice caps or the rise of right-wing populism. Sure, I can donate and agitate, drive less, organize, and vote my conscience, but is this *really* going to make a difference? So much of what happens in the world falls beyond our narrow sphere of influence, and so our grip tightens on what we think we can control, on everything within reach. If one sees fear in this context, not as a passive state but as a thing we produce, a thing we do to soothe our feelings of helplessness in a largely indifferent world, the child-rearing style that Frank Furedi calls "paranoid parenting" begins to make sense.

My father told me a story once about a nightmare he had when I was small. He dreamed he was back in upstate New York, where he grew up, and he was driving in a snowstorm along a deserted highway, I a baby asleep in the back of the car. He pulled onto the shoulder to check on a tire. A minute later, when he tried to get back into the car, he realized he'd locked himself out and that I was trapped inside in my car seat. It was freezing. The snow swirled down around him in wild eddies. He banged on the window, trying to break it. He screamed for help, but there was no one near, no one to help, only empty fields and darkness.

In "Fatal Distraction," Gene Weingarten describes how one father whose infant perished in his office's parking lot as he went about his work relives the horror again and again in dreams. In reality, he could see his car that morning as he walked between office buildings only as a blinding glare of sun on chrome. In his dreams, he is walking back and forth past the car and can see his child inside. He reassures the child that he'll be right back. He's coming back.

These nightmares speak to something deep inside us, our darkest fear as parents: the fear of failure, the fear that we can't protect our children, or ourselves. But maybe this fear goes deeper than parents and children. Maybe it is what makes us suffer most as humans. Knowledge without power, foreseeing things we can't forestall. We now live in a moment where it is infinitely easier to know than it is to do. We are living in an age of fear.

When I was a child, I believed that a wolf lived in the back of my closet, up near the black plastic bags of old clothes. The wolf was going to eat me, though I begged him not to. He could not be reasoned with. He could not be appeased. The wolf was clever and well-spoken, and one day, amused by my pleading, he told me that if I counted to fifty before I fell asleep every night, he would stay in the closet; he would not come out. I still remember how I lay in bed, tight beneath the covers, counting slowly in my head. It made no sense, but I believed it. I knew that if I counted, I'd be safe. One, two, three, four, I counted every night, all the way to fifty. I never doubted or wavered in my counting. I wanted to be safe.

4

NEGATIVE FEEDBACK

The lawyer my father-in-law put me in touch with said that all there was to do was wait. He had explained my "lapse in judgment" to the detective in Virginia and I was supposed to sit tight, wait for him to contact me and tell me if they planned on formally pressing charges or if they had decided to drop the case. But waiting is harder than it sounds. Late at night, after Pete and the kids were asleep, I'd go downstairs, sit at the dining room table, and open the browser on my computer, always looking for some information, some clue that would help me solve this puzzle. *Leaving children in cars,* I Googled. *Letting children wait in cars? How long can a child wait in a car? Laws about children and cars? Mothers arrested for leaving kids in cars. Is it a crime to let a kid wait a car?* I read of parents, usually women, arrested for letting a child wait in a car outside a coffee shop, a convenience store, a post office, or a Rite Aid. Sometimes they left babies or toddlers, sometimes older children, but almost always for a few minutes, a single errand. They ran in to get one thing, to drop off a letter, to grab a coffee, to pick up a shirt. They left children playing with an iPad, or reading, or studying their spelling words, sometimes with an older sibling in the car, and they came out to see a police car, an angry bystander, an officer holding up his badge. But the stories got even stranger. I read of parents arrested for letting children play alone in a park, or for allowing them to walk to a neighbor's house or to soccer practice down the street, or for letting an older child babysit a younger one while a parent walked the dog. I read these stories and didn't know what I was reading, if they were real or make-believe. I read late into the night, and as I read, my obsession grew. I felt myself falling into something, trying to orient myself, to figure out where I was and how and why this was happening.

There was a part of it that didn't make sense. The moral panics surrounding children had peaked in the late eighties and early nineties. If policies and public sentiment about dangers to children were tied to these panics, then the laws regulating child supervision should have leveled off or even decreased over the past twenty years. Instead, it seemed, they'd escalated. Surveys suggested that children of each decade were afforded fewer freedoms than the one before, that the age in which parents allowed children unsupervised time continued to rise. The panics came and went, but the anxiety lingered, and there was no clear reason. At dinner one evening, another mother and I were discussing our children, the question of how much freedom to give our children came up, and she said that even though her kids were teenagers now, she still couldn't bring herself to let them out of her sight in a store. She knew it was irrational. She knew it made no sense, and yet still, something stopped her. She couldn't explain it.

"Is it superstition?" I asked her.

"Not exactly," she said.

"Are you afraid someone will hurt them?" I asked.

She lifted her fork, paused for a moment, seemed to be considering. "No," she said. "Well . . . I don't know. I guess it's other people.

I worry that if I let them out of my sight, other people will see us and think I'm doing something wrong. I feel like it doesn't matter what *I* think; that if *other* people think I'm doing something dangerous, then it's dangerous. I suppose I can't quite tell where my own anxieties end and other people's begin. I don't know if I'm afraid for my kids, or if I'm afraid other people will be afraid and will judge me for my lack of fear."

It took me a moment to understand what she was suggesting—that for her, risk assessment and fear of moral judgment are intertwined. I didn't know it at the time, but it turns out that she is not alone. According to a 2016 study by a team of social scientists at the University of California–Irvine, fear and judgment go hand in hand.

Barbara W. Sarnecka is a cognitive scientist and a professor of logic and philosophy of science at the University of California–Irvine. She has spent much of her career studying the way young children learn and the development of numerical cognition. Sarnecka is a researcher, a teacher, and an author, but she's also a mom, and like most other moms, she loves her children and strives to listen to and treat them like people worthy of consideration and respect. And so when Sarnecka's son came to her at the beginning of the third grade and told her that he hated being in the school's after-care program, that it was boring and not at all fun; that after a long day at school, he didn't want to spend another two hours sitting in a classroom but wanted to be outside to see his friends and play, she listened. She paid attention and tried to make a change.

Her son was enrolled in the third grade of an elementary school in a quiet neighborhood, and each afternoon at 2:30 the school would dismiss its students to their parents, and when the weather was pleasant (not so uncommon in Orange County), many of the parents would take their children to play in an adjacent park. An assistant professor at the time, Sarnecka had a schedule that was full but flexible, so she made some space in her afternoons and withdrew her son from the school's after-care program. Each day, she would pick him up with the other parents, walk him to the park, then sit on a bench and watch him play for an hour before taking him home. She continued to do this for a number of weeks, rushing to finish her work and arrive at the school in time for dismissal. Then one day, struggling to get through everything in her office, she began to wonder why she was hurrying; she saw how absurd it was. The park was literally next to the school. There was no street to cross, only a grassy field. Normally there were dozens of kids there, always adults within calling distance. Wasn't it a bit ridiculous for Sarnecka to leave work early to walk her son across a small field and watch him play with other children? She might not have afternoon classes, but she certainly had plenty of work to do. She decided to try something new. She told her son that after school he should simply walk to the park with his friends and play there for forty-five minutes. She'd pick him up at 3:15.

For around a month, that was what he did. Then one evening, Sarnecka's husband received an email from another parent who was concerned. The mom had seen their son playing at the park, and at one point he had been throwing pinecones with a couple of other boys. The parent asked Sarnecka's husband if he aware that his wife was leaving their son unsupervised after school. When she heard about the email, Sarnecka was astounded. "It was like she was tattling on me or ratting me out to my husband."

A few days later, Sarnecka herself received a call from the school principal, who asked Sarnecka if she realized that the school did not provide childcare in the park after hours. Sarnecka said yes, she understood, but that in her view, her son was responsible and capable enough to have an hour of unsupervised play with other children in a safe, public space. The principal disagreed, and after a brief back-and-forth, Sarnecka relented. She still thought it was ridiculous. She still believed that she wasn't putting her son in any real danger by allowing him a tiny bit of freedom, but she also recognized that there's a social cost to conflict within a tight-knit community, that this was her son's principal and that this was his school. And so she let it go, doing her best to put it out of mind.

The story might have ended there, but in the years that followed, as Sarnecka came across more stories like mine, she kept recalling her son's time in the park, turning it around in her mind, feeling exasperated and confused, but also curious. She was still thinking about it when her son turned fourteen and began driver's ed: "It seemed amazing," Sarnecka told me, "that not one person said, 'Are you crazy? You're letting him drive? Do you know what the accident rate for sixteen-year-old drivers is?' I thought, *He's in much greater danger driving a car at sixteen than he was playing in a park at nine, in the middle of the day, next to his school, in the safest big city in America*." That was when it occurred to her that maybe what had happened, and what was happening around the country, stemmed not from fear or risk, but from something else.

Sarnecka teamed up with two colleagues at Irvine, Ashley Jo Thomas, a PhD student in the Department of Cognitive Sciences, and P. Kyle Stanford, a professor and chair in the Department of Logic and Philosophy of Science. In a group of experiments, the researchers presented subjects with a series of vignettes in which a parent left a child unattended for a period of time, and participants indicated their estimation of risk of harm to the child during that period. For example, in one vignette, a ten-month-old was left alone for fifteen minutes, asleep in the car in a cool, underground parking garage. In another vignette, an eight-year-old was left for forty-five minutes at a Starbucks, one block away from her mother's location.

To measure participants' moral attitude toward the parent, the researchers varied the reason the child was left unattended across a set of six experiments with more than 1,300 online participants. In some cases, the child was left alone unintentionally (for example, in one case, a mother was hit by a car and knocked unconscious after buckling her child into her car seat). In other cases, the child was left unattended so the parent could run in to work, do some volunteering, relax, or meet a lover.

Not surprisingly, the parents' reason for leaving a child unattended affected participants' judgments of whether the parent had done something immoral. On a ten-point scale, with one being not at all immoral and ten being a hugely immoral act, participants usually rated leaving a child unattended as a three, even when the child was left unattended unintentionally even for a moment. But the ratings skyrocketed to nearly eight when participants were told that the parent left the child to meet a lover.

The more surprising result was that perceptions of risk followed a similar pattern. Although the details of the cases were otherwise the same—that is, the age of the child, the duration and location of the unattended period, and so on—participants thought children were in significantly greater danger when the parent left to meet a lover than when the child was left alone unintentionally. In other words, participants' factual judgments of how much danger the child was in while the parent was away varied according to the extent of their moral outrage concerning the parent's reason for leaving.

Sarnecka summarizes the findings this way: People don't think that leaving children alone is dangerous and therefore immoral. They think it is immoral and therefore dangerous. "It's clearer and clearer that it's not about safety," Sarnecka told me. "It's about enforcing a social norm, a moral and social norm. You're not ever supposed to leave your kids alone; I caught you doing it; you better be sorry. Now I have power over you . . . Humans are a social species, and we tend to want other people to approve of us. We tend to want to do what we think will be approved of, what everybody agrees is okay to do. What's more surprising, however, is that people also adjust their factual beliefs to bolster our moral judgment." Fear and judgment form a kind of negative feedback loop. Parents seem to have become more judgmental of parents' not watching their children. To justify their moral outrage, they form a belief that an unsupervised child is at risk, and then the perception of increased risk intensifies their moral judgment yet again. Sarnecka's colleague Kyle Stanford describes this loop as "a recipe for rapid social change."

Stanford's theory is that "suddenly, there's an availability heuristic that makes people think something like kidnaping is more common than it is, more of a risk than it is." When a passenger plane crashes, for example, and the crash is covered by the news, people will invariably assess the risk of air travel to be higher than they would when a major crash hasn't occurred for a long period of time. That's an availability heuristic. Similarly, a spate of widely publicized child abductions, the kinds of horror stories that haunt us and come to mind with little effort, increased the seeming likelihood of the threat. "This sudden shift increased people's moral outrage when they saw people breaking those moral rules or taking what they perceive now as risk." Stanford explains that as people's "moral outrage increases; they think it's even riskier and it keeps going around and around, a downward spiral, until the action at last is entirely taboo. The increasing beliefs about risk and increasing moral outrage or condemnation are mutually supporting; each time you raise one, there's pressure to raise the other."

Intellectually, I could grasp what he was saying. If a group's mode of thinking about a certain subject is a closed system, normally following a set of particular rules, the kidnapping panic of the eighties and nineties, or the public awareness campaigns surrounding hot-car deaths in more recent years, served as a sudden disruption to the system that initiated a feedback loop. I wanted to understand it in a different way, though, to grasp on a more personal level how risk perception and moral judgment interact in an individual's thinking.

I wanted to know at some level, even if only a neural one, why someone pulled out their iPhone to record my son in the parking lot of a Target in Virginia.

For this, I turned to the psychologist Paul Bloom, who'd explored similar questions in his books *Just Babies: The Origins of Good and Evil* and *Against Empathy: The Case for Rational Compassion*. I asked him about this peculiar connection between moral judgment and irrational belief: If he could explain why, psychologically speaking, the two seem to be inextricable.

"When we judge something as morally wrong," he told me, "I think we realize that at some point we're going to have to justify that judgment to a neutral third party, and the problem we face is that the language of morality doesn't translate. You can't say to a parent doing something you don't like, 'I morally disapprove of your behavior. You're behaving in a way that offends my core values.' People would think you were nuts. And so what we do is we use faulty reasoning to fabricate faulty causality to convince people of the wrongness." He offers a few examples that have nothing to do with parenting, but show the same psychological mechanism at work. "Let's say you don't like trans people. It just feels wrong and scary to you that people are openly identifying as transgender. But you can't just say, 'I don't like trans people,' so you say, 'Hey, if we give trans people rights, they're going to assault little kids in bathrooms.' Or maybe a certain politician doesn't like Mexican people. He just doesn't like the idea of all these Mexican people coming into our country. He can't say that, exactly. So he says, 'Mexican immigrants are dangerous. They're murderers and rapists. If we let them in, they'll commit terrible crimes.' Or someone doesn't like gay people, so they say, 'Everyone knows gay people cause earthquakes, and we all know earthquakes are bad.' " Bloom laughed a little as he said this, even as he admitted it's not funny when you think of the implications of this kind of thinking, this attempt to justify what can't be justified with reason or "facts."

I asked him if he thought the problem was worse now than in the past, if social media or other changes in modern life were making people more judgmental.

"I don't think our psychology has changed," he answered. "I think people are prone to judgment because as social creatures, we're very focused on social hierarchy, how we compare to others, where we each fall on the ladder and whether we're moving up or down. People have always used outrage or disapproval of others as a way of advancing in the hierarchy. I think what's changed is that it's just so much easier to do it now."

"Easier to . . . ?"

"To judge each other, to condemn or critique. Technology has vastly increased our ease and access to judgment. Our opportunities to disapprove of each other, to feel outrage at what others have done or are doing has become unlimited. At any moment I can plug myself into a community and try to manipulate my place in the hierarchy by expressing judgment. We don't have to go out and kill a buffalo and bring it back for the tribe anymore to move up the hierarchy. We just open our browser.

"And," Bloom continued, "I think mothers in particular are very attuned to the hierarchy of where they stand with other mothers."

As I waited to hear from the police officer in Virginia, I found myself wanting to believe that in the course of a generation, every parent in America, and not only parents but legislators, educators and school administrators, pediatricians and social workers, police officers and bystanders and store clerks and neighbors, had somehow lost the faculty of reason when it came to protecting children—that we were all caught in the negative feedback loop that the Irvine psychologists had identified. This was what I needed to believe to keep going—that our culture was in the grip of mass hysteria, that I was a victim of this hysteria, knocked over by a wave of anxiety and uncertainty, and that I was not alone.

There was only one problem with this point of view. The problem was that I clung to irrational fears as tightly as anyone else.

Some things seem dangerous and others don't, and often, this distinction has little to do with statistics or data or even reality. No matter how many people reassure me that flying is the safest form of travel, I will always be more nervous at thirty thousand feet than I am en route to the airport. There was a time when I felt nothing but elation when plunging into a cloud, seeing the sky go white, then back to blue, and a bout of turbulence was no more frightening than the rumble of driving over a rutted road. I can remember these flights without fear, but no matter how hard I try, I can't resurrect them. Now a short domestic trip involves sweating, nausea, moderate sedation. *It's safe, it's safe, I know it's safe,* I want to yell at all those well-meaning people who try to reassure me with statistics. *But it doesn't feel safe!*

When I later made this observation to Barbara Sarnecka, she said she understood my fears completely—but it isn't fear per se that is so troubling to her but what we, as a society, are *doing* with those fears. "You're afraid of flying," she says. "It's a fear for you, you know it doesn't make sense, you know that it's actually more dangerous for you to get in your car, but you have the fear, and so my feeling is, fair enough, you don't like to fly. That's your choice. Maybe it will affect your life; maybe you rearrange your travel so you don't have to fly. Maybe you take a fear-of-flying class and move beyond it. Whatever. It's your quirky little thing and it's not really other people's business. But when it comes to this fear about leaving children alone, which is equally irrational and equally not based on data or risk, the fear has become both common custom and law. Everyone is being compelled to share the phobia and if they don't act like they share it, they are literally subject to litigation. You can be arrested and jailed and your kids can be taken away if you don't behave in this way that's demonstrably irrational. That's what seems totally nuts to me. It doesn't seem crazy when people have fears. It doesn't surprise me at all that some mothers or fathers have some superstitious feeling that if they never take their eye off the kid, then nothing bad will ever happen to the kids. People are prone to superstition. Throw salt over your shoulder three times and the devil will never take your baby, that kind of thing. It is what it is. But to make it the law? To make it something we all have to participate in under threat of prosecution? That's when I step back and say, 'What is happening here? Why have we all bought into this assumption that the parent who is the most cautious, the most irrationally afraid, the most risk-averse, is the best or most loving parent? When did a good parent become a parent who is constantly, obsessively focusing on risk, and not just any risk, but the wrong risk?' "

Sarnecka points out that the greatest enduring risk to children in America right now is not strangers and not pedophiles and not overheating cars, but obesity and all the health disorders related to it. "What used to be called adult-onset diabetes is now just called type 2 diabetes because kids now get it. They get it because they're fat, and they're fat because they never get to go outside and run around, and they're never allowed to go outside and run around because they're never allowed to be unsupervised." She goes on to say that if we feared rationally, we'd worry about obesity and diabetes, we'd worry about how to keep our kids far away from sugary juices, we'd worry about young drivers killed in moving-vehicle crashes, we'd worry about things like teen depression or cigarette addiction. Instead, we tend to focus on occurrences that are far less likely, and yet somehow more frightening. "The fact is," she says, "having your kid get fat and develop heart disease and die before her time is sad, but it doesn't scare people. There's no *Law and Order: Diabetes Unit*. Instead, the media fixate on these nightmare scenarios with fascination because they scare us in a delicious way, like horror movies. The Centers for Disease Control warn that if current trends continue, one in three US adults could have diabetes by 2050, whereas a child's chances of being abducted and murdered are way less than one in a million. On average, you'd have to leave your kid outside, unsupervised, for 750,000 years for this to happen. But abduction is titillating, it's exciting, it has something to do with sex, something to do with violence. And the part of our brain that deals with assessing threats did not evolve to see threats like diabetes and heart disease, things that kill you slowly over a long period of time."

Sarnecka's study seemed to be confirming what I'd sensed without seeing, that this process I'd been caught up in was not about risk and safety and legal protections of children or even the statistical likelihood of particular dangers. It was not about my own incompetence as a mother, or about a lapse in judgment or a concerned stranger or the dangers of the modern world. It was not about things happening in the world at all. It was about the awesome and terrible power of our imagination.

5

SELF-REPORT

Almost a year passed before I found out what would come of that day in Virginia. For a mentally sturdy, easygoing person without a generalized anxiety disorder or a tendency to fixate on unlikely worst-case scenarios, it would have been a long time to wait. For me, to not know if I was going to be charged with a crime, visited by DCFS, or summoned to court, it was an eternity. Luckily, I had other concerns to distract me. This was the year that Felix turned five and Violet turned two, and many days I felt like I was manning a ship that was taking on water. I was trying to keep my kids healthy and happy, my marriage intact, my career extant. When it came to my unfinished business in Chesterfield County in the Commonwealth of Virginia, the mania of juggling the mundane pursuits of family life proved useful. My worries distracted me from my worry.

Then one morning that spring, the kind of morning when everyone in Chicago staggers out of doors, drunk on sun, disoriented by the warm air, the almost foreign scent of trees and shrubs or just any sort of unfrozen plant life, I received a phone call. I'd made it through the usual marathon of waking, dressing, and feeding the kids, then dropping them off at their respective schools. To nonparents, or to the parents of those mythical calm and compliant children about whom I've heard so much but never observed in the wild, this might not sound like much of an accomplishment. For me, it was a feat.

To be a youngish, able-bodied, mentally functional adult is not to think about the thousands of small miracles of brain and muscle and willpower and concentration that take place each morning just to get a human body out of the house. To wake, for example. To move from sleep into consciousness without screaming or sobbing or crying out for a bottle of milk that has not yet materialized in one's grasp. To go to the toilet and empty one's bladder. To not have defecated in one's bedding in the middle of the night. To drink or to eat without complaint. To eat a piece of buttered toast without worrying about how well the crusts have been removed, how evenly the butter has been spread. To put on one's clothes the right way, not backward and not inside out. To put on socks without feeling tormented by the placement of the seams, the padding of the heel. To comb one's hair. To blow one's nose. To accept the necessity of wearing a coat when it's cold outside or, God forbid, mittens. To make one's own lunch, to wipe one's own butt, to brush one's own teeth, to spit out rather than to swallow the fluorinated toothpaste. To not require the presence of a particular stuffed animal to soothe one's self into the jarring routine of the day. To put on shoes. Only when you become a parent and have every increment in this process illuminated by a small, adorable creature that simply cannot yet perform it independently, do you realize the greatness of what we humans do each day, the impossible majesty of what we must accomplish before we've even started, what we must learn and be taught, what our hulking, unfinished brains must master.

On this particular morning in May, I had just completed the marathon and miracle of morning rituals and was still basking in the afterglow, planning to spend the rest of school hours working on my novel at my favorite coffee shop. I parked the car on a nearby side street, gathered up my computer bag, my purse, my cell phone, scooped up some empty juice boxes and granola-bar wrappers that had fallen to the floor. I was making slow progress down the sidewalk, scanning the street for a trash can, thinking how one day very soon I was going to implement a no-eating-in-the-car policy like the one my father had enforced—not today, not tomorrow, but soon, soon. That was what I was thinking when my phone began buzzing. I stuffed the garbage into my pockets so I could answer it. A Virginia number, but not my parents, not my sister.

"Hello?" I said.

The voice on the other end was warm, polite, not at all official or unkind. "Hello. Sorry to bother you. I'm trying to get ahold of Miss Kimberly Brooks. Do you know where I might reach her?"

"This is Kim," I said.

"Miss Brooks, I'm an officer with the Chesterfield County Police Department. I'm following up on outstanding arrest warrants. Are you aware that there's a warrant out for your arrest?"

I stopped walking. For a moment, I stopped hearing. My body became impossibly heavy, my arms and legs felt loose. I let my computer bag drop to the ground. Then I let myself drop. I sat down half on the sidewalk, half on the grass, leaned into my knees, tried to breathe. "Excuse me?" I said. "I'm sorry?"

"You're not aware that there's an outstanding warrant for your arrest in Virginia?"

"No. No. I was not aware of that."

I heard papers shuffling, a hand over a receiver, something muffled. "Looks like it was issued back in May of last year. About a year ago. I'm just doing some housekeeping here, following up on open files. So do you know what this is in regard to? Can you tell me a little bit about what happened?"

It occurred to me for the first time that I was talking to the police. *Never talk to the police without a lawyer*, I remembered my father telling me. Or was it a character on *Homicide* who'd said this? "I'm sorry," I said, my voice hardly more than a whisper. "I need to have my lawyer call you back."

"Oh, I doubt that's necessary. Up to you of course, but I'm just trying to gather information here, to follow up."

"I'll have my lawyer call you."

I hung up the phone. I tried to put it back in my pocket, but there was an empty juice box in my pocket. *Pete*, I thought. *I have to call Pete.* My fingers were shaking as I dialed. I don't remember if I was crying or screaming when he answered, only that he was saying he couldn't understand me, that I needed to calm down, to tell him what happened.

"There's a warrant out for my arrest in Virginia," I said. And then something happened that I wasn't expecting. I started laughing. I was crying and I was laughing and I was still sitting on the sidewalk with my purse and my computer bag beside me on the ground. A woman walked by with her poodle. A man rode by on his bike. People were getting out of cars, talking on cell phones. But no one stopped. No one slowed down. They looked, and then they looked away, seeing this woman unraveling, sprawled out on the sidewalk, laughing and crying. I don't blame them for averting their gazes. I would have done the same.

Where do our fears come from? How do we decide, as a culture, as a country, as an individual, what we're going to worry about? When do we wring our hands and take every precaution, and when do we throw up our arms and say, "What can you do?"

At some point very early in my life, it was impressed upon me that the worst thing a human being could endure was the loss of a child, that there is no cost too high to pay if it protects one's child from harm. I never questioned or doubted this assertion. But what happens when this same way of thinking is used to shape policy and law? A number of legal experts I spoke to pointed out to me how frequently legislators and advocates of various stripes will say things such as, "There should be no cost too high to pay if paying it will save even one child." It sounds obvious. It sounds like the kind of statement no humane person could challenge. The only problem with such a statement is that of course it's not true. We, as a society, decide that the cost is too high to save people all the time. In 2015, 35,992 people died in car crashes, and 938 of them were children under the age of thirteen. We could reduce moving-car fatalities to almost zero if we reduced all speed limits to ten miles per hour. But we don't do it. In 2008, the CDC found that there were 234,094 nonfatal bathroom injuries treated in hospital emergency rooms for people older than fifteen. Many people suffer serious or even fatal injuries falling in the shower. We could reduce this to almost zero by making protective headgear a part of our bath routine. Drowning is one of the leading causes of death for children. We could save so many if we never let children near water. But we don't resort to these measures; we don't take these precautions. The cost is too high, the benefits too great to forfeit.

This kind of cost-benefit analysis is unavoidable. It's simply a part of being a person with a functioning prefrontal cortex living in a dangerous and unpredictable world. But what I began to see after talking to Sarnecka and Bloom was that something had happened in recent decades to weigh the analysis toward the side of risk, away from the benefits, especially when it came to children.

In the five years since I'd become a mother, I'd heard about or read about or watched news segments about babies who'd stopped breathing in their cribs, who'd developed horrible, incurable, degenerative diseases, who'd been hit by cars or fallen out of windows or stumbled down stairs or choked on checkers, who'd been maimed by a family dog, scalded by a cup of instant noodles, drowned in the backyard swimming pool when a parent turned away for just one minute. One day my father said to me, "Want to hear a horror story?" He told me about a malpractice lawsuit one of the doctors at his hospital was facing. A two-year-old had been brought into the emergency room with loss of appetite, stomach pain, and vomiting. "Gastroenteritis," the attending concluded. "Stomach flu's going around." The parents were sent home. The symptoms worsened. A day or two later they returned to the hospital. X-rays were ordered. A small, flat round object was visible inside his intestine. A penny, they thought. "Happens all the time," they said. "He'll pass it." A few days later they returned when the child began vomiting blood. They took him into surgery. It wasn't a penny but a lithium battery. It was leaking acid into the child. He died a few hours later.

What is the moral of such a story for a concerned parent? What is one supposed to learn? There is no moral. The moral is fear.

Over the course of the next week, I tried to figure out the best way to proceed. I spoke with the new lawyer, asked him how so much time could have passed, why I'd never been informed of the charges. He was flummoxed, said he didn't understand it either, that perhaps it had to do with my living out of state, that maybe the Virginia police couldn't find me.

"Couldn't find me?" I yelled into the phone. "They called me on my cell phone. They showed up at my parents' house when it happened. I'm not exactly hiding in a cave."

He told me there was a particular prosecutor he wanted to approach about the case, someone with whom he had a good relationship, "a reasonable fellow," he called him. But the next day, he told me the call hadn't gone well. The prosecutor wasn't as amenable as he'd expected because of the amount of time that had passed since the incident. "He wants to know why you didn't come forward earlier. Why we're dealing with this now, a year after the fact."

I felt the situation spinning out from under me. *This is how bad things happen*, I thought. A speeding ticket goes unpaid, a court summons goes unanswered. Shit escalates. Incidents become ordeals. I tried to speak slowly, to keep my voice calm. "We're dealing with this now because I was never notified about the charges, because when I emailed you about it a year ago, you told me no one was pursuing it."

There was a long pause. I dropped my head onto the table.

"I don't suppose you still have any of those emails?" he asked.

"You mean *you* don't have them?" It occurred to me that I was definitely not on an episode of *Homicide*. I hurried home, dug the emails out of my inbox, and a few minutes later I forwarded them along.

"Now we're in business," he told me the next time we spoke. "This proves it; they're the ones who dropped the ball on this, not us."

"That's terrific," I said. "What now?"

"Now, we need to plan a time for you to come back to Virginia so you can self-report."

Self-report. I imagined holding out my hands for cuffs, my fingers for prints. Then I instructed myself to stop imagining. I needed to keep myself rooted in reality if I was going to get through the next few weeks.

"And what does self-reporting entail?" I asked.

"Well," he said, as though this were all the most common thing in the world. "It involves you coming back to Virginia to be arrested."

A few weeks later, I stood in front of my closet, staring at the blouses and skirts I no longer wore now that I'd stopped teaching, wondering what one wears to be arrested. Nothing I owned seemed quite right; every outfit seemed too dowdy or too casual, ill-fitting or overly bright. I had one pair of taupe trousers, but buttoning them would result in broken blood vessels. My friend Beth, who was my kids' occasional babysitter, sprawled across my bed and tried to comfort me.

"They must have shrunk," she suggested.

"Yes, everything is shrinking. I'm staying the same." I stepped out of the pants, dropped them into my suitcase. "Do you think it's still baby weight when the baby is almost three?" I asked her.

"Who cares what you wear? I think you're overthinking this. It's going to be like paying a speeding ticket."

I hoped she was right; at the same time, I doubted it. It wasn't only the warrant I had to see to, but my initial arraignment in court. Because I lived out of state, my lawyer arranged for it to happen in a single trip, a process that would normally take weeks. I would meet him at a local jail where the charge would be processed. Because I was self-reporting, because I didn't pose any immediate threat to my victims, I'd be released without bond, given a time and day to appear in court for the arraignment, where my lawyer would present to the judge the agreement he'd made with the prosecutor. He'd told me about this agreement a few days before with a great deal of excitement. It was exactly what he'd hoped for.

I also found out what I was being charged with. This apparently had taken the authorities some time to determine—because there is no statute in Virginia (lots of other states too) for dealing with a case like mine. But you can't just charge someone with misdemeanor Lousy Parenting or Behaving in a Way We Don't Like. There needs to be an actual law on the books being violated. They went with contributing to the delinquency of a minor. The buying-beer-for-teens rap. It's item 18.2 in the *Code of Virginia*. Part i pertains to anyone who "willfully contributes to, encourages, or causes any act, omission, or condition that renders a child delinquent, in need of services, in need of supervision."

The prosecutor would agree not to pursue the charge of contributing to the delinquency of a minor if I completed one hundred hours of community service and twenty hours of parenting education over the course of nine months. I would be allowed to meet these terms in the State of Illinois. If I stayed out of trouble during this period and provided documentation of having met these requirements, it would demonstrate that I'd learned my lesson. The charge would be dropped. It would disappear, and I could put it all behind me.

As I listened to my lawyer describe the terms, I felt relief, but also awareness at the absurdity of it all, a feeling that I still didn't fully understand the legal context of what was happening.

"I don't get it," I told him. "Contributing to the delinquency of a minor? It makes no sense."

He told me it wasn't so unusual. In 2007, the state had tried to pass an ordinance that would penalize civilians who left a child under six alone in a vehicle if the conditions within the vehicle, including temperature, or in the immediate vicinity of the vehicle presented a risk to the health or safety of the child, and make it a misdemeanor for multiple offenses. The penalty for a first offense would be a hundred-dollar civil penalty—in other words, a ticket. But the legislation didn't go far and never came to pass; instead, the act of leaving a kid in a car would continue to fall into a legal gray area. The extent of this grayness became clear to me only later, when I spoke with other mothers who'd been charged with half a dozen different crimes for similar acts, everything from felony child neglect to misdemeanor child endangerment.

"Although historically a matter of state law, the child welfare system has become increasingly federalized through a series of statutes passed by Congress since 1974," writes David Pimentel, a lawyer who has written about the legal issues of parents' rights, in *Fearing the Bogeyman*.

In 1995, the Senate Committee on Labor and Human Resources issued a report finding that the rate of unsubstantiated reports of child abuse and neglect had skyrocketed and was "overwhelming an already overburdened child protective system." Congress settled on language that is in effect today, defining child abuse and neglect as any "recent act or failure to act which presents an imminent risk of serious harm." In this regard, I was lucky. Contributing to the delinquency of a minor was only a misdemeanor. It might keep me from getting another teaching job. It might prevent me from ever adopting a child, or it could be held against me should I ever be involved in a custody dispute, but at least it wasn't a felony. My lawyer explained that the charge was a bit of a stretch given the offense, but technically "contributing to delinquency" included the act of "rendering a minor in need of services."

"So for example," he said, "if you'd left your son there and not come back, someone from social services would have needed to come, bring him in, make sure he was safe and such."

"But I did come back. I came back after a few minutes."

"A gray area," he repeated. Then he went on to remind me that in my case, it wasn't just that I'd left my son, but that someone had seen me do it and stood there and recorded it and called the cops and given them the video. In cases like these, the judgment of a stranger, a neighbor, any person passing by was as, if not more, important than the judgment of the parent.

"A Good Samaritan," I said. "They couldn't have just talked to me directly? Am I so intimidating?"

"Look," he said. "Here's how I see it. I'm glad we live in a world where people are watching out for kids. I'm glad that when a concerned someone thinks they're seeing something wrong taking place, they get involved. No one wants the kid they pass by in a parking lot to end up on the six o'clock news. That's a good thing. But in your case, what you did wasn't malicious. It wasn't neglectful. It was a temporary lapse in judgment. This is what we need to stress."

"A concerned someone," I repeated to the lawyer.

I picture this concerned someone standing beside my car, inches from my child, holding a phone to the window, recording him as he played his game on the iPad. I imagined the person backing away as I came out of the store, watching me return to the car, recording it all, not stopping me, not saying anything, but standing there and dialing 911 as I drove away. *Bye, now.* At this point, almost a year had passed since it happened. I could hear my lawyer shuffling papers. I looked down and saw that my hands were shaking. My hands were shaking, but unlike before, I wasn't afraid. I thought of Lenore Skenazy: *It's not rooted in any true change or any real danger.*

"I don't know," I said. "It doesn't sound to me like I committed the crime I'm being charged with. I didn't render him in need of services. He was fine. He was perfectly safe in that car for a few minutes. Maybe I should go to trial."

The lawyer's response was instant and unequivocal. "I don't think you want to do that. This is going to be handled in juvenile court, and the juvenile courts are notorious for erring on the side of protecting the child. I would strongly advise not taking any risk."

I can't remember if he said it or only implied it, but either way, the warning took root. *You don't want to lose your kids over this.* It was the first time the idea had skulked out of the darkest, most anxious corners of my mind. My lawyer and I said we'd talk later. I thought I was going to be sick.

For my day in juvenile court, I finally decided on a pair of tailored trousers and a shapeless, lavender blouse. I wanted to look composed but not businesslike, educated but not urbane, feminine but not sexy; in other words, I wanted to embody the almost unsexed softness of motherhood. In conservative, rural-suburban central Virginia, this is how a good mother was supposed to look. The good mothers I had grown up with were quiet, gentle-mannered Christian women. In the winter, they wore sweaters with reindeer on them. In summer, they wore loose, floral blouses. They wore Mary Kay lipstick and permed their hair and rolled hot dogs in crescent buns on special occasions and deferred to their husbands. My household was different. My mother, a loving, frenetic New York Jew with wild mood swings and a poorly calibrated social sensor, was a different story. She would be of no use in helping me dress for court.

"You ready, Kimmy?" my father called from down the hallway, the same way he called for years to make sure I was awake and dressing for school. I was staying with my parents for my self-reporting visit. My dad had taken the day off from work to take me to the Chesterfield County Jail, where the lawyer would meet us.

"Ready," I called back, applying the lightest shade of lipstick I could find.

My father was wearing one of his work suits—gray, wool; he already looked uncomfortable in the summer heat even before we'd stepped out of the house. When he asked the day before if I wanted him to come with me, I'd said he didn't have to, that I'd be fine on my own. Then a few minutes later I realized how much I needed him. Nothing too terrible was going to happen to me if my father was there beside me. I recognized this way of thinking as a holdover from my childhood—but at that moment I experienced it once again as fact. I remembered Felix's self-assured words: *I think it's your fault.* I remembered the car accident I'd been in as a child, the thought that my mother shouldn't have let us get hurt. I remembered an Israeli friend whose brother had died in an accident in the desert at the age of sixteen. She'd been twelve at the time, and she told me the hardest part of the grieving process was trying to convince her parents that it was not their fault, that they were not omnipotent. "I was just a kid," she told me. "I wasn't ready to learn that lesson, but I had to." How awful it is, this realization we all must come to, that our parents are not, in fact, gods; that try as they might, there are times when they can't protect us.

We drove across town (if you can call the expanse of unconnected suburban developments a *town*) to the courthouse. It was a beautiful day. Sunny. Clear. I'd lived in Chesterfield County for the first eighteen years of my life. I'd been to its schools, its parks, its hospitals, its malls, but I'd never been to its jail. Growing up, I was the kid who didn't go out with friends to a party until we'd designated a driver. If my friends were smoking pot, I wouldn't inhale for fear it would irritate my asthma. The one time I was caught by a local cop making out in the back seat of a car with my boyfriend, I appeared so mortified and stricken that the officer tried to comfort me and told me it wasn't that big a deal. Now here I was, almost thirty-four years old, pulling into the sprawling suburban complex that included the Chesterfield County Jail. I'm not sure what I expected a jailhouse to look like, but it wasn't this.

"Where are we?" I asked my dad. "I keep looking for a Gap Outlet." There was an empty drive with a wide, manicured median, oak trees planted at equal intervals, a roundabout separating off four large parking lots filled with SUVs, silver and black. "It looks like a strip mall."

"Better than it looking like a jail."

We were early, so we went to a Starbucks, got cups of coffee, sat in his car, futzed with our phones. I texted Pete that we were there, waiting.

Are you in handcuffs? he texted back.

Not yet. How are the babies?

Violet says she won't poop until you get home. Other than that, fine.

I tried to respond with something snarky, but didn't have the heart.

I'm sorry about all this. I'm so sorry.

Stop.

I still can't believe this is happening. I feel so ridiculous.

You're not ridiculous. The State of Virginia is ridiculous.

I love you, I texted back. Then I looked up and saw my lawyer standing on the sidewalk, waving for us to come over.

I soon learned that if you are going to be arrested for child endangerment or child neglect or contributing to the delinquency of a minor or any other crime against your own child, or really if you're going to engage with the criminal justice system period, it is very beneficial to be like me: white, educated, professional, and middle class. It is very beneficial to look like a person with resources, a person of privilege.

We walked up to the front of the jail. There was a steel-reinforced door with a number-code lock, high bulletproof windows. In front of the door, a fence wrapped around the building, so to approach it, you had to first use an intercom, announce your visit, and be buzzed in. My lawyer pushed on the intercom. "Hello?" No one answered.

The parking lot was perfectly quiet. So many cars. No people. The building was a box of gray cement and cast wide shadows. I stood in the shade, my back to the heat. As the lawyer buzzed again, another family approached, a man, woman, and girl who looked to be eleven or twelve years old. All three were morbidly obese, their expressions pained. They didn't speak as they approached. I tried to guess what had brought them here. Were they visiting a prisoner? Had one of the parents come to self-report like me? The man sat down on a low, stone bench a few feet away from where I stood. He sat with his legs parted and leaned his head over, letting it hang between his knees. A few moments passed before I realized he was crying. "What do you want to do?" the woman was saying to him, leaning over him. "What do you want to do?"

He answered without looking up. "I don't know. I don't want to go to jail."

I turned to my father. We were both listening and trying not to listen. The man continued to sob. The girl kept her distance, looked at the ground. Whatever this man had done, whatever had happened, could this place possibly be the answer to this family's problems? Could this place possibly be the answer to anything? The sun beat down on the pale cement, reflected off the coils of razor wire surrounding the building.

The lawyer buzzed again. "I have a client who's here to self-report. I called ahead and spoke to Janet. She said it might be possible to take care of this quickly."

Yes, I thought, *let's please take care of this quickly.* Even as this idea took shape, I recognized it as code, shorthand for: There is a person here with paid legal representation, a person in an expensive lavender blouse, holding a Starbucks latte; a person who often goes through the expedited security line in airports and is accustomed to things moving smoothly. This is not a black person or a poor person or a morbidly obese redneck with a string of DUIs waiting here. Can we move things along?

I saw what was happening, the way my privilege was shielding me from the more unpleasant elements of the process, and a part of me recognized that it was wrong to quietly and gratefully accept this protection. Another, stronger part of me was fine with this. I was too scared to choose fairness over my being able to avoid being fingerprinted or having to wait for hours alone in a cell while my case was processed.

"Hold on one sec," a voice answered.

While we waited, the lawyer turned to me. "Now, they won't let us go in with you. But don't worry, we'll be here waiting. There shouldn't be any problem. You'll go in, hand them the warrant. They'll get you registered, fingerprinted, assigned a court date—which should be tomorrow 'cause of the calls I made—then they should release you without bail. Shouldn't be any problem."

"And what if there is a problem?" I asked, somehow only now truly understanding that I was walking into a jail, alone, to be arrested.

The intercom buzzed again. "Send her in."

"There won't be," he said.

And then the fence opened and I walked inside.

So here is jail, I thought when I entered the waiting room. It looked like a post office or DMV but without the frills. It was just a space. A cement floor. Cinder-block walls. A few vents along the ceiling blowing cold air. Across the room, a black desk sat behind a pane of bulletproof glass with a small, round, metal intercom in the center. There was an empty chair before the desk. "Hello?" I said.

No one answered. After a moment, the door beside the glass opened and a young, male officer came toward me. "You Kim Brooks?" he asked.

I nodded, held out my warrant. "I'm here to—"

"Got it," he said.

He couldn't have been much older than twenty-two. He had short-cropped hair, a boyish blush to his cheeks. He looked like one of the kids I'd known in high school, and for a moment I considered asking which one he'd gone to, then thought better of it. We were standing beside a narrow desk against the wall, the kind with pens attached on chains, plastic bins of forms. I handed him the creased sheet of paper. He looked at it, jotted something down, pulled up a schedule on his phone. "All righty. What do we got here? Wow, you came all the way from Illinois? You work up there?"

I nodded again, mystified but also grateful that the person arresting me should be so friendly, so polite.

"What sort of work you do up there?"

"I'm a writer," I told him, and then instantly wondered if that was the wrong thing to say, if I should have stuck with teacher or stay-at-home mom. But before I could backtrack, he was nodding, saying, "Very cool. Don't know many writers. What kind of things you write?"

"Oh, this and that. Mostly I stay at home with the kids."

He smiled as he filled in the form. "All right, looks like I got you on the court schedule for tomorrow at 8:30 A.M. The address is written here at the bottom."

He handed me back the paper, smiled in a way that told me we were finished.

"That's it?" I said. "No fingerprints?"

He made a dismissive gesture with his hand. "I don't think that's necessary, do you? You're not gonna flee the country, are you?"

"No," I said. "Definitely not. I have two little kids. No fleeing for me."

"Just make sure to get there on time tomorrow. It's the juvenile courthouse. Show up when you're supposed to. Bring your lawyer. Smile. And wear something nice." He pointed to my blouse. "Like that."

I think he winked at me. Maybe he was only blinking. Maybe it was the light. Yes, it would be okay. I realized for the first time that I'd been shaking, but now I felt calm. It wasn't such a big deal after all. A momentary lapse in judgment. A misunderstanding.

When I left the building, my lawyer was gone; only my father remained, waiting. The lawyer had another appointment and had to run, apparently. So did my father, for that matter, but he would never leave me in a moment like this.

"How was it?" he said, his usual ironic smile creeping up.

"Brutal," I said. "Full-body cavity search."

"Another Starbucks, then?" he asked.

We were walking toward the parking lot when I said, "Hey, what happened to that other family, the crying guy?"

"Eh, not so good."

I thought he was going to say more, but he didn't. I was in my thirties and my father hadn't yet lost the impulse to protect me from all the unpleasantness of the world.

The next day, both my parents accompanied me to the juvenile courthouse for my arraignment. My mother found the ordeal too upsetting to endure without sedation. She popped a Xanax and rode in the back seat, half sleeping. The courthouse, again, was not what I was expecting. There were kids there, first of all. Lots of them. Somehow, I hadn't seen that coming—juveniles in a juvenile courthouse—but there they were, teenagers, tweens, toddlers, and infants in their portable car seats, and every age and stage in between. Most of them seemed bored or oblivious. They looked the way kids looked in waiting rooms. Only the parents seemed different, more anxious, pacing, whispering to one another, staring at the sheets of paper that told them when and where they were supposed to be. There was a long hallway and at least a dozen different courtrooms, numbered and lettered above the door. 7D was my room. My time to appear, 8:30. At 9:00, the bailiff still hadn't called my name, which was fine with me, because to my horror and amazement, my lawyer was running late.

"Where the hell is he?" my mother asked, opening her eyes for a moment. "For the money you're spending, he couldn't be on time?"

I took a deep breath. I tried to think of what I would say to the judge if the lawyer didn't show up. *A lapse in judgment. A temporary lapse in judgment. Regret. Remorse. Never again! No, that was the Holocaust. Never before. I had never done this before. A terrible mistake.*

We were called into the courtroom along with thirty other people. Again, they weren't what I was expecting. This was juvenile court, and I was expecting juvenile delinquents and the parents of juvenile delinquents—these people surrounding me were just parents. Tired, nervous, flustered, struggling parents. What were they all doing here? What was I doing here?

The judge entered the courtroom. I'd been hoping for a wise and magnanimous-looking woman, an older woman with a mane of silver hair and compassionate hands and searching eyes. I'd been hoping for Marilynne Robinson with a robe and gavel. Instead, a wan middle-aged man came into the room, small and bald and moving quickly, like a squirrel. His hands were not compassionate and his eyes were not searching. At first, his goal seemed to be to move through his list of defendants as quickly as possible, calling names, assigning public defenders, scheduling arraignments. He spoke with a thick Chesapeake drawl that reminded me of a sixth-grade social studies teacher I hadn't thought of in twenty years, a man who'd yelled at a classroom full of twelve-year-olds that "the Civil War was fought over secession, not slavery, and don't let any damn Yankee ever tell you different." I remembered this, and then suddenly the judge was yelling in exactly the same tone, chiding a young black man for having shown up in his courtroom—*his* courtroom—in improper attire. The man was wearing long shorts and a T-shirt. "There are certain judges who will not even hear a case when the defendant is dressed in improper attire," he lectured. "I don't happen to be one of those judges, but you should know that there are many, sir, in case you find yourself in this situation again."

My father turned to me. We exchanged a look. I glanced back at the door, and at that moment, my lawyer appeared. When my name was called, a few minutes later, he stood and explained to the judge what had happened, that I'd self-reported all the way from the state of Illinois, that he had discussed my case with the prosecutor involved and that the prosecutor had agreed to a continuance, a period of nine months during which I'd be allowed to complete one hundred hours of community service and parenting education. I'd agreed to these conditions. I had no record, no strikes against me. I had a husband who worked at a university, a father who was a physician in the community. I'd attended the University of Virginia. I was a good mother who'd had a temporary lapse in judgment.

The judge nodded slowly as my lawyer presented this information. His lips turned up slightly in an expression that seemed to indicate approval. He seemed to particularly approve of the fact that I'd self-reported from Illinois. "Very well," he said, signing the paper, moving on to the next case.

PART II

THE COST OF FEAR

6

WHAT A HORRIBLE MOTHER

Sometimes I think about how the story might have ended here. I came home from Virginia more than a little embarrassed, more than a little ashamed, but basically grateful that there would be no more waiting and wondering; that in nine months, if I completed my one hundred hours of community service and twenty hours of parenting education, it would all be over and I could put what had happened behind me. Maybe in a few years, Pete and I would even joke about it. Most parents have their own examples of parenting-fail family folklore, stupid mistakes that could have ended really badly but didn't, and so over time, they become funny.

Don't get me wrong. One hundred hours of community service seemed like a lot, especially since I'd been struggling to squeeze writing into the limited hours my children were at school. But it wasn't as though I was going to jail. It wasn't as though I was losing custody of my kids or being placed on a registry. In the grand scheme of things, I told myself, it was closer to annoyance than tragedy, so the best thing was probably to get it over with and then move on. As my lawyer had pointed out, I wasn't being forced to pick up litter along the side of the road—although in retrospect that might have made me feel more useful than what I ended up doing. Picking up litter is something that needs to be done. It benefits everyone, beautifies a shared public space. What *I* ended up doing instead was more of the things I'd already been doing, more of what it seemed every parent I knew was doing. I volunteered for the organizations from which my own kids benefited—their soccer leagues and schools. I attended bake sales and fundraisers, supervised practices and organized snack assignments. My lawyer assured me that these were perfectly acceptable activities for fulfilling my volunteer hours, since they involved giving time to nonprofit organizations, and that the judge would find them appropriate, since, after all, my crime was not against the larger community but against my own "endangered" children. If my failing had been inattention to my kids, then hyper-attention seemed a suitable punishment. And so as I put in my time and logged my hours, it occurred to me that I was finally becoming the thing I'd never wanted to be: a housewife.

On a few occasions, I did wonder aloud to friends or family if perhaps the ordeal might be something I should consider writing about (I'd been writing essays about domestic life and motherhood for a few years), but they were quick to point out all the ways that might backfire. People went nuts when it came to these kinds of parenting issues, one friend told me. The discussions were always so black and white, so combative. I had no desire to become some kind of parenting-rights advocate, so what could be gained by writing about my experience? Also, my lawyer had made it clear that under no circumstances was I to publish anything about the case until it had officially concluded. "Hell hath no fury like an embarrassed prosecutor" was how he put it.

Also, even beyond legal constraints, there was the simple matter of stigma. I was beginning to understand that it didn't matter if what I'd done was dangerous or wrong; it only mattered if other parents felt it was dangerous and wrong. When it comes to kids' safety, feelings were facts, and such "facts" often led to disapproval and judgment. If all this wasn't enough reason to keep what had happened to myself, there was the additional issue that, well . . . the whole thing was just so weird. Surely, I thought to myself in the weeks after my court appearance, it took a rare and special kind of fuckup to allow this kind of thing to happen.

It reminded me of how, during my freshman year of college, I'd kept a Costco-sized jar of dill pickles on top of my bureau, and one day, opening the bureau to find a pair of jeans, it crashed down right beside me, an inch shy of falling on my head. I still remember how my dorm room reeked of garlic and dill for most of the semester, and also how my roommate had said at the time as I stood there amid the shards of glass, "Only you, Kim. Only you could come that close to being killed by a falling jar of pickles." What had happened in Virginia felt like the emotional equivalent of a falling jar of pickles. Best to try to forget about it or pretend it never happened. I well might have, if it weren't for one conversation.

A few years earlier, a friend introduced me to a woman named Sarah Ahlm, a clinical social worker who worked with many families around the city. She had three kids of her own, and often we'd chat about parenthood and family life. I liked Sarah. Also, I trusted her. And so one day when she asked if I had any fun plans for the weekend, I told her that I was going to be spending it baking cookies for my daughter's preschool fundraiser. "Look at you," she said. And then, because, as Pete had so astutely put it, I've never not told anyone anything, I found myself explaining to her that it was not exactly something I was doing out of the goodness of my heart.

I summarized the whole ordeal for her as succinctly as I could, then braced myself for whatever reaction might follow. But instead of judging, Sarah said simply, almost offhandedly, that almost the exact same thing had happened to a friend of hers, and that after a year, her friend was just finally getting off of Illinois's DCFS child neglect registry.

I was taken aback by the coincidence and told her so.

"I know," she said, but then she added, "To tell you the truth, though, I'm not sure that it is a coincidence. I think this kind of thing is happening more than anyone knows."

I told Sarah I'd read about a few cases that year, heard about a number of them from Lenore Skenazy, but not enough to suggest any real frequency or pattern.

"Right," she said. "But then again, it's not exactly the kind of thing people talk about. My friend certainly didn't tell many people when it happened to her. No one wants to be the neighborhood mom accused of neglecting her children. I think there are probably a lot of people who have similar things happen to them but who don't come forward."

As I drove home that day, I kept turning her words over, and in the months that followed, they'd come back to me from time to time. What if Sarah was right? What if what had happened to me was not an isolated incident, but a trend? How could anyone begin to grapple with the implications of this kind of criminalization if we couldn't even admit that it was happening?

All that year, while I baked cookies and manned fundraiser booths and learned how to dribble a soccer ball so I could fill in as an assistant coach at a youth soccer league, as I signed up for and recorded my hours of mom-unteering, I thought about Sarah's friend, and about other women like her. I thought about how lucky I'd been in the end, lucky that I had family who could help me pay for a lawyer, lucky that I had the resources to go back to Virginia and self-report, lucky that at the last minute, my lawyer had shown up in the courtroom, lucky that I'd been able to fulfill my volunteer hours in activities that didn't force me to miss work or spend less time with my children. I thought about what might have happened if my lawyer hadn't made it there in time and I'd been thrown into the position of all the other parents in that room, those who couldn't afford their own defense attorneys and had to depend on the counsel of whatever overworked public defender the system sent their way. What if I'd had to defend myself? What if I didn't have a nice, professional outfit from Ann Taylor Loft in my closet and had shown up in this judge's court in dress he deemed inappropriate? What if I'd never made it to *his* court at all because I couldn't afford to fly back to Virginia, or to take days off of work to do so, or to find someone to watch my children? What if by some circumstance or misfortune I'd missed my court date? What if my record wasn't perfectly clean and, like many people, I had some minor past infraction? What if I was in the middle of a custody dispute? What if I lived in the Commonwealth of Virginia, and in addition to this criminal process, I was also facing a separate investigation from Child Protective Services?

In the weeks and months after my court date, I continued to fixate on these what-ifs and the other women like Sarah's friend who might be facing them. And I continued to wonder what, in the end, the cost of these fear-based policies was for the individuals being charged with crimes, for parents in general and mothers in particular, and for society as a whole. And just as important, I wondered, how exactly was this cost being distributed among us? Could it be that the cost of fear was different for mothers as opposed to fathers, for single parents as opposed to married ones, for the poor, middle, and upper classes? After all, it's one thing to insist children can never be unsupervised to an economically privileged, partnered, professional woman who can afford nannies, babysitters, a barrage of organized enrichment activities—a woman who has the means to absorb any burden. It is quite another to say it to a single mother, a poor mother, a mother who struggles to pay for housing, health insurance, food, and clothing, much less quality childcare. What, exactly, was the price of fear and who exactly was paying it?

In June of 2014, months after I'd appeared in juvenile court in Virginia, after the prosecutor had formally agreed not to prosecute my case, and after I'd completed my mandated community service, I wrote an essay for *Salon* titled "The Day I Left My Son in the Car," in which I told the story of my experience in that parking lot in Virginia. Within a few days of the story's publication, it had been viewed six million times. It elicited tens of thousands of readers' comments, readers eager to express their sympathy, or to elaborate on my overall unfitness as a mother and as a human being.

Many readers sympathized with me and voiced horror at the kind of vigilante parent policing I'd described. Other readers echoed my frustration, lamenting how many of the freedoms parents had given their children a generation ago had now become impossible. Some parents recalled moments when they, too, had felt judged or self-conscious or unable to parent the way they wanted to because of their own irrational beliefs or broader social pressures. These commenters generally argued that I hadn't done anything wrong, and that my arrest revealed more about our shared state of media-fed paranoia and culture of misogyny than about my own competence as a mother.

Others, meanwhile, viewed me as a symbol of everything wrong with parents, mothers, women, and the world.

"Try being a parent," one commenter suggested. "That is what you are, it is your job."

"If you didn't want to be responsible and parent your children, why did you have them?" wondered another. One reader reasoned,

"People get hurt, people get shot. Because people are stupid enough to leave a child in the car." And still another reader wrote, "Watch your freaking kid. Period," and declared, "God bless the person who calls the cops!"

The tone of the comments varied from indignation to disgust to enlightened disbelief. Some readers took an edifying tone and tried to explain to me what I had somehow missed: "When you left your four-year-old son in the car, you abandoned him in public. Of course someone called the police." The reader went on to wonder why this wasn't obvious to me. Others used my story as a call for increased vigilance on the part of bystanders: "WAKE THE HELL UP PEOPLE AND DO SOMETHING WHEN YOU SEE AN UNATTENDED TODDLER IN A CAR!!" or "You made a mistake. You were wrong. What you did could have resulted in a tragedy. Anyone who puts their child in harm's way is irresponsible and those that defend them are pathetic."

Other readers offered me advice on how to be a better mother in the future, noting (fairly) that I never should have allowed my son to whine his way out of coming into the store with me in the first place: "Train your child to listen to you; it's your job to teach them about life. Not to cater to their whims. P.S. I'll report you for leaving your DOG in the car."

Another reader wondered, "How many kids have to be abducted, for us as parents to get it to our bleeding heads . . . that we are the guardians of our children's well being and we should not even for a bleeding second compromise it!" And many responded anecdotally, like the woman who confided, "Once I left my 4 year old in the car, in front of a grocery store in small town while I ran in for a head of lettuce. When I came back . . . she was gone! I raced around the parking lot frantically, only to notice another woman parked in back of me with my daughter laughing away and waving. She said she wanted to scare me for doing such a stupid thing. She did! I never did THAT again!!!!"

If these commenters felt they had something to teach me about parenthood, others took a less patient, more excoriating tone. "What a bitch she is!!!! . . . She is a bad mother!!! . . . What a piece of shit mom. What a dumb, lazy moron. What a dumb cunt. Shame on her!! Shame on you. Shame on any woman who doesn't want to take care of her own kids. What a horrible mother! Shame!"

And yet, in response to these comments, there were still others who not only came to my defense, but went on to point out the toxicity and cruelty of others' judgment. One reader noted how "in my mother's time, you sacrificed a significant portion of your life in order to raise kids. These days, it seems you're expected to sacrifice your entire life. No thanks. Parents used to be responsible for providing basic necessities and keeping kids reasonably safe. Now parents deal with constant judgment up to and including people who want to throw you in jail for leaving your kid out of your sight for a few minutes. This is why I don't have kids."

As I skimmed the various Facebook page skirmishes that seemed to be igniting around my essay and the response pieces that cropped up in other publications, I realized that my story, unusual as it might seem, had tapped into a common and long-established tradition of mother-shaming, the communal ritual of holding up a woman as a "bad mother," a symbol on which we can unleash our collective, mother-related anxieties, insecurities, and rage. I guess, at some level, I had expected it. Sanctification and public shaming are two sides of the same coin. A culture can't venerate and idealize the selfless, martyred mother as much as we do without occasionally throwing an agreed-upon bad mommy onto the pyre. I'd practically lit the tinder and sharpened the skewer for them.

What I hadn't expected, however, were all the other "bad mothers" who reached out to me for support and guidance in the months after I published my essay, all the mothers who contacted me to say how grateful they were, because they had thought they were the only people in the world to whom this had ever happened, because they'd been so scared and so ashamed.

It turned out Sarah was right; there were more of us than I suspected.

The day it happened to Debra Harrell, she wasn't worried and she wasn't running late.

She wasn't stressed out about catching a plane or buying a pair of headphones. For her, it was a day like any other day; she was up early, heading to the McDonald's, where she'd worked every morning for the previous five years. Harrell was on the clock when it happened, trying to support herself and the nine-year-old daughter she was raising on her own, but the fact that she was working didn't help her when a concerned citizen noticed Harrell's daughter at the park, playing contentedly but without supervision, and decided to call the police.

Debra grew up in Atlanta. She moved to Florida as a young woman, married, became pregnant. By the time of the girl's second birthday, it was clear that the marriage wasn't working and Debra decided it was time for a change, time to go someplace new. She filed for divorce, packed up her daughter and all of their belongings, and took a bus north, back toward her home state of Georgia. Now that she had a child, she wanted to be close to her mother who still lived in Atlanta, but she decided against returning to the city itself. Raising a toddler, city life no longer appealed to her. She preferred the country—a small town where she could become friends with her neighbors, feel like a part of a community, give her daughter peace and quiet and space and fresh air. The two of them settled in the town of North Augusta, rented a small apartment in a complex where there seemed to be a lot of other families with kids. Debra didn't have a car, so shortly after settling in, she walked down the street to a McDonald's and applied for a job.

For five years she worked at the restaurant, first as a clerk and then as a manager. While she worked, her next-door neighbor, a woman who stayed home with her own children, watched Debra's daughter. Eventually, her daughter started school. "She was always a good girl," Debra told me. "Never any trouble. Lots of friends, an honor-roll student."

The day that it happened, school was out, her daughter on summer vacation, which, as any working parent in this country knows, can be a logistical nightmare. American children often have ten, even twelve, weeks of summer vacation. Working parents often have two or three. In another era, parents might have relied on a network of extended kin, neighbors, or older siblings to keep an eye on vacationing kids who'd spend their days romping through sprinklers, playing sports, swimming, or exploring. But now, as K. J. Dell'Antonia noted recently in *The New York Times*, "in 2014, parents reported planning to spend an average of $958 per child on summer expenses . . . Those who can't afford camps or summer learning programs cobble together care from family members or friends, or are forced to leave children home alone."

Debra fell directly into that trap. On this particular day, her daughter didn't want to stay home, where the neighbor could keep an eye on her. It was a beautiful day. Her friends and schoolmates were outside, attending day camp, going to the park. She wanted to join them. The park where many of her friends played was close to the McDonald's where Harrell worked, about a mile away. It was a safe neighborhood, lots of kids, a big playground, water jets to keep cool; some volunteers from her church even brought snacks. Her daughter had a cell phone to call her mother if there was a problem, but Debra couldn't imagine what kind of problem there would be beyond a scraped knee. And so she was perplexed when she received a call not from her daughter but from the local police department.

The officer was calling from Richmond County Sheriff's Department.

"What's this about?" she asked them. "Is everything okay?"

He wouldn't give her any information. He'd tell her only that the North Augusta County sheriff wanted to see her in the precinct.

By the time Debra arrived, she was terrified. She'd been frantically trying to call her daughter's cell phone, but the phone was turned off. When she arrived at the precinct, she begged for information and was told that yes, her daughter was there, but she was not allowed to see her or talk to her. Her daughter was being held in a separate room, alone. Later, she would tell her mother that she'd assumed she had done something wrong at the playground and was going to be sent away to jail for it. Knowing her daughter would be terrified, Debra asked if her boyfriend or her neighbor could come pick the girl up. She was told this was not possible, that her daughter would be sent to foster care while the case was processed. After that, an officer told Debra that he wanted to hear from her what had happened, that he was going to film her and that she'd better tell the truth.

"I've got nothing to lie about," she said. "Why would I lie?" The officer then interrogated her in a private room, without an attorney present, filming the interrogation. I watched this video long before I spoke to Debra. It was aired on a local news channel soon after I wrote about my own experience. In the video, Debra is sitting on a chair in a dark room. She's crying, but she holds her voice steady, wipes her tears discreetly, her head bent forward.

"You're her mother, right?" the officer says to her.

"Yes, sir," Harrell answers.

"You understand that you're in charge of that child's well-being?"

"Yes, sir."

"That's not other people's job to do so."

"Yes, sir."

He tells Harrell that workers at the "feed-a-kid program" at the park have reported seeing Harrell's daughter there unattended several times. Harrell replies that she has not left her daughter "every day," as she doesn't work every day, to which the officer responds, "Don't give me that one-day-only crap."

"Yes, sir," she answers. "Yes, sir."

It is not possible to talk about the history of child-saving in America without also talking about race and class. When the officer interrogating Debra Harrell lectures her with almost palpable disdain—"You're her mother, right? You understand that you're in charge of that child's well-being?"—it's easy to imagine *the kind of mother* he sees before him: unemployed, dependent on state and federal benefits, maybe a substance abuser, maybe domestically abused; a dropout, multiple kids by multiple dads, none of whom are anywhere to be found. It's likely he does not see a mother working full-time to support her daughter, a mother who has weighed the risks and benefits of her own limited options for childcare. Instead of a person, he sees a symbol, an easy scapegoat to stand in for the complex web of economic, educational, and racial inequality that led to Debra Harrell's having so few options in the first place.

Unfortunately, there is nothing new about using child-centered sentiment as a cover for class-based hostility. The historian Paula Fass notes that it was after the Civil War that Americans first began to focus on the plight of threatened, neglected, and abandoned children, and to seriously question, "What after all was a child's due, and what were society's obligations to provide it? When did the interests of children override the authority of parents, and who determined this? What did it mean to be forced into an early adulthood, and how was this related to what Americans understood as a proper childhood?" By the end of the nineteenth century, rural to urban migration and industrialization stoked fears about the spread of "children of the streets"—the abused, orphaned, undernourished, and exploited foundlings that came to be seen as a grave threat to modern, American life.

Charles Loring Brace, a nineteenth-century reformer, founded New York City's Children's Aid Society in 1853, an organization dedicated to saving children from "hereditary pauperism" as well as the criminal consequences of maltreatment, homelessness, and abandonment. The society is largely remembered for initiating the "orphan train," from 1853 to the 1900s, an initiative that resettled more than 120,000 children from urban slums to new and more "suitable" homes in the West. Fass describes how, "in salvaging children from isolation and neglect, Brace and the Children's Aid Society hoped in the long run to save American society from the criminal consequences" of maltreatment and indecency. In 1875, New York passed the Children's Act, which aimed to remove children aged two through sixteen from poorhouses, including those who lived with their families. Reformers reasoned that protecting such children from the harmful influence of their parents was sufficient reason to break up families, and this trend continued through the end of the nineteenth and the start of the twentieth century, as "well-educated, well-connected, and well-raised" child-savers and reformers sought to teach the urban poor and newly immigrated how to better care for their children, and to rescue these children when their families did not prove up to the task. Thus, by the end of the nineteenth century, Fass writes, "the reconstruction of family life took place against a backdrop of abandoned children who were assumed to be the detritus of the new immigrant and working classes' lack of responsibility . . . The new standards of the family were class standards, as the reformers incorporated class ideals into the very notion of family decency. Indeed, the middle classes defined themselves in terms of these distinctions embedded in the very nature of family life."

As I read about these distinctions, I find myself recalling the conversation I had with David, my first lawyer, the night I returned to Chicago. "Listen," he'd said. "Try not to worry too much. I don't think you're the person they're after. You're not the kind of mom they'll throw the book at."

He'd been trying to reassure me, and I'd been so desperate for reassurance that I didn't stop to think about what he was implying. Now I wanted to ask him, "Well, what kind of person *are* they after? What kind of mother *do* they throw the book at?"

I decided to ask Diane Redleaf, founder and legal director of the Family Defense Center. She told me that they've represented parents from all socioeconomic stratums and that in her view all parents are vulnerable, but she concedes that "the cases tend to go away more quickly if they involve upper-middle-class or middle-class people . . . the whole way the police and prosecutors interact is different when they know there's going to be a fight about it." As Redleaf sees it, the biggest problem is that individuals, the people who called the police on Debra Harrell, are trusting a system that is inherently biased (as most systems are in this country) against poor people and people of color.

"There's an assumption," Redleaf told me, "among the general public, that it's always better to make a call, even if you're not sure what you're seeing, because these people are professionals and if there was no real neglect, then the system will sort it out. Well, what we find is, they often get it wrong when they try to sort it out. The caseworkers at protection agencies aren't licensed social workers. They often have minimal training. Police certainly aren't experts on parenting or childcare. So basically we as a society have entrusted people who have no real training or serious knowledge about children and families with critical issues involving children. And they are making decisions about who gets to be a parent and who gets to raise their children and whether you'll be labeled a child-abuser and unable to work."

In other, more ubiquitous words, if you see something, say something.

As I spoke with her, I began to understand what I'd first been able to ignore. I knew perfectly well what kind of parents they went after, what kind of mother they threw the book at—the kind who works at McDonald's and hasn't gone to college and can't hire a lawyer the moment she senses danger—the ones, like Debra Harrell, who aren't in a position to fight back.

When I contacted Harrell, almost two years had passed since she was arrested, but her case had only recently been dismissed. Even after so much time, she still found it difficult to talk about the incident and the emotional toll it had taken on her and on her daughter. She was held at the jail for only one day, but her daughter was sent to a group home, a foster care facility, for fourteen days. Eight days passed before the nine-year-old was allowed to speak to her mother. The hardest part, Harrell told me, was that until that day, her daughter had never spent the night away from her. She was in fourth grade, but still a mama's girl. Harrell slept in her daughter's bed, crying, every night that she was gone.

It's possible that no one outside her own circle of friends and family would have ever heard about her experience if it weren't for the fact that a few days after her arrest, the North Augusta Police Department shared the story of Harrell's prosecution with a local news station. The station aired the video of her interrogation, along with the tagline "Mother Confesses to Letting Her Daughter Play Alone in the Park." People were appalled by this public shaming, and the case came to the attention of Lenore Skenazy, who helped find

Harrell pro bono legal representation with Robert Phillips, a South Carolina attorney.

But even with Phillips's services, her case dragged on for nearly two years. After all this time, when I spoke to Harrell, it was clear that she still didn't entirely understand why this had happened, what purpose it had all served. "When I was a child," she told me, "I would walk two miles to the park. We rode our bikes up there every day with no problem, me and my friends. I don't see why parents shouldn't have the say-so if their own child is ready to go out there in the world. My baby, she's very responsible, so I wasn't worried. And when Robert, the attorney, came down and went to the park on a Friday to see what it was like, there were seventy-five people in that park. They had cameras. My daughter knows everyone there. Everybody knows each other at the park."

It simply never occurred to Harrell that one of those seventy-five people would assume she had abandoned her daughter and would call the police.

Now, finally, her case has been dropped, but still, the ordeal has had a lasting impact on Harrell's and her daughter's lives. After the arrest, Harrell was out of a job from the McDonald's where she'd worked for almost five years. The court proceedings took longer than she could have imagined.

"It was just a waiting process," she told me. "Everything was a wait. We went to court. They passed it off and we'd have to come back thirty days after I went to parenting classes. I was trying to go every day to get through it faster, but they wouldn't let me. I had to go once a week. I had to go there and listen to them tell me how to talk to my daughter, how to treat my daughter. But I didn't mind doing it. I just wanted it to be over."

At first, Harrell worried that she wouldn't be able to find another job. She applied for a position as a nursing aide, but when a background check was ordered, they found that she'd been charged with abandonment. Luckily, the woman interviewing Harrell remembered hearing her story in the news.

"Arrested for letting your daughter go to the park," Harrell remembers the woman saying. "I thought it was ridiculous then, and I think it's ridiculous now." She got the job and was able to move on with her life.

But for Harrell's daughter, the episode has had a more lasting impact. "It affected her more than it affected me," she told me. "She's been wanting to go on a vacation, go on a summer trip with me. But I still can't leave the state after two years. She's scared to go outside too, to walk up the street. She won't go nowhere. She won't go away with friends. She's too scared. They put fear in my baby's heart, and I don't like that, but I just talk to her and say, 'Baby, you're old enough now to go outside and live your life. You don't have to be in this house on a computer.' "

A case like Debra Harrell's, or like Shanesha Taylor's, the homeless single mother who was arrested and charged with two counts of felony child abuse in 2014 in Scottsdale, Arizona, and sentenced to eighteen years of supervised probation after leaving her two children in the car while she went on a job interview, demonstrate how class, race, and cultural bias can both motivate and complicate trends toward the criminalization of parenthood.

After I wrote about my arrest, I was surprised to find my story was being retold, sympathetically, in libertarian publications, such as *Reason*. The Free-Range Kids movement and the parents' rights movement has been adopted by this corner of the political universe as yet another example of how hard it has become to exercise one's freedom—in my case, the freedom to parent as one sees fit, within the confines of an oppressive and infantilizing nanny state. The problem with this argument, the movement's detractors are quick to point out, is that parenting, by definition, involves the well-being of minors whose rights must also be considered. We don't parent in a vacuum, just as we don't own guns in a vacuum or waste fossil fuels in a vacuum. Our actions as individuals affect other individuals and communities. The parent-child relationship makes it impossible, in other words, to talk about parenting strictly in terms of individual liberty. But cases like Harrell's reveal the issue to be more complicated than a conflict between individual freedom and parental responsibility.

David Pimentel explained it this way: "If you make it a crime to leave a child out of your sight or the sight of a nanny or another paid professional for a second, then you're basically saying that poor people can't be parents."

In a country that provides no subsidized childcare and no mandatory family leave, no assurance of flexibility in the workplace for employees, no universal preschool or early childhood education, and minimal safety nets or state-subsidized support services to parents and families, it is impossible to make it a crime to take your eyes off your children without also making it a crime to be poor. And not only does such a mind-set criminalize poverty and single, working-class parenthood, it also criminalizes Latino parenting cultures, European parenting cultures, African American parenting cultures, and all parenting cultures with a tradition of sibling care or informal community care or independent childhood activities.

"When you make it a crime to let your child play in a park or wait in a car," Pimentel says, "you're saying that good parenting is the kind of parenting practiced by affluent white people in suburban America at the beginning of the twenty-first century." Civil libertarians might disapprove of this criminalization because they see it as impinging on individual freedoms, but those on the other end of the political spectrum should be incensed by it too. I think of Debra Harrell sitting in that room with a white, male officer hovering over her, lecturing her on how to be a responsible mother, taking down her "confession" as she sits there crying, asking to please be allowed to speak to her daughter.

Pimentel is never surprised by such "confessions." He describes the immense fear and intimidation parents feel in these situations, their tendency to play it safe when it comes to the possibility of losing their children: "People are being intimidated into waiving their constitutional rights," he says, "which means, in effect, that they have no constitutional rights." This, I realized, is one of the most damaging consequences of new, intensive parenting mores. It is the price we pay for our fears.

Class-based animosity may be a strong motivating factor in the desire to teach "bad mothers" such as Debra Harrell a lesson, but in an odd way, it has also led to a different kind of vilification of middle- and upper-middle-class mothers. One mother who reached out to me not long after I wrote about my experience epitomizes this other kind of hostility. A white, affluent, stay-at-home mother living on Manhattan's Upper East Side, she was charged with felony child endangerment when, on the way home from visiting family in Connecticut, she left her sleeping four-year-old daughter in the car with the windows open for five minutes while she ran into a store. She hired a lawyer, traveled back and forth to Connecticut numerous times to appear in court, was subjected to a thorough investigation by Child Protective Services (which found no evidence of neglect or abuse), and eventually pleaded her case down to a lesser charge that could be satisfied with education and volunteering. She knew that it could have been much worse, but told me that all in all, it was one of the most humiliating experiences of her life. And perhaps the worst part of the whole ordeal came when she had to go to the local precinct to be fingerprinted and formally charged. "There was this female officer working at the station," she recounted, "who had to interview me for the report. And I could tell from the moment she realized what I was there for, she had decided I was a worthless, terrible person. She literally looked me up and down, looked at my clothes, my car. 'Stay-at-home Mommy's too busy shopping to take care of her kid?' she said. 'Does your husband know that's how you take care of his child while he's out earning the big bucks?' "

One of the findings of Barbara Sarnecka's study on risk assessment and moral judgment, the study in which people were asked to evaluate the danger children were in when left alone under different circumstances—and the moral "wrongness" of the parent who had left them—was that when participants were told a father had left his child for a few minutes to run into work, the level of risk to his child was equal to the risk when he left the child because of circumstances beyond his control (when he was struck unconscious by a car). When a woman was running into work, the moral judgment was closer to the level expressed at her going shopping or having an affair. I'll admit it—I love this finding. I relish the way it makes plain and undeniable something we all sort of know but aren't supposed to say: We might accept that mothers occasionally want to do other things besides mothering, that they might want to have a career, a social life, a full human existence. But we don't like it. We hate it, in fact. A father who is distracted for a few minutes by his myriad interests and obligations in the world of adult interactions is being, well, a father. A mother who does the same is failing her children.

In *Perfect Madness*, Judith Warner describes a similar strain of thinly veiled hostility toward working mothers in the coverage of one of the nineties' most publicized child-abuse cases, the trial of British au pair Louise Woodward for the murder of her eight-month-old charge, Matthew Eappen. Warner writes that "public sentiment turned most angrily not against the sullen-faced au pair but against Matthew's mother, whose crime, in many commentators' eyes, was that of having hired an au pair in the first place." She notes how the columnist Mike McManus wondered why the mother wasn't at home with her infant son when her husband, a physician, clearly earned enough to support them, and talk-radio callers accused her of being self-absorbed and materialistic, one going so far as to say, "Apparently the parents don't want a kid and now they don't have a kid."

When examining cases like these alongside those like Debra Harrell's, it becomes clear that motherhood has become a battleground on which prejudice and class resentment can be waged without ever admitting that's what we're doing. Middle- and upper-middle-class mothers can be excoriated for failing to appreciate the support that so many others lack. Working-class and poor mothers can be pilloried for their ignorance and inattentiveness and inability to provide the kind of care middle-class children receive. And those who criticize them can rest assured it's not women they hate, or even mothers; it's just *that* kind of mother, the one who, because of affluence or poverty, education or ignorance, ambition or unemployment, allows her own needs to compromise (or appear to compromise) the needs of her child. We hate poor, lazy mothers. We hate rich, selfish mothers. We hate mothers who have no choice but to work, but also mothers who don't need to work and want to do so.

You don't have to look very hard to see the common denominator.

I said as much to a friend not long ago, and he pushed back, wondering if *hate* was the right word.

I asked him what word he thought would better describe it, and he wondered if *contempt* might be more accurate.

"Hate," he said, "is personal. It's intimate. You hate the bully who picked on you, the boyfriend who dumped you, the person in the Mercedes SUV who cut you off and gave you the finger. Contempt, on the other hand, is more removed. It involves a level of condescension, a power differential. You feel contempt for the colleague who got the promotion she didn't deserve, or the panhandlers driving your property value down, or your lower-class relatives who don't know any better than to put the ketchup bottle on the dining room table with the tablecloth and nice china."

"So we feel contempt for those beneath us?" I suggested.

"Or those above us who we think belong beneath us."

As he said this, I thought about all the jabs and digs and thinly or not-at-all-veiled insults I'd heard directed at women throughout my life. I thought of all the mother-directed criticism I'd received, read, uttered, and overheard in my years, too wide-ranging in subject to categorize—and yet, I could, sort of. The mother (and maybe the woman) most vulnerable to attack is the one who doesn't know her place, the one trying to have or do or be more or less, higher or lower, than she is *supposed* to be. We want her to know her place, and we have no sympathy if any misfortune befalls her when she leaves it. We might not hate the rich mother, the poor mother, the ambitious or lazy mother, but we fear and scorn her refusal to stay put inside our notions of what a mother should be. We want her to know she should be careful, cautious, conscious that she is not so free to make and remake her own story.

After my article was published, after I had spoken with Debra Harrell and had heard from so many other "bad moms," I began to understand what Lenore Skenazy meant when I spoke to her that first time: *You don't have to tell me your story; I'll tell you your story.* After a while, it begins to feel as though these scenarios follow a script. But for one woman I spoke to, the script was different.

"I am the horrible Starbucks mother!" Julie Koehler wrote to me in the subject heading of her email. The Starbucks in question was located in Evanston, a suburb of Chicago. The "horrible" act to which she referred had occurred in a parking lot a few months before when

Julie let her three daughters wait in her minivan, watching an episode of *Dora the Explorer* while she ran into a strip-mall Starbucks to grab a much-needed cup of coffee. By this point, you know how it goes. A concerned citizen. A phone call. A nearby cop approaches the vehicle. *Where is your mother?* he demands. Julie's daughter gestures toward the Starbucks, but the officer misinterprets and walks instead into the adjacent nail salon, because of course, there's nothing a lazy, self-centered mother loves to do more than get her nails done while she's neglecting her children. Judgment comes first; risk assessment follows. When he doesn't find her in the salon, he goes back to the car just as Julie is returning with her coffee. She sees him, sees her children are upset. "What's going on?" she asks. But here is where the story diverges, because Julie is not a writer or a stay-at-home mom or a secretary or a professor or a McDonald's manager. Julie Koehler is a senior public defender with twenty years' experience in Chicago's criminal justice system, and unlike me, unlike Debra Harrell, unlike any of the other mothers I spoke to, she knew what her rights were as she approached the officer; and, as she would tell me later when we spoke in person, smiling a little, almost laughing, "I cross-examine cops all day long. I'm not about to be intimidated by a badge."

There is nothing about Julie's person or children or two-story suburban house in Evanston, Illinois, that reveals her to be a woman who spends her days defending people accused of murder, rape, assault, larceny, and a potpourri of other violent crimes. We'd been planning to meet at her office, but after a late cancellation of a trial, she invited me to talk in her home. The kids had a day off from school. They had friends coming over. "You know how it is," she said. "They're at the age where they keep themselves busy while we talk."

The first thing I noticed when she showed me inside her house was how clean and organized everything was. Toys in the basement. Kitchen stuff in the kitchen. Living furniture in the living room. The whole place was sitcom-tidy, which both amazed and embarrassed me. I followed her into the kitchen, accepted a cup of tea, and was about to sit down at the table when I noticed the ducks, four of them, waddling around her backyard, circling the swing set at its center, wandering in and out of a coop.

"Ducks!" I said. "You have ducks."

"We do," she said. "Everyone talks about chickens now. Chickens are the new big thing, backyard chicken coops. I was ready to do it; I ordered the coop. I put it together. We were excited, and then, at the last minute, my brother—he's a wildlife biologist—says to me, 'No, no. Forget the chickens. Get ducks instead.' They're so much better. Cleaner, friendlier, less chance of disease. And the eggs. Duck eggs cost twenty dollars a dozen at the farmers' markets. We have them for breakfast. Plus, the kids are crazy for the ducks. They wanted a dog, but I grew up on a farm, and I can't get past the feeling that animals belong outside. So I said, 'You can pretend the ducks are dogs,' and that's what they do. Occasionally I even let them put a diaper on one and we let it in the house for a few minutes. Only occasionally."

I was still admiring the ducks when Julie handed me my tea and said, "The ducks were really helpful during the DCFS home visit."

She explained to me that when the social worker arrived at her house to investigate, the thing she was most concerned about was the emotional toll it would take on her kids. So when the caseworker arrived, Julie met her outside and persuaded her to agree to play along with the story she had devised. They had just set up the coop for the ducks, and she told her girls that a lady was coming from the city to talk to them and find out if their home was in good enough shape to get the permit to keep them. "They have really high standards in Chicago," she told them. "She needs to make sure there's enough space, enough light, for the ducks to be happy."

We both sighed after she said this. The mutual feeling was more exhaustion than disgust. The kids were laughing and squealing from the rec room below us. The afternoon had gone gray, and it began to drizzle outside. I glanced a little wistfully at the ducks in their puddles as we talked.

"People are just nuts about this issue," Julie said as she recounted her story. She told me that the afternoon it happened, she'd left the side door open on her minivan so she could keep an eye on the girls while she stood in line for her coffee.

I asked her if she wasn't scared about a man driving a white van coming to snatch them.

"No," she said. "I don't worry about the man in the white van, and I'll tell you why. I'm a Cook County public defender. I have been for twenty years. And never in my twenty years of working there have I ever seen a single child abduction case. Not one. I've seen parents who abused their children. I've seen parents who killed their children or whose relatives or spouses killed their children. But I work in the building where any case in Cook County would come if someone abducted a stranger's child, and there just aren't any. In twenty years, I have never seen a child abduction case."

And yet, as Julie walked back toward the car that day after buying her cup of coffee, an officer was leaning against her vehicle, barking at her kids. He was having what seemed to her an aggressive conversation with them. The oldest of them was covering her ears, the middle one was crying, and the youngest, the four-year-old, was frozen in her seat.

"What did you think was happening when you saw this?"

"At that point, I saw him as someone attacking my kids. It doesn't matter if he's a police officer or whoever the heck he is. He is an individual who is making my kids upset. 'What are you talking to my kids like that for?' I asked him. I acted like any mother would when they see a man who is making her kids cry."

The officer asked where she had been, and when she lifted her cup and said she'd been getting coffee, he said to her, "So you abandoned your children?"

Julie began to laugh. "I didn't give him the deference that he thought he needed, which is what most people do because they're intimidated by the uniform. I'm not. So I challenged him. I don't want a police officer telling my children that they could be snatched at any opportunity. I told him I knew for a fact that I was not doing anything wrong here. It's not against the law in Illinois to leave your children unattended. You have to prove that I'm willfully endangering their life by going into Starbucks and getting a cup of coffee where I can see them. Good luck getting that case approved by a state's attorney."

The officer replied that he could take her kids if he thought she was putting them in danger, and Julie replied, "You know what, let me call my husband down here in that case. Let me call my mother down here too. Both of them are also attorneys."

At that point, the officer walked away and contacted the Department of Child Protective Services, who could investigate Julie without his pressing charges.

It's not lost on Julie that her ability to stand up for her rights and to refuse intimidation is largely the result not only of her professional background but also of her privilege as a white, suburban mom. In her view, this fact makes it all the more important that mothers like her, mothers like me, stand up for our right to parent our children without public shaming or investigation or prosecution.

"Your view is that people who have more privilege and more power have an obligation to stand up."

"Yes, for all the people who can't. If this had happened to anyone of color, they could have been shot in the street for doing what I did.

My color is protecting me, so I have to push the envelope so that it gets out in the news that this can happen to white moms too."

"Because if it's happening to white moms, then people might care."

"Yes. Let's be honest. I'm a privileged white woman who left her kids in a $30,000 minivan watching *Dora the Explorer* to go in for a Starbucks. Is there any clearer picture of privilege than that? But no matter what color you are, no matter how much money you have, you don't deserve to be harassed for making a rational parenting choice."

It's funny, but in all the time that had passed, I had never thought about what was happening in quite those terms—as harassment. When a person intimidates, insults, verbally abuses, or demeans a woman on the street, in the bedroom, at the office, in the classroom, it's harassment. When a woman is intimidated or insulted or abused because of the way she dresses or her sexual habits or her outspokenness on social media, she is experiencing harassment. But when a mother is intimidated, insulted, abused, or demeaned because of the way she is mothering, we call it concern or, at worst, nosiness. A mother, apparently, cannot be harassed. A mother can only be corrected.

"You can call it what you want, but it's harassment," Julie insisted. "There's no better word for it. It's harassment by people on the street; it's harassment by the system, by the police. And frankly, there should be consequences for people who harass parents."

I asked Julie what, as a woman and as a defense attorney, she would tell all the other mothers I'd talked to if she were standing beside them as it happened.

"I would tell them to ask the officer what law she was breaking. I would tell them to ask why and how going into a store for a few minutes meant she was abandoning her child. I would tell her to ask if she was under arrest and if not, if she was free to go. And if it's a person on the street, calling them names, yelling at them, scaring their kids, threatening to call the police and have their children taken away, then I'd tell them to be extremely calm and clear with that person. I'd tell them to take out their own phones and start recording the interaction. I'd tell them to say calmly and assertively, 'I haven't done anything wrong; I haven't broken any law. I don't know you. So please step away from us. You are harassing me, and you're harassing my children. If you don't stop harassing us, then I'll have to call the police and file a complaint.' "

Of course, it doesn't always become so contentious. There are plenty of times when a child is left for a few minutes in a car, when a passerby becomes concerned, but when nothing so ugly ever comes of it. Julie knew this as well as anyone, that so much of the tenor of our interactions is determined by circumstance and by all of our unconscious biases. Julie revealed to me near the end of our talk that day, that a few years before this happened to her, something very similar but not quite the same had happened to her husband.

The day it happened to Julie's husband, she had taken the kids to a museum in nearby Skokie. "They have food for kids there, but they don't have anything for an adult, so we were there all day and I got hungry, so my husband brought me some food. He had the baby with him in the car. He pulls up to the building, puts the blinkers on, leaves the baby in the car, gives me the food, we maybe talk for two or three minutes, then he comes back out and there are two women and a police officer standing there in front of the car. He asked the officer what the problem was, and the guy says very matter-of-factly, 'You've left your child in this car unattended. These two women have called me.' Then he turns to the women and says, 'Okay, ladies, I've got this now,' and he sends the women away. Then he turns to my husband and says, 'Listen, you can't do that in Skokie; these women will call and complain. You've got to take your kid in everywhere, because I'm telling you, these women will call the police on you."

Julie's husband was too surprised to say anything. He just stood there until the officer softened and said, "Don't worry about it this time. And don't be too hard on yourself. We've all done it. I get it. But just a heads-up that these women are crazy and will call the police."

"I didn't know," her husband said. "I had no idea."

The officer told him not to worry about it. "I've got kids of my own," he said. "I know how it is."

7

QUALITY OF LIFE

The majority of mothers are not going to be arrested or harassed. The majority of mothers are not going to be charged with contributing to the delinquency of a minor or child endangerment; they are not going to be placed on a registry of neglectful parents. It might be happening far more than we realize, it might be a new form of harassment, but it's not going to impact the lives of the majority of American parents the way it impacted me or Debra Harrell or Julie Koehler or any of the other mothers I talked to. And since this is the case, you might wonder if the cost of fear is really so prohibitive, after all. If arresting and harassing and publicly shaming a few dozen parents, even a few hundred parents each year, would make kids a tiny bit safer, maybe it's worth it. I'd be willing to say it well might be if it weren't for the fact that there are other costs, costs not just for mothers like me or Debra or Julie or Lenore Skenazy—mothers who assert their right to make rational parenting choices that go against convention—but to *all* parents attempting to raise children in an atmosphere of fear. What about the typical, not horrible, perfectly responsible, good-enough mothers or fathers who would never, ever, ever take their eyes off their child, not even for a minute, because you just never know? What is the cost of fear for them?

A few months after I published my essay in *Salon*, I decided to visit a friend in New York. My two kids, by then seven and four, were at home with my husband and my parents, so the vacation involved all the small, rejuvenating pleasures and indulgences that children make impossible. I stayed up late talking with my friend and then slept until eleven, rising slowly and lingering over coffee. I took long showers and shaved my legs. I dined in restaurants where the food was coursed and there wasn't a single chicken finger on the menu, and through it all, I walked around the city carrying a purse that felt slim and impossibly light for its lack of sticker books and Goldfish crackers and wet wipes and crayons. The second day of my visit, my friend asked if I wanted to meet some of her other friends for dinner.

We met them at a macrobiotic restaurant in the East Village. The place was shaped like the cabin of a passenger jet, a row of bamboo tables against a wall, a narrow passage for the servers to pass. There was not a child in sight. I squeezed into the booth side of the table and found myself doing two things I hadn't done in years: eating a bowl of beans with a pair of chopsticks and sitting at a table with a group of childless women.

They were around my age—intelligent, sophisticated, independent women. One was an editor, another a professor, the third was working at an art gallery, and the friend I was visiting had just published her first novel. They were all beautiful and interesting and funny. And I, the only mother at the table, felt like a creature from outer space. It wasn't so much *what* they talked about—jobs, men, books, parties—as it was *how* they talked about it. They spoke slowly and thoughtfully. When they sought advice about decisions that lay before them about love interests or career changes or friendships or just the direction of their lives, they did so with seriousness, but without the urgency to which I'd grown so accustomed. They wanted to know what the others thought, and I sensed no fear of judgment, no hint of anxiety in their voices. They seemed to me open, vibrant, free. But more noticeably than any of that, their lives seemed to possess a fullness, a roundness, that I'd forgotten was possible. If they were struggling in one area, there were other areas in which they were thriving. They had jobs, friends, sex lives, hobbies. They had different kinds of relationships with different kinds of people. Their identities were still malleable, multidimensional. They were still, in some essential way, the heroes of their own stories.

I could remember a time when my own life had been like that, when my anxieties about my children and about motherhood had not crowded out all the other parts of my identity, but the memory was fading. For more than six years, I'd been embracing, or at least blindly accepting, the assumption that a woman who has small children doesn't just become a mom. She becomes *Mom*—that is her name, her station, first and foremost the essential thing she is. In a *New York Times* op-ed, Heather Havrilesky wrote, "Motherhood is no longer viewed as simply a relationship with your children, a role you play at home and at school, or even a hallowed institution. Motherhood has been elevated—or perhaps demoted—to the realm of lifestyle, an all-encompassing identity with demands and expectations that eclipse everything else in a woman's life."

For six years, I'd assumed this was an inevitable transformation, an inherent part of parenthood. It seemed to be what most parents (but especially women) did, moving their children to the absolute center of their lives and pushing everything else—marriage, friendship, civil engagement, creative work—out to the distant edges where maybe, possibly, it could be revisited in fifteen or twenty years. Or at least, I thought it was parenthood we were moving to the center, but what if that was only part of it? What if the thing taking up so much space was not the fact of parenthood itself, the actual relationship with our children, but the feeling surrounding that relationship, the fearful feeling that we could never quite do enough?

Halfway through the meal, the woman who was an editor turned to me: "So you have two little kids?" she said.

"It's true," I replied, growing nervous, wondering if she knew my secret, which was no longer a secret, since I had published a widely read article about it.

She took a sip from her bowl of miso. She was recently married, thinking about starting a family herself. "Would you say," she asked in an impartial journalist's voice, "that having children changes your quality of life?"

I sat without moving, a single black bean clenched between my chopsticks. I expected laughter, but instead there were stares. They were all looking at me, waiting for an answer.

"Well," I said as the waiter came by and refilled our glasses. "I guess I would say that when you have small children, you have no quality of life."

In *Perfect Madness*, Judith Warner begins her exploration of motherhood and anxiety by contrasting the experiences of American mothers with the experiences of mothers she encountered during her years living in France. She writes, "I had friends in France who were full-time stay-at-home moms with three or four children, but I had never once encountered a woman whose life was overrun by her children's activities. I had never met a mother, working or otherwise, who didn't have the 'time' to read a book . . . Only an unbalanced person would be doing something like that. A woman insufficiently mindful of herself. A woman who was, perhaps, fearful of adulthood."

Upon returning with her children to America, Warner describes her amazement and horror at "the breakdown of boundaries between children and adults and the erosion, for many families, of any notion of adult time and space." She remembers feeling angered by the beating-up on working mothers, the pressure to breast-feed and to endure natural childbirth, to give herself over to "attachment parenting," to baby-wearing, to co-sleeping, to the constant and endless subjugating of her own needs as an adult woman to the real or at times imagined needs of her child. She writes, "I was amazed by the fact that women around me didn't find their lives strange. It appeared normal to them that motherhood should be fraught with anxiety and guilt and exhaustion."

Of course it did, I thought when I first read this. It certainly did to me. When all of the parents you encounter have rearranged their lives to make room for a style of parenting that demands total control, micromanagement, endless monitoring and measurement and observation and intervention, when you've never known a different way, you accept that this is what parenthood is. Most of us join the stampede without ever bothering to ask or wonder what we're chasing.

Right up until the moment Felix arrived, I had a clear idea of how I wanted his first few minutes in the world to transpire. I'd read the books, taken the birthing class, discussed the details with my husband and midwife and doula, and we'd all decided how we wanted it to go. We'd wait for the umbilical cord to stop pulsing, as the latest research showed was beneficial, then my husband would cut the cord, then the baby would be immediately placed on my chest to bond and nurse. This birth experience, or "birth plan," as we had been told to call it, would be the best entrance into the world for our son, but would also, I felt but did not admit, reflect positively on me and my preparedness. His birth was not something that was happening to me, to us, but something we were doing—consciously, with love and care. Right from the beginning, I would prove myself to be a conscientious parent. That was the plan.

But after two days of mind-numbingly painful labor, I begged for the epidural I had spent six months swearing off. Then, when our midwife announced that it was time to push, her brow furrowed, her expression hardened, and she called for the doctor.

"What's wrong?" I asked.

"Probably nothing. But I see some meconium, so we want to have help in the room just in case."

"Just in case what?" Pete asked.

She didn't answer. A physician whose face I don't remember came into the room and stood beside the midwife. My body was hoisted, my legs raised. I pushed once, twice, three times, and then he fell into their hands, gray and silent at first, then flushing pink and screaming.

"It's in his lungs," the doctor said. "We need to suction."

When he handed Pete the scissors, it was with urgency in his eyes.

"Can I wait until the cord stops pulsing?" Pete asked.

"No, we have to clear his airway. Cut it now."

Pete did as he was told. I lay back on the bed, numb and sweaty, watching him fumble. The baby was whisked off, suctioned, given oxygen, hooked up to monitors and taken for a few hours of observation. I dozed off, exhausted. I opened my eyes sometime in the middle of the afternoon, looked around the unfamiliar room. For a moment, while my mind cleared, I felt so happy, so content, so relieved that the hours of labor were finally over and I'd made it through, that I hadn't managed to jump out the window as I'd threatened to do at the height of the pain. Yes, I was alive. And I was not in agony. I'd made it. And the warm September sun was filling the window.

And everything was good. That was what I felt for about five seconds. And then, following this contentment came another, unfamiliar feeling. I looked over at the roller crib beside the bed and saw that it was empty.

"They're monitoring him in the nursery to make sure he's breathing well," Pete said before I could ask. And as soon as he said it, I began to understand. There was now a *he* (my son) and a *they* (his world) that mattered to me more than myself, more than the most deeply seated notion of who I was. And what I had wanted for him—an easy, hitchless birth—had not come to pass. And furthermore, all the things I wanted for him or would ever want for him—joy, love, belonging, a meaningful life—might come to pass and might not. It wasn't up to me. This new kind of love, which seemed to take up all the space inside me, was not limitless in its power to determine the future or to protect him. And in realizing this, that feeling I'd had upon waking, that feeling of relief and contentment, dissolved.

I pushed back the hospital sheets and stumbled out of bed toward the hallway to find him. He was in the nursery, asleep in a cradle, a few wires streaming from his head, but breathing, sleeping, healthy. I'd like to say that this was a moment of pure tenderness and joy, going to check on my son for the first time, realizing that I was his mother. But that would be an omission. There was joy, of course, but beneath it, and above it, and around it on every side, was fear.

Felix was born on a Monday morning, and Pete and I took him home from the hospital Tuesday afternoon. In another era, I would have stayed for the better part of a week, resting and recovering, but hospital costs and managed health care had made such indulgences the stuff of fairy tales. We'd planned to stay our state-mandated two nights, but the hospital where I gave birth had no nursery for healthy babies. Parents were expected to room with their infants to promote bonding (and cut costs). This sounded wonderful when I was pregnant. What I hadn't anticipated then was a baby who would spend his first days on Earth screaming as though he were on fire. The room was small and hot, the bed narrow and uncomfortable, the nurses curt and overworked. Breast-feeding was not going well. The lactation specialist so lauded on the tour was nowhere to be found, and after one night, Pete and I decided that if we were not going to sleep, we'd rather not-sleep at home.

A few months earlier, an acquaintance at a party described to me her childbirth homecoming. In the hospital, she'd told me, her baby had been a sleepy, sweet-tempered bundle of quiet. He'd been like the babies you see on toilet paper commercials and inspirational greeting cards. But once home, he'd moved his half-open eyes from one parent to the other as though to say, "My God, there's been some horrible mistake. They didn't really send me home with these people." Then he cried for a month.

Since Felix began expressing his distaste for existence so urgently and immediately upon entering the world, Pete and I thought at least we'd be spared this sort of surprise. What we didn't anticipate was that once at home, among the many fruits of our anticipation—plush nursing pillows, unopened boxes of pacifiers, vibrating bouncers, towers of burp rags and bibs and blankets—amid this oasis of infant plenty, Felix would howl ten times louder than he had at the hospital. He howled when we fed him, when we burped him, when we rocked him, when we put him in his crib.

"He's just not a happy guy," my aunt said when she came to visit. Pete and I passed him back and forth, exhausted. *Where the hell is everybody?* I wanted to scream. But then I remembered warning them away, laying the groundwork for that nebulous endeavor that had seemed so important—taking ownership of my birthing experience. For two days, we cared for our child in a fog of sleepless terror. Then I called my mother and begged her to get on a plane.

"I can't do this," I said. "I'm so tired I feel nauseous. I feel like I could fall asleep walking. Everything's sore. The sink is full of dishes, and we haven't eaten in days."

"I thought you wanted time to yourself," she said.

"I was wrong. I want help. I don't know what to do. He won't let us put him down."

"You need to stay calm. He has a little colic." She was looking at flights while we spoke. "It's so expensive to come last-minute."

I was trying to nurse him. He'd suck for a moment, then cry, suck a little longer, then cry harder.

"Listen to me," I said. "I'll pay you back for the ticket. I don't care how much the flights are. I don't care if the ticket costs a million dollars. At this moment, if Adolf Hitler knocked on the door and offered to help me, I'd invite him in and pour him a cup of coffee. So charter a jet if you have to. Bum a ride with an escaped convict. I don't care how you get here as long as you come and as long as it's now."

"Kimmy! What is wrong? What is the problem?"

I hardly knew. I couldn't say. "I'm scared," I told her. "I have this awful feeling that something terrible is about to happen." This was a laughable understatement. The truth was that it was even worse than I let on. The anxiety that began with my pregnancy was spreading and growing stronger.

Why does he cry so much, so ferociously? Why can't I soothe him? Why, fifteen minutes into feeding, does he arch his back and shriek as though in pain? Is it colic? Is it acid reflux? When he was six weeks of age, we started giving him Prevacid, and the crying abated. We were relieved, but within a week, there were other worries. He had his first upper respiratory infection, fever, runny nose, but why was he wheezing like a leaky balloon? The pediatrician said it was reactive airway disease and a double ear infection. He'd need nebulizing treatments of albuterol, oral steroids, antibiotics. He got better, but a few weeks later, it happened again. Then again. Why was he always sick? Was it because I'd given up on exclusive breast-feeding and supplemented with formula? Was it all the germs he encountered during his two days a week of day care? Should I even have him in day care? Was I prioritizing my writing over my child, doing him irreparable damage? Would he be better off if he stayed with me at home every day? And yet at home there were more worries. Was I giving him enough tummy time, enough playtime, enough visual stimulation? He hated sleeping on his back, but if I put him on his stomach would he die of SIDS? He loved being worn, but I'd read a story of a woman whose baby suffocated in its sling, so when I wore him I held my hand by his lips to make sure he was breathing. Was he nursing enough, napping enough, smiling enough, babbling enough, meeting all of his developmental milestones? Were all the asthma steroid treatments damaging his brain?

These were the thoughts that met me when I opened my eyes in the morning. They were with me when I was with him, and they followed me when I tried to work. He was not a hardy baby, but would he be sickly forever? He wasn't putting words together as much as expected or engaging in extended play. Did he have autism, a hearing problem, some other mysterious deficiency? Could I help him by doing something differently, giving him more time, more attention, by reading a book on new parenting styles or making my own baby food or learning the art of infant massage? Was I doing everything I could for him? Would he get into a good preschool, a good grade school, a decent college? Would he find a job, a calling, friends and lovers and eventually a mate? Would he have a rewarding career that paid the bills and filled his soul? Would he continue to love and value me? When he thought of me twenty years from now, or thirty, or fifty, would he think I'd done well? Would I be a point of pride and affection or of loathing and shame? And would any of this even matter? Would there still be colleges when it was time for him to go to school? An economy when it was time for him to get a job? Drinkable water or breathable air? One question led to another, which led to another, an endless train of worry chugging along.

When I remember those first years of motherhood, it is not so much memories or moments I return to; it is this feeling, this constant gnawing, on-edge-ness, this vague but persistent sensation that something wasn't right, that I was doing something wrong. And the feeling was different from what I'd experienced during pregnancy. It was not only an intensification of fear but a multidirectional expansion. Where there had before been a straightforward fear of something bad happening, there was now fear of something bad happening as well as a fear of my own incompetencies, of present mistakes, future failures, the omnipresent possibility of not measuring up.

Looking back, it is clear to me these feelings were not within the range of normal anxiety. I'd been reminded repeatedly about the warning signs and dangers of postpartum depression. At the same time, I didn't think that's what I was experiencing. But I had no idea. Awareness of postpartum depression has increased in recent years, but the reality is that while depression is distinct from anxiety, there's a significant amount of overlap. Trying to untangle the emotional and mood-related changes I experienced after the birth of my son, I spoke with Emily Miller, a maternal-fetal medicine specialist at Northwestern University, who explained that the overwhelming majority of women with perinatal depression will have anxiety symptoms and vice versa. Miller became interested in the subject of perinatal mood disorders when she noticed a significant number of patients coming to her with symptoms, not of depression but of anxiety disorders and obsessive-compulsive disorders that began during pregnancy. "One patient," she told me, "had these obsessive thoughts that her kid's car seat would turn over and the kid would suffocate.

Another woman had obsessive thoughts when she was cooking that she would accidentally put the baby in the oven. She didn't want to put the baby in the oven. It was very disturbing to this woman, but she thought she might accidentally do this or this might happen and then these obsessive thoughts and compulsions like, okay, let me check the oven twenty times (or the more standard of washing hands fifteen times, checking that the doors are locked). Things that would be fine if done once or twice but were now happening enough to disrupt these women's ability to complete other tasks."

It was only when Miller started sharing these stories with other obstetricians, and learned that they'd also had patients who'd begun having similar symptoms around pregnancy, that she began to wonder if what she was observing was part of a larger phenomenon that wasn't being talked about enough by the obstetrical community. "I spend so much time teaching my medical students and residents about preeclampsia and postpartum hemorrhage," she told me, "but mood disorders are more common than any of these other things and we don't focus our medical education on them."

Later in the conversation, I asked her why she thought there was more awareness around perinatal depression than anxiety.

"That's a good question," she said. "Maybe it's because with depression, there's a potential effect on maternal mortality. Depressed people sometimes kill themselves. Anxiety is more about quality of life."

Of course, women don't usually kill themselves from chronic anxiety; chronic, gnawing perfectionism; and self-consciousness and isolation. Mothers don't often die of fear. What happens, I think, far more often, is that we simply, slowly disappear. We become something less than we thought we'd be. We see things less clearly, experience things less intensely; as fear expands, the world recedes. The more minutiae a mother has to worry about, the more unlikely disasters she's charged with preventing through her infinite maternal wisdom and foresight, the less mental, emotional, intellectual, and spiritual energy she has for herself, her work, her community. Feminists frequently debate which elements of systemic and internalized sexism most need to change in order for more women to run for political office or rise to the top of their companies or colonize professions from which they've been historically excluded. Undoubtedly, there are many. But maybe not expecting and encouraging women to worry about every fucking thing that happens in their household might be a solid place to start.

I've been reminded of this many times since I began writing about parenthood and fear, but maybe never so much as a few months ago, having coffee with a woman a little older than myself whose kids were finishing college. When she learned that I was writing about parenthood, she asked if we could chat. I was excited for the meeting, as she seemed to me not just any mother but exactly the kind of mother and woman I hoped to become. She had two kids who seemed not just successful in a looks-good-on-the-college-application kind of way, but also genuinely interesting and curious and connected and thriving. She had a successful career, a strong marriage, a circle of intelligent and interesting friends. *Here is a success story of American motherhood*, I thought to myself as I'd gotten to know her. And yet after we'd chatted for a few minutes, she said something about her memories of motherhood that startled me in a way not much else had.

When I asked her to tell me about the role that fear had played in her life as a mother when her kids were babies and then as they grew, she sat quietly for a moment, then she said, "I don't remember."

"You don't remember how fear affected you?" I asked.

"No. No. The effect, I think, is that I don't remember much of those years. It's so strange. I wasn't an absentee mom. I was there. I tried my best to be present, to give them so much of myself. But now it seems what I mostly remember of those years is the worrying, the anxiety, the uncertainty. Always feeling afraid that if I did the wrong thing, made the wrong choice, something bad would happen to them. I never chose to parent that way. It's just what we all were doing. Now they're gone, those babies and little boys of mine are all grown, and what I remember most of my time with them is feeling afraid, feeling like I didn't measure up. I remember the other stuff too, the sweetness, but somehow it seems more muted than it should be, obscured by something."

It seemed to me, as I sat there, that perhaps this was the greatest cost of fear, the way it blots out everything it touches—drowning out the joys of parenthood, deadening the very thing we hoped it would protect.

I asked her what advice she would give, now that she'd scaled the wall, to today's mother of small children. Somehow, after all that had happened in Virginia, after all the women I'd talked to and things I had read, it was her response, the beautiful, brilliant simplicity of it, that most changed me. She said it with a little shrug, as though the answer was so obvious, impossible to miss. "Try to be less afraid" was what she said.

And so that was what I did.

As spring arrived in Chicago that year, as I began writing and thinking more and more about my experience and the questions it raised for me and for all parents, I decided to make another trip to Virginia—this one not to go to juvenile court, but instead to do something I'd wanted to do for years but hadn't been able to bring myself to do. I went alone, without my children, to an artist residency near Charlottesville to spend a week writing.

As much as I'd always wanted to do this, I wavered. After all, responsible, nondegenerate mothers didn't ditch their small children for a week of writing and going on long, meditative walks and talking to other writers and artists around a communal dinner table. What if Felix's asthma flared up while I was away? What if Violet got an ear infection? Pete could handle it, certainly, in a baseline way. No one would die, probably. But he couldn't handle it the way *I* would handle it. My children, I imagined, would become inconsolable without the one person (me) who was the most attuned to their wants and needs. Pete would feed them macaroni-and-cheese and grapes for seven days. Violet would grow constipated and get dreadlocks in her unconditioned hair. Felix would forget to use toothpaste when he brushed. They loved Daddy. Daddy was fun. Daddy was terrific. But Daddy was no Mommy. Or so I told myself, buying into one of the lamest tropes of the cult of motherhood.

"You have got to be kidding me," my friend Amelia said when I called her one evening to talk through my doubts. By this time, she'd become a mother herself; she was both working and raising a little girl on her own and had little patience for my laments about how Pete wouldn't be able to hold down the fort in quite the way that I could.

"I can't even process what you're saying," she told me. "That's how much rage I feel right now. The rage is literally breaking my brain. Are you living in like 1850? Are you wearing a crinoline right now and stirring porridge on the hearth? Fuck that. You go do your writing residency and you leave those kids in the care of their perfectly able-bodied, mentally competent biological father. This is your duty as a writer and a woman. Tell me you're going to go or I'll have to hate you. Okay, maybe I won't hate you, but I definitely won't respect you anymore."

This was not a threat I could take lightly. I told her I would do it. I promised her I would. But then, almost before I'd hung up the phone, I sat down in front of my computer, opened up Facebook, and went about seeing if anyone else, any of the other parents I knew without really knowing, might have a different opinion.

Hey writer/artist/mom friends, I posted. *I'm thinking of going to do a writing residency for 10 days, but I've never left the kids for this long. I'm scared! Guidance? Suggestions? Am I going to scar them?*

Within an hour, the thread showed twenty comments.

Do it! one friend encouraged.

Go, Kim, said another.

When I went back full-time and had to start traveling, one woman posted, *it was definitely an adjustment, but they'll be fine.*

Other responses were more measured. *Hmm*, said one woman. *How old are your kids again? 10 days IS a long time. It's so hard when they're young. But I'm sure it will be fine. Can they Skype with you?*

Wow, said another. *You're so brave. Claire is four and I haven't even left her over night yet! She's super attached though, and every kid is different!*

Oh man, I can't imagine, wrote someone. *I'd miss them too much.*

I'm not sure where these other folks are coming from, someone else responded. *I run away from my kids whenever possible. :)*

I think this is really a personal choice, someone else added. *I wouldn't personally be comfortable with it but that's just me. I'd miss them too much. I'm a wimp.*

I'm sure she'll miss them too, said someone else. *But that doesn't mean she shouldn't go.*

Just pretend you're a man, suggested another friend. *I mean, would we even be having this discussion if we were dads? Has any father in the history of the universe ever felt guilty about going on a work trip for a week?*

Maybe you could go for a shorter time, someone else posted. *Or is there any way you can take your kids with you? 10 days is a long time to a four-year-old.*

Kim, another friend replied. *I do a lot of travel for work. Message me privately. Too much judgment here.*

Who's judging? She asked for advice and we're all just offering it, another person wrote.

I closed my computer, pushing it away from me. I took a deep breath, stood up from the table, walked to the other side of the room. It didn't matter; it was too late. The internet oracle had unleashed the voices of discord, and now they were sparring inside my head, leaving me feeling more confused and conflicted than I'd been when I opened my browser.

For five years, I'd indulged this kind of masochistic relationship with social media. When it came to questions about my pregnancy, my baby, my toddler, my preschooler, I wanted to know what other people were doing. I wanted their different perspectives, their advice. This desire made sense to me. If people used crowdsourcing to figure out how to lose weight or find a new apartment or build their own urban chicken coop, why not use it to get information about one of the most important things in life—raising children? And so I asked. I consulted. I browsed and lurked and got a good eyeful of everyone else's sepia-tinted, beautiful, happy, well-adjusted families. And at the end of peering through the virtual living room windows of all these people I sort-of-but-didn't-really know, I always, invariably, was left feeling . . . what's the word I'm looking for? *Unsettled*? *Uncertain*? No, the word is *shitty*. Just generally, undeniably shitty.

In the end, I made the decision the old-fashioned way. I put Violet in her stroller and took a long walk around our neighborhood and weighed the pros and cons, the complex negotiation of my children's needs, my needs, Pete's needs, and then I made a choice. I decided that guilt and anxiety or no, I would go to the writers' colony for a week because this was my career, after all, and I was lucky enough to have a partner who really could man the ship perfectly well, and also no one ever dies from a week of mac and cheese.

. . .

I arrived at the writers' colony in early June. The place was located on top of a hill at the foot of the Blue Ridge Mountains. It was invisible from the main highway, so I drove past it, back and forth for fifteen minutes, before I finally spotted a turnoff, marked by a sign that read REAL WORLD ENDS HERE. Past the sign, the road narrowed, then angled steeply upward, asphalt loosening to gravel. There were cows grazing in a pasture, clusters of wildflowers, shallow ponds, a long stretch of weathered, white-wood fence. At the top of the hill sat a long, two-storied building, a structure all window and dark brick, not entirely unlike a 1970s motel or a college dormitory in need of renovation. This was where I'd live for the week. And beyond this structure, farther up the hill, a stone farmhouse with a grain elevator, sun-washed and surrounded by writers' and artists' studios where I would spend my days working. That was it. Bed. Desk. A dining hall for meals. A small pool and a few communal bikes for getting around or seeing the countryside. No cars. No car seats. No strollers. No high chairs. No toys. No diapers. No diaper bags. No sippy cups. For a week, I'd be equipment-less. I'd have that antigravity sensation known only to parents who are suddenly away, not just from their children but from all the modern contraptions of parenthood that are supposed to make children safer and happier, that are supposed to make parenting easier but that collectively inhibit our every movement through space. Getting out of the car, I felt eighty pounds lighter, almost buoyant. I also felt for the first time in a year like maybe everything was going to be okay, the awfulness of what had happened in Richmond falling away from me.

At the colony that August, I became friends with a visual artist who had two kids in college. I became friends with an Israeli guitarist my own age, recently married but not yet a parent. I met single people, married people, gay people, and straight people. I met people who were parents, people who were grandparents, people who never wanted children of their own. I met a woman in her late forties, both a psychiatrist and a writer, who'd lost her husband to skin cancer two years before and was now raising two teenagers by herself. I met a novelist in his fifties going through a divorce, trying to persuade his twenty-year-old daughter not to hate him. I met an artist somewhere in middle age, raising two kids in a large city, and one evening when we went for our after-dinner constitutional, walking up the crest of the foothill on which the colony sat, she asked me about my writing. I told her that a lot of it was about my experience as a mother, and she said, very casually but a little out of breath, "So interesting. You know, I came close to killing myself twice after my children were born."

At first, I wasn't sure if she was speaking figuratively—in my family, "I'm going to kill myself" is synonymous with "The day is not going well," so I kept pace, kept a neutral face. "Oh, no. Really?" I said.

"Yeah. I had terrible, terrible postpartum anxiety and depression. The first time I had to be hospitalized for a few months. The next time a little less, but still . . . it was awful. I don't talk about it much. In fact, you might be the first person I've told in years."

She went on to say more about how dark that time had been for her, how unhinged and lost she'd felt, even after the acute, depressive period had passed. She talked about how isolating it had been, because in addition to feeling terribly depressed, she'd also felt alone. "When you're struggling with parenthood, no one really wants to hear it," she said. "At least that was my experience. There's this silently enforced code of contentment. Mild complaining is fine, but only to a point. It's one thing to say, 'I'm so tired because my kid's still not sleeping through the night.' It's another to say, 'Having children made me want to end my life. I feel like I don't exist anymore.' Or maybe there are people out there who are comfortable saying things like that, but I was never one of them. And it's funny, because it sort of snuck up on me. It was like I didn't expect to feel so anxious about it, about what kind of mother I was. It never occurred to me that becoming a mother would make it hard for me to keep being the other things I'd always been and wanted to be: an artist, an activist, a person with a lot of different kinds of friendships. I mean, look at me. I've considered myself a feminist since first grade. I make art for a living. I'm a left weirdo who has never had any desire to keep up with the Joneses. I've never even owned a car. I'm just, you know, not in the race. Except when it came to motherhood. Motherhood somehow dropped me right into the middle of the stampede. It was the one place where I felt this incredible pressure, this mania to get everything right, to be all in it. If I'd become anxious and depressed because I'd lost my job or gotten dumped or whatever, that would be one thing. I could have owned it. But to say that motherhood had triggered my depression, it felt like such a profound failure. I felt unsexed by it. You know, people are talking more and more about the pressures women face to have children, how hard it is to choose to not be a mother. And I have total sympathy for these people. But you know, it's not as though that pressure stops the moment a woman gives birth. It's not as though everyone says, 'All right, job well done. Let's all get back to work now.' That pressure and judgment and scrutiny are still there. Maybe more than ever, because for the woman who chooses not to have a kid, people can say, well, so what? Let the selfish bitch do what she wants. Not hurting anyone. But when there's an actual child . . . when how a woman mothers is impacting a human being, it's suddenly a free-for-all. Even after you've decided to become a mother, there's enormous pressure to *be* a mother, not just to take care of your kid but to totally embrace the role."

"Do you think people made you feel that way?" I asked her. "Or do you think it came from inside yourself?"

We'd reached the top of the hill and slowed our pace. The humidity in the air lifted. The sun sank lower in the sky. The air tinged newly blue with shadows as the first stars pressed through. It felt good to be sweaty and out of breath, and to be talking to this woman I'd just met about parenthood without the usual posturing and insecurity and thinly veiled boasting. "I don't know," she said as she sat down to rest on the guardrail. "We think we're doing things on our own even when we're not. Did others make me feel like an inferior parent? Or did I feel inferior from the start and project that feeling onto others? I don't know the answer. Maybe a little of both. I only know that in those early years, even after I made friends with other mothers, even after I went on medicine and got help for the depression, I felt constantly anxious and insecure. Now that my kids are in their twenties and doing fine and I have a strong relationship with them both, I look back and understand how bad it must have been, how hard."

"How did you get through it?" I asked her. I was hoping she was going to recommend a book, a pill, some quick fix to make this feeling of inadequacy go away.

Instead, she looked at me kindly, quite earnestly, and said, "You know, I think after years and years, I learned to stop giving a fuck. If people I knew, friends or relatives or strangers or whoever, had an opinion about what kind of mother I was or wasn't, if they thought I was making mistakes, or doing things the wrong way, being too this or too that, being selfish by not giving all of myself to my kids, I eventually decided, fuck 'em. I'm doing the best I can in a culture that offers parents little material or emotional support. If people have a problem with the way I'm doing it, fuck every last one of them. And it's funny—that anger—that was what got me to a place where I could finally stop caring and enjoy the little monsters. That's when I started feeling better."

8

GUINEA PIGS

I was having coffee with a friend and former teacher not long ago, when after a few minutes, the conversation turned to parenthood. He was about ten years ahead of me. His children were in high school and college—and he asked me how I was finding the whole parenthood gig, if it was everything I'd expected it to be.

"It's basically nothing I expected it to be," I said. "It's much better and much worse, wonderful and impossible at the same time. But," I added, "I do think it's a hard time to be a parent in this country at this particular moment."

He thought about it for a second, then said, "Maybe. It's sure as hell a horrible time to be a kid."

I asked him what he meant by this, and he went on to say that it simply didn't seem that kids got to be kids anymore. Something was different. Something felt wrong.

"I grew up in the seventies in California. And one of my best memories of childhood was going out in the afternoons to play baseball with my friends. It sounds so simple. But, God, I loved it. I'd grab my glove. We'd meet at the park. We'd play until dinner. That kind of thing just doesn't happen anymore. Now they've got to call in a coach from the Dominican Republic to work on hitting technique even before the kids step foot on a field. Everything they do is organized, supervised, observed. Stop and think for a moment what that must be like, that total lack of freedom. Imagine how awful that must be."

I asked him if he had any theories about how this change had come about.

"No," he said, "it just seems that somewhere along the way, Americans gave up on the idea of childhood."

On the one hand, the traditional markers of adulthood now arrive later than ever before for middle- and upper-class people. Financial independence, home ownership, marriage, parenthood, full-time employment: milestones achieved most often in the early or midtwenties a generation or two ago are now commonly postponed by up to a decade. Attending college, once an entryway to early adulthood, now, for many children of privilege, seems to mark the beginning of a second phase of extended adolescence in which young people make a series of attempts at independence while often enjoying the financial and emotional support and intervention of parents. In this way, childhood has not vanished but expanded. And yet the quality and nature of this childhood has been permanently altered by the rise of intensive and fear-based parenting. It turns out that it isn't possible to change what it means to be a parent without also changing what it means to be a child.

In his history of American childhood, historian Steven Mintz describes this change, writing, "Young people spend an increasing number of years in the company of other people their same age, colonized in specialized 'age-graded' institutions. Young people's interactions with adults are largely limited to parents, teachers, and service providers. Children spend more time alone than their predecessors. They grow up in smaller families, and nearly half have no siblings. They are more likely to have a room of their own and to spend more time in electronically mediated activities . . . because fewer children attend neighborhood schools within walking distance, most children live farther from their friends and play with them less frequently, experiencing a greater sense of isolation. Meanwhile unstructured, unsupervised free play outside the home has drastically declined for middle-class children . . . Unstructured play and outdoor activities for children three to eleven declined nearly 40 percent between the early 1980s and the late 1990s. And from 1997 to 2003, unstructured time continued to decline for children aged six through twelve, with playtime dropping off more dramatically for girls than for boys. Because of parental fear of criminals and bad drivers, middle-class children rarely get the freedom to investigate and master their home turf in ways that once proved a rehearsal for the real world."

I connected to one mother whose family was caught off guard by these changes after living abroad. Elizabeth had been living abroad with her husband and children for more than fifteen years when they returned to the wealthy suburb of New York where Elizabeth had grown up. She was shocked by the changes that had occurred in her absence. "Europeans," she said, "are much more relaxed about parenting. . . . They love their children, but they don't seem to live for their children in the same way [we do], to define themselves by them." They also didn't seem determined to manage their children's lives in quite the same way. In Elizabeth's experience, American parents manage every aspect of their children's existence. In Europe, a family still seemed more like a family, less like a corporation. Despite living in a large city, all of her kids had enjoyed more freedom abroad. By the time they were eleven, they were walking to and from school by themselves, taking cabs, going to each other's houses on their own or going to the park. At thirteen, her son was in charge of his own schedule in a lot of ways. And his social life was all around him.

Elizabeth had imagined that upon returning to the States, the kids would enjoy the same unstructured, suburban lifestyle she'd had as a child. But it didn't take long for her to realize how much things had changed in the intervening decades. "I felt a little like Rip Van Winkle," she said. In wealthy American suburbs in 2016, "the mothers drive the kids everywhere. Every playdate is scheduled by a parent, or at least the parent is involved because of the driving. And in general, I find the parents are terrified—of what, I don't know." Her dominant impression upon returning was that "American parents were expected to wear their kids in a BabyBjörn until at least the age of eighteen." It was an adjustment for all of them, but for her oldest son, Shep, it was something worse. He immediately became anxious, depressed, withdrawn, and developed a video game addiction for which they sought psychiatric help.

In the months that followed, their son's anxiety and depression worsened. He struggled at school, withdrew from friends and family, couldn't get excited about anything that didn't involve a screen. The family took him to see assorted therapists—the problem seemed, in some way, shape, or form psychological. A psychiatrist diagnosed him with an internet addiction.

I asked Jason, Shep's father, what an internet addiction looked like in a fourteen-year-old.

"It looks exactly like it does in a forty-year-old," he said. "He couldn't sleep. He couldn't focus on anything else. He had total exhilaration when he did just that one thing to the total exclusion of everything else in his life. He fell into it like crack, stopped sleeping regularly, was staying up all night, which made the ADHD worse."

When Jason and Elizabeth began restricting how much time and money Shep could spend on *Mobile Madden*, he stole their credit cards, at one point racking up a $10,000 charge.

One night, after confiscating his computer and iPad, Elizabeth woke at two in the morning with a feeling of dread. She made her way down the hallway to Shep's room and found his bed empty. She discovered her son in his closet, playing on an old, broken Xbox he'd restored himself, the discarded iTunes gift cards he'd stolen from her office littering the floor. It was at this moment she realized they were in over their heads. Soon after, an educational consultant they'd hired suggested something that at first seemed extreme, a new company that had quickly developed a reputation for helping children just like Shep get through problems like these. Their rates were GDP–high, but Elizabeth and Jason weren't sure what else to do. The company was called Cognition Builders.

The idea is simple, Elizabeth and employees of the company explained to me later, though at first it sounds strange. The idea is that if you want to truly change the way a person parents, you need to *be there* as they're parenting.

To this end, Cognition Builders offers its clients a team of trained, on-the-ground professionals, or "family architects," as it calls them, who are essentially highly trained parenting coaches who embed themselves in a family's home. These architects, with the help of recording technology—mainly webcams—observe, scrutinize, and analyze a particular family's dysfunctional (or, as they would put it, "maladaptive") culture and style of communication. Embedded in a home over a period of months or even years, a Cognition Builders team, for the cost of several college educations, aims to help parents succeed in whatever capacity they feel they're failing their children.

The mere existence of such a company came as a revelation to me. The time I first heard about it, through a friend of Elizabeth's, I was already eyeball-deep in my research on the modern state of anxious parenthood, and I'd assumed at that point that I'd more or less seen it all. In the course of my research, I'd come to the conclusion that the average American parent was devoting more time, money, resources, attention, and planning than at any other point in American history; that we had literally reached a moment of peak parenthood, and that there was simply no way to further escalate or intensify our communal quest for parental control without resorting to the development of exo-uterine technology and retrofitting mothers as marsupials. I'd read about and interviewed parents who spent well into the five figures each year on childcare, private school tuition, enrichment activities, tutoring, educational consulting, therapy, specialty summer camps, and life coaching. I knew parents—and I had been one myself—who spent their negligible amount of free time reading books and consulting experts about the best way to shepherd children into adulthood. I'd internalized the fact that if you were struggling with a particular parenting challenge, there was probably a product or service designed to fix that specific problem. Cognition Builders, however, stretched the limits of my imagination.

A small company that, every year since its founding, has grown exponentially by nothing more than word of mouth, Cognition Builders rests on the premise that whether one is dealing with a neuroatypical child's debilitating outbursts, an adolescent's internet addiction, a teenager's refusal to go to school or poor study skills, or the more universal challenges of temper tantrums and sibling rivalry, a solution can be achieved through an unprecedented level of parental intervention.

To many parents, these problems—and problems very similar to them—are unavoidable, even predictable, or not even problems at all but rather standard bumps in the road, and the idea that someone might spend in the neighborhood of a gazillion dollars to make them go away would seem the pinnacle of capitalist indulgence. Not only are the parents indulging their children when the matter could be settled with a firm hand and some tough love, but the parents are indulging themselves, refusing to be the bad guy, refusing to believe that whatever plagues their child *must* be clinical in nature.

But it's also not hard to understand how for a family with sufficient resources who feels sufficiently overwhelmed, a service such as Cognition Builders would feel nothing short of lifesaving. The experience of despair over a child's struggles certainly varies by socioeconomic status, but it cannot erase the despair. And like anxiety, despair is an emotion we'll give almost anything to get rid of.

On the first day the assigned family architects were scheduled to arrive in her home, Elizabeth had worked hard to prepare her children for their arrival. Shep had just returned from two months at a therapeutic wilderness camp out West, and she'd explained to his three younger siblings that the architects were coming to help him settle back in to their home, but also to teach them all how to get along better as a family. The team would be in the house whenever the kids were there, and sometimes they'd come along when they went out to do errands or activities. The "FAs," as they're called, would spend a lot of time watching the family, but they'd also help Jason and Elizabeth establish and enforce a set of house rules. They'd put in place a system of positive reinforcement (points) for when rules were followed and contingencies (strikes) for when they were broken. They'd help everyone learn to communicate better and more effectively and would provide the kind of structure Shep needed to live successfully at home.

"Are they going to live here?" her youngest son had asked.

"No," she told him.

Some family architects did live with families, but theirs would be around only during the day. However, even when they weren't physically present in the house, they'd still *be there* in a sense. Nest Cams would be installed in all the home's common areas. The cameras would record everything the family said and did, and at any time the family architects or other members of the Cognition Builders team could log on to a computer and see how things were going with Elizabeth and Jason's family. If the kids' behavior went south—a tantrum, a meltdown, a sibling fight, or a refusal to do homework—the FAs could see for themselves just what had happened and how it had been handled. They could even offer, through the speaker function of the Nest Cam, real-time verbal feedback on their parenting, in addition to a more detailed follow-up by email or text.

For weeks, Elizabeth had tried to imagine what it was going to be like, this immersive, super-intensive parent coaching. She was still trying to get her head around it when the doorbell rang. Shep followed her into the front entryway. The women at the door were in their early twenties, pleasant, professional, energetic. Elizabeth greeted them. Shep said nothing. He looked down at the floor, then retreated to the back of the house.

"Interactions with adults have always been hard for him," Elizabeth would later tell me. "He's fine with kids, but his social anxiety spikes when he's around adults."

She'd gotten in the habit of warning him to go upstairs when a friend of hers was coming over so he wouldn't have to endure the awkwardness of a greeting. It was such a long-established habit that she didn't even think about it anymore, not until one of the architects called her out that very first day.

"Hold on," the architect said. "What just happened? An adult you've invited into your home comes inside, and without any greeting or acknowledgment, your fourteen-year-old runs away. This is not acceptable behavior."

Rule number one was thus established. When an adult comes into the room and says hello to one of the children, the child stops what he or she is doing, looks the adult in the eye, shakes his or her hand, returns the greeting, and asks the adult how she is doing. This is the new expectation. If any member of the household fails to meet this expectation, he receives a strike.

Elizabeth was stunned, but also impressed. This dual impression of admiration and disbelief would persist for much of the time she worked with Cognition Builders. It persisted when they printed out, laminated, and posted house rules all around their home. It persisted when they installed the Nest Cams that would record her family's every move. It persisted when they intervened in the multitude of small misbehaviors she would have typically let slide. It persisted when they told her that the family architects needed to be there with them not just in the house but also as they went about their business in the world, riding with them when they drove to Staples for school supplies, observing them as they went to sports practice or a playdate.

As mentioned earlier, their idea, as Elizabeth explained to me later, is that to truly change the way a person parents, you need to be there as they're parenting. She told me it reminded her of running: "I can run sprints, but only if a workout instructor is standing over me. If no one's watching me, my sprints look a lot like an intense jog with a lot of arm movement."

Elizabeth wanted to clarify that it wasn't as though she hadn't had rules for her kids before Cognition Builders: "I never had kids who played video games whenever they wanted or ate whatever they wanted out of the pantry. But what Cognition Builders pointed out to me was all the ways I was basically turning my children into mass negotiators whenever I let the rules slide." Family architects didn't allow for such sliding. They insisted that from now on, Shep would greet adults politely when they arrived. "While they were telling him this," Elizabeth recalled, "I was cringing, like, 'Oh my God, he's going to be in the corner shaking—he doesn't do this well.' But they forced my hand. They oversaw that I was following through. [Cognition Builders] basically comes in and they point out to you all those times the kids are running the show, all the times the kids have all the control. They're right there beside you to talk you out of all your bad parenting habits."

"And how did the kids respond to these changes?" I asked her.

She told me their reaction was mixed. Shep was nervous, but he knew that if he was going to continue to live at home instead of going to a therapeutic boarding school, he and his parents needed help. Their daughter, the youngest, was too little to really understand what was happening. Shep's twelve-year-old brother was probably the least accepting of the project, the one most likely, as Elizabeth put it, "to rattle the cage."

One afternoon, not long after the family architects settled into their home, he was feeling rebellious and decided to grab a footstool and put his face right up to one of the Nest Cams. "Hey, buttholes!" he said. "Why don't you leave us alone?"

At first, nothing happened. Then, a crackle of static followed by the voice of a Cognition Builders employee on the other end. "That's a strike," it said.

As I interviewed different families who had used Cognition Builders, all of them well educated and affluent, I couldn't help but think about how many people around the country were struggling terribly to provide their children with food, shelter, a decent education, basic health care, the most basic necessities for a decent life and future. Who in the world did these Cognition Builders parents think they were, paying strangers hundreds of thousands of dollars to come live in their home and set up cameras to help them monitor and manage their every interaction with their child in the hope of somehow ensuring their child's happiness and success? The very existence of such a company seemed to demonstrate something deeply wrong not only with American parents, but with America. This was what one part of me thought about Cognition Builders.

The other part thought, if I had a gazillion dollars, I would absolutely pay these people to come and help me figure out how to handle my kids. I thought of all the difficult moments—the grocery-store meltdowns, the bedtime tantrums, the challenges at school, all the small hurts and failures I'd experienced, the feelings of inferiority I'd had when comparing myself with other parents, all the moments as a parent when I didn't know the right thing to say or do and had to just make it all up to the best of my ability. How amazing it would be to have a family architect of my very own to help me become the best possible parent I could be. I admit it. I was horrified and covetous all at once.

Luckily, this contradiction was resolved by the fact that I didn't have a gazillion dollars to spare. I didn't even have enough money for the new vacuum cleaner I'd been eyeing, much less a family architect of my own. And so, at the end of my visit, after interviewing Elizabeth and Jason, the nanny and the manny, after talking to the family architects and the educational consultants and the director of curriculum and on and on, I asked if, before I left, I could speak with Shep, the little boy at the center of the storm. I hoped that in talking to him, I'd come to some conclusion about what my own kids were missing and what the future might hold for the next, most affluent generation of American children.

He came across as a sweet, sensitive kid, small for his age, a little shy and awkward, but bright and good-natured. He sat across from me on the large leather sofa in his ten-bedroom home on his family's plot of attractive, fallow land.

"What did you think about the people who came here, the family architects?" I asked him.

"I liked some of them," he said. "There were four of them."

"What kind of stuff did they do?"

"They mostly just made me write down what I had to do all the time. They helped me be able to do better in school and behave better."

I told him that sometimes I argued with my own kids and asked if he and his parents ever argued.

"Mostly just about doing my homework. Getting on my back about doing my homework. Because I didn't do it last year."

I asked him if it was hard coming back to America from abroad, how things were different.

"When I lived abroad, I could always take a walk to my friends' houses. I could do more stuff on my own. Here, everyone lives miles away. Here, we have to drive and organize way long before. The only really socializing I get here is at school or on my phone or video games or Xbox. In the games, I can play with my friends. That's where I talk to my friends the most. There, I could see them every day, but here I can't."

I asked him what he thought the best thing about being a kid was, and the worst.

"I think the best thing is being able to talk to my friends and my family. And the worst thing is definitely having a lot of homework. I'm taking a lot of honors classes and it's really stressful. If I don't have a quiz or a test, then I have two to three hours a day. And then I have therapy once a week, drums once a week, tutoring twice a week, and an executive functioning tutor once a week."

I was going to ask him another question, but for some reason, I couldn't. I sat there for a moment. A terrible sadness came over me. I told him it was great to meet him and thanked him for chatting with me, and then I sat back on the soft leather sofa and sipped the glass of Pinot Grigio Elizabeth had brought me, and I tried to breathe in and around the immense sadness welling up inside me.

I looked at this little boy and tried to smile, to ignore the feeling I had at that moment that something was wrong, not with him but with all of us; that something, as my friend had put it, was amiss. *A kid*, I thought. He should be out wading in rivers and climbing trees and learning the world with his arms and legs and senses, not at a wilderness camp for $500 a day, but always. Sitting there on the sofa amid his schoolwork and devices, he seemed so frail and uncertain, a creature better suited for a setting starkly different from the place he'd ended up. I wished there were some way I could help him escape it all—or help my own kids escape it, or myself. I felt my whole soul rattling the cage.

But what could I do? The interview was over. Phones were beeping and screens were buzzing and cars were starting and the family's life swirled onward, outward, hurrying and reaching toward everything and nothing, as did my own. The moment of sadness passed, or morphed into something closer to compassion. He was just a kid, not bad but lost, and yet sitting there, it wasn't a child he resembled, but a small, frightened animal, moving through a machine. And as he spoke, I recalled what Elizabeth had said about how badly Shep had resisted coming back to America. How he told her he'd rather stay in Europe on his own, that he'd run away and live in the subway tunnels, getting his friends to sneak him food—a young boy's fantasy of freedom and danger, the fantasy of being unobserved.

I was still thinking about Shep and about Cognition Builders when I reached out to Barbara Sarnecka, the social scientist at UC–Irvine, for the second time. I'd originally spoken to Sarnecka about the role of judgment on risk assessment, but I wondered what she had to say about the role that our excessive monitoring and intervention might be having on kids themselves, if this fear and judgment could be impacting children as well as parents and parenting culture. Was it possible these new expectations surrounding child supervision were impacting the way children develop psychologically, that in our determination to protect them, we were exposing them to other, less obvious dangers?

"We don't know for sure," she said. "But as a developmental psychologist, I think it's plausible."

She described to me the concept of self-efficacy, which, in simple terms, involves an individual's ability to navigate the world, to experience a problem, a challenge, a setback large or small, and to deal with it effectively. "When something unpleasant or frustrating or disappointing or even really painful happens to you," she explained, "but beneath those negative feelings you have a sense that you're going to be okay, that you can ultimately deal with these problems—that's self-efficacy. And related to this concept is the difference between an internal locus of control versus the external locus of control. Adults who are depressed often feel like they don't have control over things. They feel that the world is the way it is and they're at the mercy of all these forces. The more you feel in control, the happier you usually are. So that's called having an internal locus of control."

"I think I have the most external locus of control that is humanly possible," I admitted. "I feel like my locus of control is on one of those distant moons of Jupiter. I basically feel like I have no control over anything."

She told me that if that's true, research would suggest that I'm not a very happy person.

"Research doesn't lie," I said.

"Right. People assume that having money makes you happy or having children makes you happy or being married makes you happy . . . but actually the thing that makes people happy is how much control they have over how they spend their time."

I was digesting what she'd said, testing it against memory and experience, when something struck me.

"Wait," I said. "If what you say is true, then children must be miserable these days. They have so little control over their time now. They're so structured. We take them to school. We take them to lessons. We take them to summer camp. We take them to playdates. They get to control when they go to the toilet and that's about it."

"Yes," she said, "they're never responsible for anything themselves or in charge of anything. We never even let them go to the store to get a loaf of bread because it's too dangerous. So they never have the ability to do the right or the wrong thing. Nothing ever happens. They're being raised like veal, never allowed to take any risks or to be responsible or independent in any way. Or to develop a feeling of worth, of resiliency, of efficacy. Of self-confidence or self-worth or of the excitement of life."

"And you think there's an emotional or psychological cost to this?"

"Well, again, I haven't studied it. No one has. But I think it makes sense. I mean, it's like one of the basic joys of growing up, gradually getting to do more and more on your own. I used to be too little to walk to school or to ride my bike to the store, but now I can. It's exciting to become more confident and able and free to explore the world. When we massively underestimate what children are capable of or massively overestimate the danger they're in, when we effectively end up locking them in their houses like prisoners because we're so afraid . . . or we surveil them and monitor and manage them all the time, when they're always under watch, then it seems very plausible this would lead to at least unhappiness if not clinical levels of anxiety."

Sarnecka didn't seem surprised when I mentioned how the National Institute of Mental Health indicated that one in five children either has or has had a seriously debilitating mental disorder, and that anxiety disorders affect as many as one in five kids from thirteen to eighteen years old at some point in their lives.

"It's not surprising at all," she said. And then she tried to illustrate her point with a hypothetical scenario. "Let's imagine," she said, "that you're so terrified of your kid falling down and getting a concussion that you decide it's just too dangerous to even let them stand up. So you eliminate all danger of them ever falling down by keeping them in a wheelchair. If you're in a wheelchair, you're not going to fall down. And even if it's extremely rare that kids just fall down and die, we say, it happens. There's 74.2 million kids in America. Somebody fell down and hit their head and died this year. So if we wanted, we could focus on that. Let's say the media covered it 24/7 and *Law and Order* made shows about it and fictionalized accounts of it and every time it happened, even in another country, you heard about it, and there were pictures on milk cartons of kids who had fallen down and died. If you can imagine this, you can imagine a situation where parents become so terrified of that situation that they say, whatever the cost, if I can eliminate the risk of this happening to my kid, then it's worth it. So I'm going to make my kid stay in a wheelchair all the time just to be safe, because better safe than sorry. And so eventually you have a bunch of kids who aren't disabled being confined to wheelchairs, and at some point you can imagine schools and cops saying, well, a lot of the kids are in wheelchairs anyway, so if a kid falls down and gets hurt on our premises, they're going to ask why we didn't have all of them in wheelchairs, so from now on, during the school day, all the kids have to be in wheelchairs. You can imagine it getting to the point where it becomes unusual to see a kid not in a wheelchair, and where you start calling the police saying, 'I saw a parent walking down the street with a child. The child was not in a wheelchair and could fall down at any moment.' Let's just all be grateful that I caught you in time before the kid fell down and died.

"Now, this is a fantasy. This is a thing we don't do because we understand that healthy physical development requires children to do things that are risky, things like walking around. We understand that there's some risk in standing up or climbing or running or jumping, but we think it's an acceptable risk because it doesn't happen very often that a kid falls down and dies, and we think the benefits of letting our kids walk and run around are worth the small risk that every once in a very great while a kid falls and dies. We're willing to take the risk."

"For now," I said.

"For now. But let me tell you something. As a developmental psychologist, I think the benefits of kids having age-appropriate amounts of independence and unsupervised time is just as important as the physical benefits of letting them walk around. I think the benefits are worth the very small risk that at some point a child has a tragic accident or a crime committed against them. I think we are grossly underestimating the benefits of independence and overestimating the risks."

"And doing so is taking a psychological toll on our kids?"

"Well, again, we don't know for sure. We don't know how much. But to put that in perspective, we also don't know exactly what the toll would be on forcing nondisabled kids to stay in wheelchairs all day. We don't do that experiment because it would be unethical. But in a way, we're *doing* the experiment to see what happens when you don't let kids have any independence. We're doing it *right now* to an entire generation of children."

"Using them as guinea pigs."

"In a sense, yes. And you could argue that what we're seeing in this experiment we're doing on our children is acute amounts of obesity, acute amounts of depression and type 2 diabetes, acute amounts of anxiety, and all kinds of other very, very bad things."

There's an increasing amount of evidence to support Sarnecka's claim. In her book *How to Raise an Adult*, Julie Lythcott-Haims highlights a number of recent studies on the connection between overparenting and mental health problems in teens and young adults. She writes how, "In a 2013 survey of college counseling center directors, 96 percent of respondents said the number of students with significant psychological problems is a growing concern on their campus; 70 percent said that the number of students on their campus with severe psychological problems has increased in the past year; and they reported that on average 24.5 percent of their student-patients were taking psychotropic drugs such as antidepressants, antipsychotics, ADHD stimulants, mood stabilizers, and anti-anxiety medications."

In 2012, an earlier version of the same survey reported a 16 percent increase in visits to student mental health centers since 2000. And in 2013, the American College Health Association surveyed 100,000 students on 153 college campuses and learned that 83.7 percent had felt overwhelmed at least one time within the past twelve months by all they had to do; 79.1 percent felt exhausted; 59.6 percent felt very sad; 55.9 percent felt very lonely; 51 percent felt overwhelming anxiety; 46.5 percent felt things were hopeless; 37 percent felt overwhelming anger; 31.3 percent felt so depressed that it was difficult to function; and 8 percent had seriously considered suicide. A 2013 *Journal of Child and Family Studies* survey of 297 college students found that college students with helicopter parents reported "significantly higher levels of depression and less satisfaction in life, and attributed this diminishment in well-being to a violation of the students' basic psychological needs for autonomy and competence."

Lythcott-Haims writes that because these mental health crises are happening to kids who end up at hundreds of schools in every tier, "they appear to stem not from what it takes to get into the most elite schools but from some facet of American childhood itself." She concludes that "when a seemingly perfectly healthy but over-parented kid gets to college and has trouble coping with the various new situations they might encounter . . . they can have real difficulty knowing how to handle the disagreement, uncertainty, the hurt feelings, or the decision-making process. This inability to cope—to sit with some discomfort, think about options, talk it through with someone, make a decision—can become a problem unto itself."

A friend who works in the administration of a highly selective university in the Midwest echoes all of this. "There are still a lot of clever, curious, ingenious little minds out there, far smarter than I'll ever be. But so many of them come in to school already carrying burdens. This got a lot worse after the crisis back in '08, so I think there's definitely a financial factor. Tuition makes that nearly inevitable. Mom and Dad have let Johnny know he's been securitized. He's an investment. That's an incredible weight to place on the back of someone who developmentally isn't that far removed from daydreaming about playing in the NFL.

"But then there's also this feeling that these kids have been programmed to win. All their lives, probably going back as far as they can remember, they've been told how spectacular they are. You get into a college whose acceptance rate is like negative 3.6 percent. Everything that's happened to you has affirmed this idea of how awesome you are. Just set aside for a moment how damaging that can be to someone's sense of self. These kids eventually have to face the twin existential monsters of 'I got a C; this is the worst moment of my life' (I've had those exact words spoken in my office) and 'Now what? I got into this great school, everything my life has led up to, now what?' They get to campus and for a number of them the ground falls out from beneath them. *Getting in* has been the thing that matters, and it can be so disheartening to realize this isn't any sort of finish line at all. I mean, the end of youth is apocalyptic in plenty of ways, but I don't think it has to be quite so explicit."

Sarnecka wasn't surprised by my friend's experience, or by any of this data. She finds it deeply disturbing and adds that "there's a real human rights issue here. We're used to thinking it's acceptable to make rules for children that we wouldn't or couldn't make for adults. And in many ways, this is right. Kids can't drink, they can't vote, they can't drive, and it's appropriate to make these rules. But the idea that we're protecting someone from something does not give us carte blanche to take away all of their mobility and all of their independence and all of their rights. There are countries where women are not allowed to drive, and I'm sure there are people in these countries who say, 'Well, we're concerned about women's safety.' If Donald Trump announced that women were not going to be able to drive anymore because no one respects women more than he does and driving is very dangerous, people would say, 'Fuck you, Donald! We'll take that risk, thank you very much.' But when we have these debates about kids, we need to remember that there was a time in history when women were not allowed to vote and women were not allowed to drive and women were not allowed to make basic choices about how they spent their time or did x, y, and z, and a lot of the rhetoric surrounding these issues was about protecting them from a dangerous and daunting world."

"Of course," I said, "there *is* a difference between the rights of adult women and the rights of children."

"Of course there is. And I'm obviously not saying that children should have all the rights that adults have. But I do think they have *some* rights, and not just to safety. They have a right to some freedom, to some independence and efficacy. They have a right to try things and to fail at them and to try other things and succeed. They have a right, like all of us, to a little bit of danger."

We can deny them that right, as we've been doing, but as with everything, there is a cost—for us, for society, and for them. William Deresiewicz sees one of these costs in colleges that "are producing a large number of very smart, completely confused graduates. Kids who have ample mental horsepower, an incredible work ethic, and no idea what to do next." In the end, he observes that "all the values that once informed the way we raise our children—the cultivation of curiosity, the inculcation of character, the instillment of a sense of membership in one's community, the development of the capacity for democratic citizenship, let alone any emphasis on the pleasure and freedom of play, the part of childhood where you actually get to be a child—all these are gone. . . . We are not teaching to the test; we're living to it."

I couldn't get this idea of living to the test—and also, of parenting to the test—out of my mind. I recalled how Felix was not even two years old when I began noticing that he was a little behind the other babies in his developmental milestones. It was nothing drastic, but I observed that he sat up a little later, talked a little later, pointed at things a little later. He hadn't bonded to a specific transitional object when the books said he was supposed to, and in the evenings I'd sometimes hold him and talk to him about the wonderful quality of this or that special soft toy. *Don't you want to bond to soft little turtle? Don't you want to carry teddy bear around with you? Teddy would make a very good transitional object.* When my pitches didn't land, and later, when his preschool teacher complained that he seemed to be demonstrating some "sensory-seeking behavior," I did what at least half the parents I know have done at one point or another. I took him to an occupational therapist for an evaluation. Perhaps it was unnecessary. Perhaps it was a waste of time and money. But it wasn't an invasive or painful procedure. It couldn't hurt. And if it turned out that he did need it, and I didn't give it a try, imagine how I'd feel then.

I discussed this with Erin Anderson, an occupational therapist who runs a practice on Chicago's north side. Anderson's practice offers services from occupational therapists, speech and language pathologists, psychologists, and social workers. She told me that many of the parents who come to their practice do so for reasons that are similar to those that had brought me in.

I observed to her that these days, it seems as though every other parent I meet has a child receiving occupational therapy or speech therapy or social therapy or some kind of therapeutic service. I told her I suspected that practicing pediatric occupational therapy today must be quite different from how it was practiced twenty or thirty years ago. Certainly, I said, better screening and education had something to do with the ever-increasing number of clients, but I asked Anderson if she thought parental fear and this new style of intensive or anxious parenting might also play a role.

"I think it's both," she said. "I'm seeing more and more mothers who had careers, who were in business, and now they have kids and decide to stay home. And what I see is many of them doing for their children as they might have done in their job. So the kids are very scheduled, they're in classes, the parents are super-educated, reading how to parent on the internet instead of trusting instincts."

I recalled to her how nervous I had been during the first few years I spent at home with my children. "I didn't grow up in a house with five siblings or cousins," I said. "I babysat a little, but not for infants or toddlers. So I remember that when I had kids of my own, there was this anxiety about just being in the house with them. I know this sounds awful, but it's true. I mean, I wanted to be with them. But it was always easier to say, 'Let's go to Target, let's go to the music class, let's go on a playdate.' Constant movement was much easier than just sitting in a house with a baby or small kid. And so this is a big change. Where I grew up, there wasn't a lot of culture or a lot of things to do. It was hard to get around. I think there was a lot of boredom. But as a kid, I remember playing in the yard, playing in the cul-de-sac, walking over to this friend's house, walking over to that friend's house. Nobody was at camp. Nobody was doing classes. Some of the moms worked. A lot of them worked part-time. Often a neighbor would watch the kid whose mom worked. Most of my memories are just sort of hanging out, certainly watching a lot of TV, which wasn't great, but also riding my bike, going to the pool in the summer, doing weird things, trying to find our parents' porn or trying to shoplift crappy earrings from Claire's Boutique or seeing how many Krispy Kreme doughnuts we could eat before we puked or whatever. Occasionally getting in trouble, but usually not."

"So what you were doing was you were exploring, you were taking risks, you were problem-solving because there wasn't someone watching over you. You were doing time management, you were taking mitigated risks, maybe doing some things that were unsafe, but you realized that and it was within a realm of safety because you were in the neighborhood and you were supporting each other. But because our kids are in classes so much, even at young ages, because society is telling us we should expose them, if you have the financial means, to music, to gymnastics, to soccer, to ballet; because we're scheduling them so much, you do take away that problem-solving, that learned independence, that self-esteem to make it across the street with a friend, or mastering the monkey bars or figuring out how to take turns on the slide.

"And even at the parks now, we as parents are so overinvolved. I mean, I try to stand back, and I see people look at me. I stand back and watch my daughter at the top of the slide and another kid pushes past her and goes ahead. And I just wait. And the mom's right up there saying, 'Oh, Johnny, don't push in front of her, you shouldn't blah-blah-blah.' And I feel like, 'It's okay. I'm going to let her make that choice.' And my daughter looks at me, and I say, 'If you don't like what he did, you need to tell him.' I'm not going to solve that problem for her. I mean, I don't care whether she goes down the slide or not, so why would I solve that? She needs to advocate for herself.

"But the hanging back is hard to do. Everyone else is right there and hovering, so it's hard to be the only one who isn't. But again, I feel like most of the time my parents wouldn't have even been at the park. There would be parental involvement if someone was injured, or if there was something extreme. But beyond that, the little squabbles, the parents would just say, 'Work it out.'

"And the research does show that if you don't get a chance with peers in particular to do that, to figure out that sharing, that action-reaction, that cause and effect of behavior, then you don't learn appropriate assertiveness. You don't learn what is okay and what isn't, how much is too much to push someone. These interactions are the beginning stages of negotiation and problem-solving and social-emotional development. Even two-year-olds can do it."

"And if the parents are managing it, the kids don't learn it in the same way?"

"No, they don't. Because it can't be taught. It has to be learned experientially. And with all the technology they're using, they don't learn the facial expressions of these interactions. They don't know the tone of voice and the cues. We're not giving them enough practice because they need to do it in kindergarten, not when they're twelve. And I think by putting them in all these classes, by being so, so, so present, we're not giving them time to build that self-esteem because that's how you build it. When you negotiate. When someone is trying to push you out of the way to go down the slide before you and you tell them to cut it out. And so you got to go down the slide, you learned to speak up, you solved a problem. That's a good day at the park."

"Because they learned something."

"Right. Like my son is two now. He climbs up on the stool, falls off, cries. Does he want to try that again? Yes. Yes, he does. One more time. *I wonder if that was a fluke*, he thinks. He tries it again. Falls. And then the third or fourth time, he gets it. It's only a step or two. It's basically safe. But he's learning from experience. Why would I take that from him?"

"I wonder," I said. "If part of the equation is the quantity of products out there we can buy to make it easier. We all want to be good parents, so we buy all these things that are supposed to help, or to protect them, but that really promote a lack of development."

Erin offered the example of a new infant chair on the market. "They sit in this little chair where they can't get into any trouble. But then they're not learning to use their core muscles; they're not learning to explore their environment. We have to try to accept that it's okay for them to have some quiet time, to explore on their own, to get frustrated, to cry. We don't want it, not even the moment they're born. We want them to be contained. We want them to be like people. We want them to be like us."

I recalled to her those early months, going to the pediatrician and hearing about all the terrible risks—the choking hazards, the dangers of falling, the risk of letting them sleep on their stomachs, and on and on. I recalled to her what a relief it was to strap my child into a bouncy seat and feel like he was contained. "But then I wonder if in solving for that anxiety you create another problem. You manage one risk and produce another."

"I think there's some of this going on across the board," she said.

"I feel like more people are starting to go back to their instincts, to the basics. But still, my kids have no one to play with because there's no one around. They're all in camp. The streets and the parks are empty."

"I know. We moved into our first house a few months ago. We live on a block with single-family homes, thirty kids in a three-block radius. And so often, none of the kids are around. The streets are quiet. Once or twice a year we have a block party and all the kids come out and play and ride their bikes and scooters and have a blast, and I watch them and think, 'This is how it should be every day. Not once or twice a year. Every afternoon. Every day in summer.' But that's a fantasy. It's not how we live anymore. Everyone's in their own little pod.

"Also," Erin continued, "I feel like we as parents have changed too. I remember my mom having this community of mothers. And they supported each other. They'd talk about crazy stuff their kids did and one would say, 'Oh, don't worry about it. Mine did the same thing. We'll dye their hair back,' or whatever. Now I feel like you're at the park and there's so much judgment. Constant judgment. I was standing outside my office, which is five minutes from where I live. I had the kids in the stroller and was going in to get the mail and a client was inside the waiting room. I left the kids, two and four, in the double stroller while I ran in to grab the mail. Two o'clock on a Monday. And I got stopped by one of my clients in the waiting room who was very anxious and angry that I had done this. And I said, 'Well, I was just running in to get the mail. They're perfectly fine.' But she was very angry and proceeded to stand outside and wait with my kids who then were screaming because a stranger was frowning over them. And she told me she thought it was irresponsible. I was so shocked. So angry.

"And at the park, I often have to explain to parents my approach and stop them from going over if my kids are in some kind of socially challenging situation. My daughter's very shy and petite, and kids test her. And I talk to her about her options, but I don't do it for her. And I typically have to ask parents not to intervene because their MO is that they'll go and stop their kid from doing anything that reflects badly. Some are okay when I tell them not to, but plenty give me looks or they just do it anyway."

I interrupted Erin, speaking from experience. "It's like they can't help themselves. Part of it is that they're concerned for your kid, but part of it is people being self-conscious about how they look as a parent. No one wants to be the parent who's inattentive or more interested in their book or their phone than their child."

"Exactly."

"But then I wonder, isn't it incubating a sort of narcissism? Being a part of a family or a community is learning, 'Okay, I have needs, you have needs, the other people have needs, we all have to negotiate our needs.' But if we're constantly sending kids the signal that their needs are the most important, that they are the center of our emotional universe, that their needs are more important than the needs of the family as a whole—that's not a great message to send, right?"

Erin tells me about some of the teenagers she works with as volunteers, students interested in becoming OTs. "They schedule with me and then they cancel. It's disheartening. They don't seem to have a strong sense of personal responsibility or commitment or even a sense that their actions affect others. Sometimes the parents want to make their schedule with me, and I say, 'You know what, I need to hear from your daughter. She's a senior in high school, so I need to hear from her.' That's just how I was raised. My parents passed away young, my dad when I was twenty-one and my mom when I was twenty-nine. But they taught me to take care of myself, to navigate the world. And I wish they were here for me to say that to them—though of course I complained about it the whole time they were alive."

"Well, it's a balance, isn't it? I mean, we want our kids to know that we see them. I see you, and I understand your needs, and your needs matter to me. I think for my parents' generation, kids were less visible, parents less present. And so everyone wants to correct for that. We want to show our kids that we're there for them, we're in the game with them and we care. Which is all good. But it seems like we've gone so far in that direction."

"It does. But I'm hoping that now it's coming back a little. I feel like I've found a few parents who are similar to me, who believe in not doing things for their kids all the time, in letting them have some experiences, and that having them struggle now is better than having them struggle for the first time when they're ten or twelve."

"Or twenty."

"Exactly. I mean, the experience of going off to college or moving away from home for the first time is hard enough; it shouldn't also be the first time a child learns that sometimes in life, you struggle."

In *The Human Condition*, Hannah Arendt describes a process called natality. "Natality," she says, stems from "the constant influx of newcomers who are born into the world as strangers." She writes how "the new beginning inherent in birth can make itself felt in the world only because the newcomer possesses the capacity of beginning something anew." Arendt argues that this fact of natality is "the miracle that saves the world, the realm of human affairs, from its normal, natural ruin." It is not, in the end, our connection to children that saves us and offers humanity, faith, and hope; it's our ability to separate from children, to let them separate from us. Their ability to escape and transcend us, to discover their own way of being with all the pain and danger that entails, leaving us behind as they try to do better, to fail better, is what can make the world anew.

Arendt's argument on natality reminds me, oddly, of my favorite episode of *The Simpsons*, a show I watched first with my father, then with my husband, and which I will soon watch with my kids. My favorite episode, the one that still makes me cry, is the episode when an x-ray reveals that Homer Simpson has been living for years with a crayon lodged in his brain; it is this crayon that's led to his chronic and unfathomable stupidity. The crayon is removed. His IQ soars. For the first time in his life, he is able to truly see and understand and connect with his fiercely intelligent daughter, Lisa. For a few beautiful days, he is not just her father but her mentor, her friend. Of course, it can't last. To be a smart man in a stupid world is too painful for Homer. The crayon is reinserted. His stupidity returns in full force. But before it does, he leaves a note behind for Lisa, telling her that no matter how great the distance between them becomes, he'll always love her, and he'll always be grateful for the time they had together.

In the end, it's the only promise any of us can keep.

9

SMALL ANIMALS

Recently, I was looking through an old family photo album with my daughter when I noticed a snapshot of myself at about her age, five or six. In the center of the frame is a thin blue diving board stretching above the pool where my parents used to take us, and just beyond the board, a few feet over the water, I'm suspended in midair, a blurry streak of soggy girl tilted forward, arms bent, body angled right between a jump and a flop.

"That's me!" Violet said.

"Nope," I said. "It's Mommy! It's me."

I took the picture out of the album and set it on my dresser. It felt strange to see myself in it, this single moment of suspension and excitement, because I have absolutely no memory of the experience. What I remember instead from that summer was what led up to it—wanting to jump off the diving board but feeling too afraid, walking up the ladder, then back again, walking to the edge of the board, then back, over and over, all summer long, my parents watching, encouraging, urging me forward, then soothing my disappointment when I couldn't bring myself to do it. I don't remember the jump, but I remember the fear, how it felt like something holding me back, a code I couldn't crack. Until one day, apparently, I could.

Later that evening, after the kids were in bed, I told Pete I wanted to take a vacation.

"There are no vacations once you have kids," he reminded me. "There are only trips."

"Okay," I said. "A trip, then. Let's go on a trip."

"A road trip?"

"No," I said. "Let's fly."

Soon after, along with Pete's parents and brother and sister-in-law and three small nieces, we flew to New York City for a long weekend. The plane ride there was perfectly smooth and uneventful, but of course that didn't stop me from descending into my usual panic-disorder panorama of nausea, hyperventilation, clutching of armrests, and superstitious obsessive-compulsive silent counting. It must have worked, because our plane did not crash! We landed. We piled into cabs, inched our way into the city, checked our large and rowdy party into the boutique SoHo hotel that Pete had read about on TripAdvisor. Pete is the designated travel agent in our family, the one who is usually most adept at making arrangements, and so I looked at him askance as we crossed the threshold into the stainless-steel, sparkling-glass lobby, a lobby crowded with arrangements of rare orchids, bowls of exotic fruit, freestanding displays of geometric steel sculptures and European fashion models who leaned and teetered on their laser-smooth, flamingo-thin legs. We entered the holy hipness and glamour of this hotel with our brigade of poorly behaved children. All at once, they charged the elevator, sullied the glass walls with their jelly-smeared hands, initiated loud negotiations about who was going to sleep in whose room and in which bed and whether we were going to go to the Museum of Natural History first or the puppet theater in Central Park. The fashion models frowned at one another. The concierge rushed toward us with open arms, as though preparing to smother a fire.

"You said the hotel was kid-friendly," I whispered to Pete.

"It said on the website it was the most kid-friendly hotel in SoHo. You told me anything but Times Square. You said anything with a pool."

The pool, I thought. Yes, surely the pool area would be more child-friendly than the lobby. I could take the kids swimming while Pete unpacked and planned the evening. Swimming would wear them out, make them more docile and adult-like. I donned the only swimsuit I'd brought with me. It wasn't exactly a maternity swimsuit, but it wasn't exactly not a maternity swimsuit. I think maybe it was a standard swimsuit I'd worn often enough during pregnancy for the elastic in the middle section of the suit to just kind of give up. It was black nylon with a dark blue, diagonal stripe that was supposed to be slimming but wasn't slimming it all. It was not a sleek or stylish swimsuit, but really, nothing about me as I rode the elevator to the roof of the hotel with five small children buzzing around me was sleek or stylish—not my big Trader Joe's canvas bag that I was using to carry sunscreen and lip balm and pool toys and goggles; not the soft, gray half-moons beneath my eyes, larger than ever after my sleepless night thinking about the trip ahead; not my frizzy ponytail or the stubbly legs I hadn't had time to shave. Certainly not the children surrounding me, these small bodies that seemed somehow to occupy every inch of occupiable space in the very-slow-moving elevator that claimed a capacity of twenty adult humans. Nothing about me looked as though it belonged at this SoHo hotel, but what did I care, I thought. It's just a pool.

The elevator doors parted. At first, I suspected we had arrived at the wrong floor; there was no pool in sight, just a crowd of partygoers. Only as the doors opened fully did I see the open sky of lower Manhattan, the rooftop railing's sharp impression against the skyline, and on the far side of the building, past the bar, past the cocktail lounge, past the DJ and more fashion models and men in skinny pants and tailored sport jackets and the small cocktail tables made of reclaimed industrial materials, and the twenty-dollar cocktails in vintage glassware covering these tables—only then did I see that there was, indeed, a small square space of wavering blue water that I suppose could be called a pool by a person with an imagination. It was more like a jet-less Jacuzzi, really, or a very large fish tank. It was a pool for dipping or plunging. It was a pool as an accessory to drinking Prosecco or reading a Bret Easton Ellis novel or smoking some good hashish or just being seen by other people doing the same. It was not a pool for swimming. The guests surrounding it, even those in swimsuits, seemed to have no intention of getting wet. They slouched across a platform of spa-inspired birchwood, fondled their drinks and books and backgammon boards, flexed their artful and understated tattoos. The DJ began to play. Cocktails proliferated. A woman with severely cut black bangs teetered toward us in dominatrix stilettos.

"Oh no," I said, trying to hold back the children, trying to herd them back into the elevator. "We can't go swimming here, kids. Change of plans."

"Why?" they cried.

"We just can't," I said. "I think the pool is closed."

"It's not closed!" they shouted, and they rushed forward. Then they were running, charging, leaping toward the tiny speck of water. They didn't give a shit about who was wearing what bathing suit or drinking what cocktail or dancing to what music. They just wanted to swim, to play, to be submerged, to dive and float and splash. And they weren't going to apologize for wanting it, for not caring, for being kids. There was no stopping them, and so, reluctantly, I followed.

I passed the DJ, the bartender, the waitress, a sophisticated-looking French couple with a stylish baby of their own. My not-quite-but-pretty-much-a-maternity bathing suit's straps slipped down as I crossed the roof. Fixing them, random ChapSticks and change fell out of my Trader Joe's pool bag. Oops, oops, excuse me, sorry.

"Can I help you?" a waiter asked as I passed.

"I wish you could," I said.

"Something to drink?"

"Oh, a drink. A drink would help."

By the time I found a place on the deck, the kids had already forgotten about me, except for Violet, who was not yet swimming independently and waited by the side of the pool, jumping up and down. "Swim with me, Mommy. Mommy, swim with me. Swim now."

I tried to explain to her that it wasn't so much a pool for swimming. "I'm not sure Mommy can fit in this pool," I said.

"Just fit. Just fit. Mommy fit. Swim, swim," she beckoned. "Swim to me now."

And so I swam. I climbed in and stood in the middle of the tank as my little girl glided toward me, away from me, toward me again, back and forth, laughing, squealing. I stood there and watched my children occupy the pool. I watched the childless people trying to ignore us, not quite but almost containing their annoyance at having to share this obviously adult-intended space with five humans under ten. I felt a little sad when I considered the fact that there had to be so much emotional and psychological distance between us, the child-ed and the child-less, that we were all cordoned off in our own lonely worlds. And I felt relief when I saw the French couple, at least one of whom I suspected was a notable film actor—squeeze their baby's arms into a pair of blue floaties. *Thank goodness*, I thought. *One more parent in the pool.* Only I was wrong. Neither parent intended to swim. Instead, they plopped their infant into the water, watching from the side as it bobbled and waddled and drifted out of reach.

Oh my God, I thought. What the fuck? I could see the tragedy unfolding. I could see the headline: FRENCH BABY DROWNS AMID POSH SOHO ROOF PARTY; FABULOUSLY HIP SPECTATORS LOOK ON, DO NOTHING. I pushed myself out of the pool, grabbed my cell phone, and began recording this poor child left on its own in the water.

No, kidding.

What I did was I reached out and steadied the baby, along with my own daughter, though the French parents assured me again and again, *ce n'est pas necessaire*. I'm sure they were right. I'm sure it wasn't *necessaire*. I'm sure that in France, the magical land where women don't get fat and college is free, babies somehow teach themselves to swim without adult supervision. Sink or swim, their parents say to them (in French), and of course they choose swim.

How I envied them at that moment. How badly I wanted to climb out of the pool, order myself a twenty-dollar mojito, grab a novel out of my canvas sack, and live my adult life while my daughter and this strangely buoyant French baby made their own way in the world. But of course I couldn't. I simply didn't have it in me to let go like that, to look away, to feel so unburdened, so unafraid. The French couple rubbed tanning oil on each other's well-toned shoulders. The music played louder. The alcohol flowed. And I stood amid it all, a size twelve mama fish treading water in the middle of her school of swirling bodies. I was what I was—an anxious American mother. I might have spent two years thinking about the destructive ways that fear informs our parenting in this country, but that didn't mean I could now escape it. But maybe that was okay. Maybe we all are what we are, and that's okay. And besides, Pete would come looking for us sooner or later, and then I'd be able to shout over the music and the squealing children and the sophisticated chatter those words that every partnered parent delights in shouting: "Your turn!"

But not quite yet. For the moment, it was my turn. I was on. I was in it.

. . .

It might not have been a vacation, but it turned out to be a great trip. New York City, I decided, is like Disney World for people who would never go to Disney World. At Felix's request, we rode every subway line on the island. We went to the museums and played in the parks. We ate bagels on the Lower East Side and took the ferry to the marvelously emptied Governors Island. We visited museums and hung out with friends, and Pete got to spend an hour in the Strand, his favorite bookstore in the world, and remember what it was like when he used to have time to read. We did everything and went everywhere and then, on our very last day in the city, I sent a message to Lenore Skenazy, a lifelong New Yorker and faithful friend, and asked if she'd have time to grab a coffee or a drink.

"Make it a cookie and you're on," she replied.

We arranged to meet at a café near midtown. Only as I stepped inside did I realize it was run by and for the benefit of former convicts. A man in a polo shirt served us a brownie the size of a Bible, and then informed us that it was buy-one-get-one-free hour and served us a second. We paid for it and put our spare change in a box to support the human beings who, for reasons that are not always valid or clear, have spent years of their lives locked in cages in the maze of the correctional-industrial complex. Then we sat down to talk.

More than ten years had passed since Lenore had been called the worst mother in America for having let her nine-year-old ride alone on the subway. It had been more than three years since my own arrest. And yet, to both of us, the time seemed to have passed in the space of a nap.

Lenore marveled at the fact that her youngest son had just left for college, then told me, with more melancholy in her voice than I'd heard before, that the loneliness she felt at his departure had caught her off guard. She laughed a little when she spoke of it. "I miss him so much," she said, "that a couple of weeks after he left, I signed up to have a foreign exchange student live in our house. I have this nice girl from Haifa living down the hall now. Some people take up a hobby when their kids leave; I take in an Israeli." She sighed. "It's good. It's all good, but I still miss them."

"Sentimental words for a neglectful mother," I said.

"I know. Ha. Well, so it goes. How are you?"

I told her about Pete and the kids, about our vacation in New York, all we'd done and seen. I told her about their summers, their new teachers, their friends.

"And how about the book?" she asked. "It's almost done?"

Now it was my turn to sigh. "I don't know," I said. "I've been feeling discouraged lately."

She broke the second brownie in half, offered me a piece.

"You know, I have to admit, Lenore. I'm discouraged about the state of parenthood in this country. I'm not optimistic. Sometimes I think things are changing, or that they're going to change, but most of the time . . . I don't know. A few weeks ago, I was at Felix's third-grade orientation. It was right after Labor Day, and I could tell that everyone there was as exhausted from the summer schedule as I was. One friend of mine, a working mother, was bragging about the herculean feat of getting her son enrolled in some kind of camp or program every single day of the twelve-week vacation. And I started thinking how crazy it all is, that probably 90 percent of the people in the room had spent upward of four figures to have their kid in this camp or that camp or this program or that program. All that money. All that driving. It seemed crazy. And I thought about the fact that all I really wanted for my kids over the summer was for them to have a break from the structure of the classroom. To hang out, to run around, go swimming, ride their bikes. Maybe, if they're feeling particularly ambitious, make a lemonade stand or climb a fucking tree. I kept thinking, how can that be so hard, to let them do that? And so I turn to these three women, friends of mine, and I suggest that next summer, at least for a few weeks, we save time and money and do some kind of hands-off, independence camp. Like one day my house is the home base. I'm not going to be organizing the kids, but I'll be in the house. I'll be there, working from home, and they can go do whatever in the neighborhood. They'll have a radius they can stay in, but they can go to the park, go to the whatever, just do their own thing. These women are my friends. I mean, I like them. I'm friendly with them. They're smart and generally open-minded women, and I'm telling you, Lenore, they're looking at me like I'm nuts."

"Are they looking at you like you're nuts or are they looking at you like they're judging you?"

"A little of both, I guess. And they say to me, 'Kim, you can't let them go to the park by themselves. You just can't.' But why? Why the hell not? Do you think they're going to arrest us all? I say this, Lenore, and they are looking at me like I'm suggesting launching our kids to the moon."

She doesn't look surprised. She looks undaunted, leans in a little, dunks her brownie in her coffee. "All right, I get it. But don't be discouraged. You know, these panics take hold, and they don't just dissipate overnight. But that doesn't mean you should give up. Here is what you're going to do."

I leaned forward. I wanted to know.

"I've told you my theory of yuppie jujitsu?"

"Of what?"

"Yuppie jujitsu. I know, I know. 'Yuppie' is an old word, but I'm old, so there you go. Yuppie jujitsu is my name for using their own strategy against them. So this is what you're going to do. You're going to go back to these women—and as afraid as they are of letting their kids go to the park, you have to make them more afraid of *not* sending their kids to the park. You're going to say to them, 'Listen, if you don't send your kids to the park and they don't break their foot and have to get home on their bike by themselves, they will never get into an Ivy League school; they'll never run a corporation; they will never earn a Fulbright or find a cure for cancer or have their own hit series on HBO or run for Congress. They'll be fat, they'll be lonely, they'll be sad, they'll be depressed and anxious and lost, and they won't be the entrepreneurs or the problem-solvers of the next generation, and they won't have a chance to access any of those skills or feelings of basic self-worth that they need in life, because guess what—you can't give those things to kids. As much as we want to, we can't do it. They have to develop them for themselves. They have to try and fail and be scared and push through and bounce back and fail again and feel lost and then find their way home."

"Because these are the things that make us feel worthy and capable, the things that make us feel like people?"

"Yes. So you call it Independence Camp. You call it Character-Building Camp. And you tell people that if we don't start doing this, our kids are going to be in big, big trouble. I don't really believe this, by the way. I think that in the end, things have a way of working out. Or not. I don't really think we have that much control over anything. But don't say that. Not if you want things to change. You have to scare them out of their fear. You have to scare them into being reasonable and rational human beings."

"Fight fear with fear. That's what you're saying?"

"Yes," she says. "Not because we want to, but because we have to. Because fear seems to be the only thing that works."

The next day, we packed our bags and headed to Newark. It's true what Pete had said about there being no more vacations when you have kids. After a few days away, I was more exhausted than ever. I needed a vacation to recover from the vacation. And yet, despite the usual fatigue, I also felt strangely invigorated as we left the city behind. All the way under the Hudson and across the Meadowlands, I found myself thinking about Lenore, about Julie, about the other mothers I'd met and talked to, about the sociologists and psychologists and writers and thinkers who were working so hard to figure out where we are as a country, as a culture, as parents and partners and thinking-feeling beings, about how we have gotten to this place of pervasive and insurmountable fear and where we are headed. As my kids bickered and the traffic thickened and my husband checked sports scores on his phone, I found my mind wandering, then landing on a line of prose by Adrienne Rich, the radical, feminist, lesbian activist poet who, before she had children, was just a nice Jewish girl with a bad case of nerves. In her book of nonfiction, she wrote, "I was radicalized by motherhood." It had seemed a counterintuitive notion when I read it in college. I associated radicalism with youth. Motherhood happened from a place of safety and caution. Now, rereading, it made perfect sense. *After all,* I thought, *writing is rebellion.* Art takes place when we're unable to accept the boundaries we inherit, when we're compelled to reimagine or reinvent what others are willing or even eager to receive. What territory could be more fertile for reinvention than the rigid and oppressive institution of motherhood?

As we pushed onto the freeway, I reached inside my purse and took out my prescription bottle of lorazepam, my old preflight standby. I poured a dusty pill into my hand, turned it over, then put it back in the bottle. A while back, Pete had bought me a fear-of-flying app that was supposed to help with aerophobia. I decided to give it a try, to fly without sedation for the first time in almost a decade.

We arrived at the airport ninety minutes before our scheduled flight time, but we still felt rushed. There was the usual snaking line, the usual display of security theater, the dumping of water, the removing of shoes, the unloosing of belts, the collapsing of strollers, and the resigned acceptance of pat-downs and scans—all these things meant to protect us from those who would do us harm, all of us pretending to believe that this was all it would take. Once we were seated on the plane, I opened the fear-of-flying app on my phone and typed in the date and flight number. Already, my hands were trembling, my skin clammy, my heartbeat accelerating, and a familiar cramping sensation settling in my gut.

"Hello, Kim," the app said to me as I tightened my seat belt.

Hello, machine, I thought.

The app began by telling me a little bit about myself. "Fear of flying (aerophobia) is a very common phenomenon. A flight is a severe psychological problem for every third person in the world. The fear arises in people prone to anxiety and suspiciousness. It also arises in people who have problems in trusting other people and mechanisms. Sound familiar?"

Are you kidding? I thought. *Have you ever looked around? Read the internet? Watched the news? You're a piece of software, for God's sake—you must get the same updates I do.* How could anyone trust other people or the mechanisms they create? In fact, I couldn't trust anyone who trusted anyone.

"The main cause of fear of flying," the app continued, "is genetics and upbringing. It's most common in the children of anxious parents."

Right, I thought. Well, I didn't need an app to tell me that.

"In many cases, aerophobia is just a side effect of perfectionism."

I don't know, I thought as our plane pushed back from the runway. I'd never considered myself a perfectionist, but I supposed I could see his point.

"The perfectionist isn't comforted by reassuring statistics about the relative safety of air travel, the relative safety of public spaces, the relative safety of life itself. You, and other perfectionists like you, want things to be purely good, perfectly safe. You long for a certainty that doesn't exist in our universe, an assurance that no plane will ever crash, no child will ever die, no unfathomable tragedy will occur on your watch."

And what the hell is wrong with that? Doesn't everyone want those things?

The app tried to change the subject. "Conditions today are partly cloudy. Under partly cloudy conditions, the atmosphere is usually nonturbulent. In the case of no cumulus clouds. And today, we have exactly such a day—no cumulus clouds in the sky. We'll enter the clouds approximately fifty-five seconds after takeoff."

Wait, I demanded. *Who cares about the clouds? Answer my question.*

"Of course everyone wants those things, Kim. But most people accept that we can't have them, that perfection of that sort isn't possible."

I regretted not taking my lorazepam. I decided I should have taken three. Now it was too late. I looked out the window as we came to a stop before the runway, idled, then began our awful acceleration toward lift.

"Moderate wind for today's takeoff," said the machine. "The interesting fact is that the surface wind is always several times weaker than the high-level wind. But we don't feel it near the ground during takeoffs and landings."

Who gives a shit about surface wind? Oh, I hate you, machine. God, I want off, out. I want my feet on the ground where they belong. This is wrong, wrong, wrong. We aren't meant to do this. Oh, God, no. I don't want to die. Please, please, someone, help.

"Pull yourself together, Kim. Takeoff is an unpleasant moment for most anxious passengers. Control yourself, not the airplane."

Control myself? Really? That's your advice? I want my fucking three dollars back if that's your advice.

We surged. The engines roared, hurling us forward, faster and faster by the second. We tilted upward, lifted off. The belly of the bird groaned, sagged, then rose. We rose and banked, climbed and trembled through the thinning air, the lit-up clouds, the loosening atmosphere, all of us safe inside our pressurized metal tube. Without my consent, the ground pulled away from us like a yo-yo on a string. The familiar world became unfamiliar, less real, everything compressed into a model of itself. And then it was gone. I could hardly see it, and so it was gone. We were in the air, soaring smoothly, and I could breathe.

"Feel better, Kim?"

A little. But I still want you to answer my question. Is it wrong to want perfection from our world, our families, our children? Is it wrong to want control? Is it wrong to be afraid?

In my mind, the app sighed. It placed its disembodied hand on my shoulder. It was a patient app, but I was testing its patience. "It's not wrong, Kim. Fear is neither wrong nor right. It is what it is. But in the end, it can't give us the thing we most desire. It can't give us control. Nothing can. The control it offers is an illusion, a temporary distraction from the immutable fact that we're human, mortal, imperfect, and imperiled. There's no escape from that. Not for us and not for our kids. But when we accept it, there's a certain kind of freedom."

I picked up my phone, strange object that with each year felt less like an object, more like a part of myself, my mind. I felt like I was beginning to understand, like it had given me all there was to give, and so I held down the power button and shut it off. I put it in my purse, leaned back in my seat as much as the seat would let me, breathed deeply and slowly. The ascent had been bumpy but now we flew smooth. My mind emptied, then seemed to settle in a place of calm. I understood we were moving through the atmosphere at five hundred miles per hour, but my senses felt only stillness. We broke through the low cover of clouds as predicted. The sun spilled across the sea of white, the eddies of condensation. It glinted against our sheer metal wings as we angled skyward, faster, up, up and away, like it or not. Felix was sitting beside me in the window seat, and he, for one, loved the experience of flying. I'd asked him before taking off if he wanted the iPad so he could watch a movie, play a game. "No thanks," he said. "I just want to look out the window." And so he did. He looked out as I looked at him, the light on his face, in his hair, his eyes bright with nothing but the present moment, the joy of an experience that for me had come to seem dreadful and mundane. Across the aisle, Violet leaned on her father, stroked the matted fur of her pink bunny against her cheek, sucked her thumb. My precious ones. My small animals.

I watched Felix trace the view through the window with his finger. His finger ran the length of a cloud. His hand ran the width of a river. As I watched him, it occurred to me that whenever someone asked me why I was afraid of flying, I replied simply that I didn't believe in it, in flight. I couldn't believe in what seemed to me a miracle of supernatural dimensions, that human beings had found a way to lift ourselves into the sky and over the earth so cleanly. I didn't have the imagination for it, or the optimism. But maybe I was wrong. If my eight-year-old son could believe in it, why couldn't I? And was flight really any more of a miracle than this boy before me, once a nothing and soon a man?

Before he was anything, he'd been an idea inside me, an impulse, a feeling, a need and a want unmet. Pete and I had fallen in love on contact. We'd been walking along the Iowa River and I'd turned to him and said, "Wouldn't it be fun to make people?" as though I were the first person in the world to think of it.

"Sure," he said. "Okay."

And so we did. Surely that was as much a miracle as any passenger jet, the willing into existence of this person beside me, the persistence of our desire to keep going, to make things better and new, to try again. If I could believe in that, as I did, surely I could believe in flight.

For a moment, I marveled at it—and as I marveled, my fear let go of me. Then I was flying too—untethered, unafraid. And that was when my son turned to me, as though sensing and bending toward my new courage. "Mom?" he said, because to him that's what I am. "I want to be a pilot."

ACKNOWLEDGMENTS

Enormous gratitude to my agent, Maria Massie, and to my editor, Whitney Frick, as well as Bryn Clark, Amelia Possanza, Bob Miller, and the team at Flatiron Books for all the hard work that brought this book into the world.

Thank you to Sarah Ahlm, Erin Anderson, Joel Best, Joy Crane, Debra Harrell, Julie Koehler, Emily Miller, David Pimentel, Diane Redleaf and her colleagues at the Family Defense Center, Lenore Skenazy, and all the parents who spoke with me, for sharing their stories and insight that proved invaluable along the way.

Thank you to all my friends and family for their love, patience, and support, but especially Ken, Maddy, and Sari Brooks, Ann Campbell, Ethan Canin, Kevin Clouther, Gwynne Johnson, Fredrick Meiton, Kiki Petrosino, Beth Remis, Kaethe Schwehn, Ralph and Nancy Segall, Amelia Shapiro, and Benjamin Wheelock.

Thank you to my friend and amazing first editor at *Salon*, Sarah Hepola, for teaching me how to tell stories from real life.

Thank you to the Michener-Copernicus Foundation, the Yaddo Corporation, the Virginia Center for the Creative Arts, and the Ragdale Foundation for the time and space.

A very special thank you to Roscoe, whose curiosity and warmth of spirit made this book possible. Thank you to Iris for the laughter and love.

Thank you to Pete for all of the above and for everything else.

NOTES

CHAPTER 1: THE DAY I LEFT MY SON IN THE CAR

12 That March, the spring that I: Judith Warner, *Perfect Madness: Motherhood in the Age of Anxiety* (New York: Riverhead Books, 2014).

17 Margaret Mead wrote: Margaret Mead, "On Being a Grandmother," in *Mother Reader: Essential Writings on Motherhood*, ed. Moyra Davey (New York: Seven Stories Press, 2010), 31.

31 I hadn't yet memorized: Christopher Ingraham, "There's Never Been a Safer Time to Be a Kid in America," Wonkblog, *Washington Post*, April 14, 2015, https://www.washingtonpost.com/news/wonk/wp/2015/04/14/theres-never-been-a-safer-time-to-be-a-kid-in-america/?utm_term=.29896e46fe59.

CHAPTER 2: PARENTHOOD AS A COMPETITIVE SPORT

41 She highlights the multitude: Julie Lythcott-Haims, *How to Raise an Adult: Break Free of the Overparenting Trap and Prepare Your Kids for Success* (New York: St. Martin's Press, 2016), 7.

41 Likewise, in *Playing to Win*: Hilary Levey Friedman, *Playing to Win: Raising Children in a Competitive Culture* (Berkeley: University of California Press, 2016), 225.

42 "We create one for ourselves": Lisa Belkin, "Unhappy Helicopter Parents,"

New York Times, July 7, 2010, https://parenting.blogs.nytimes.com/2010/07/07/unhappy-helicopter-parents/?_r=0.

44 In 2008, 72 percent: Jennifer Senior, *All Joy and No Fun: The Paradox of Modern Parenthood* (New York: Ecco, 2015), 7.

46 As Adrienne Rich wrote: Adrienne Rich, *Of Woman Born: Motherhood as Experience and Institution* (New York: W. W. Norton & Company, 1995), 29.

48 She describes how together: Senior, *All Joy and No Fun*, 120.

48 She refers, for example: Viviana A. Rotman Zelizer, *Pricing the Priceless Child: The Changing Social Value of Children* (Princeton: Princeton University Press, 1994), 57.

48 As Hilary Levey Friedman explains: Friedman, *Playing to Win*, 13.

49 As Paula S. Fass writes: Paula S. Fass, *The End of American Childhood: A History of Parenting From Life on the Frontier to the Managed Child* (Princeton: Princeton University Press, 2016), 221.

50 In this manner, without: D'vera Cohn and Andrea Caumont, "7 Key Findings about Stay-at-Home Moms," Pew Research Center, April 8, 2014, http://www.pewresearch.org/fact-tank/2014/04/08/7-key-findings-about-stay-at-home-moms/.

50 If I'd been a citizen: Brigid Schulte, "The U.S. Ranks Last in Every Measure When It Comes to Family Policy, in 10 charts," *Washington Post*, June 23, 2014, https://www.washingtonpost.com/blogs/she-the-people/wp/2014/06/23/global-view-how-u-s-policies-to-help-working-families-rank-in-the-world/?utm_term=.9758defb2202.

53 The cost for families with: Bruce Covert, "Having a Child Will Bankrupt You," *Elle*, January 25, 2017, http://www.elle.com/culture/career-politics/a42230/cost-of-child-care/.

53 In a study of eight states: Ibid.

CHAPTER 3: THE FABRICATION OF FEAR

69 Skenazy founded *Free-Range Kids*: Lenore Skenazy, "Why I Let My 9-Year-Old Ride the Subway Alone," *New York Sun*, April 1, 2008, http://www.nysun.com/opinion/why-i-let-my-9-year-old-ride-subway-alone/73976/.

69 On her website, she devotes: Free-Range Kids.com.

83 In his book *Paranoid Parenting*: Frank Furedi, *Paranoid Parenting: Why Ignoring the Experts May Be Best for Your Child* (London: Continuum, 2008), 65.

84 "It is not surprising": Ibid.

84 "Parents," Stearns writes, "were increasingly": Peter N. Stearns, *Anxious Parents: A History of Modern Childrearing in America* (New York: New York University Press, 2004), 190.

84 Alongside these changes arose: Ibid., 165.

85 Just as experts were warning: Ibid., 192.

85 These pressures continued to build: Nathaniel Branden, *The Psychology of Self-Esteem: A Revolutionary Approach to Self-Understanding That Launched a New Era in Modern Psychology* (San Francisco: Jossey-Bass, 2001), 42.

86 As William Deresiewicz says: William Deresiewicz, *Excellent Sheep: The Miseducation of the American Elite and the Way to a Meaningful Life* (New York: Free Press, 2015), 39.

87 "Perhaps it was the luxury": Mona Simpson, "Beginning," in *Mother Reader: Essential Writings on Motherhood*, ed. Moyra Davey (New York: Seven Stories Press, 2010), 243.

87 And in an article: Hanna Rosin, "The Overprotected Kid," *The Atlantic*, April 2014, https://www.theatlantic.com/magazine/archive/2014/04/hey-parents-leave-those-kids-alone/358631/.

87 Lerner postulated that people: Jonah Lehrer, "A Just World," *The Atlantic*, September 1, 2009, https://www.theatlantic.com/daily-dish/archive/2009/09/a-just-world/196991/.

88 Burkeman cites as evidence: Oliver Burkeman, "Believing that life is fair might make you a terrible person," *The Guardian*, February 3, 2015, https://www.theguardian.com/commentisfree/oliver-burkeman-column/2015/feb/03/believing-that-life-is-fair-might-make-you-a-terrible-person.

88 Mintz suggests that: Steven Mintz, *Huck's Raft: A History of American Childhood* (Cambridge: Belknap Press, 2006), 339.

89 "Anxiety about the future": Ibid., 173.

90 In 1986, NBC aired: Joel Best, *Threatened Children: Rhetoric and Concern About Child-Victims* (Chicago: University of Chicago Press), 2.

90 "Parents could have their children fingerprinted": Ibid., 22.

90 And none of these frequent: Ibid.

91 A 1986 national survey: Ibid., 2.

91 "They frighten parents, intensify generational estrangement": Mintz, *Huck's Raft*, 339.

92 Weingarten goes on to describe: Gene Weingarten, "Fatal Distraction: Forgetting a Child in the Backseat of a Car Is a Horrifying Mistake. Is it a Crime?," *Washington Post*, March 8, 2009, https://www.washingtonpost.com/lifestyle/magazine/fatal-distraction-forgetting-a-child-in-thebackseat-of-a-car-is-a-horrifying-mistake-is-it-a-crime/2014/06/16/8ae0fe3a-f580-11e3-a3a5-42be35962a52_story.html?utm_term=.08bff6f51a9f.

93 Thirty-seven on average die: Based on US Census 2016 population estimates. Total US population: 323,127,513; persons under age five: 6.2 percent (19,387,650).

93 They are no longer afforded: Mona Simpson, "Beginning," in *Mother Reader: Essential Writings on Motherhood*, ed. Moyra Davey (New York: Seven Stories Press, 2010), 243.

94 At this time, popular magazines: Best, *Threatened Children*.

95 "And it seems that movement": Joel Best, from conversation with author.

96 "We think of nostalgia": Best, *Threatened Children*, 8.

96 "What matters is that we now": Joel Best, interviewed by author, August 6, 2015, Chicago.

96 "Salem's congregations believed they": Best, *Threatened Children,* 9.

99 Over the course of: Mintz, *Huck's Raft*, 4.

99 Yet many child-rearing tracts: Ibid., 10.

100 Puritan parents' fearfulness about: Ibid., 8.

100 As American families experienced: Ibid., *passim*.

101 "The future since 2008": Deresiewicz, *Excellent Sheep*, 41.

102 If one sees fear: Furedi, *Paranoid Parenting*.

CHAPTER 4: NEGATIVE FEEDBACK

105 Surveys suggested that children: Jessica Grose and Hanna Rosin, "The Shortening Leash," *Slate*, August 6, 2014, http://www.slate.com/articles/life/family/2014/08/slate_childhood_survey_results_kids_today_have_a_lot_less_freedom_than_their.html (October 31, 2017).

110 "What's more surprising, however": Barbara Sarnecka, interviewed by author, August 24, 2016, Chicago; Tania Lombrozo, "Why Do We Judge Parents for Putting Kids at Perceived—But Unreal—Risk?," NPR.com, August 22, 2016, http://www.npr.org/sections/13.7/2016/08/22/490847797/why-do-we-judge-parents-for-putting-kids-at-perceived-but-unreal-risk.

110 Sarnecka's colleague Kyle Stanford: Kyle Stanford, interviewed by author, September 1, 2017, Chicago.

110 "The increasing beliefs about": Ibid.

112 Bloom laughed a little: Paul Bloom, interviewed by author, February 2, 2017, Chicago.

115 "And the part of our brain": Barbara Sarnecka, interviewed by author, August 24, 2016, Chicago.

CHAPTER 5: SELF REPORT

120 In 2008, the CDC found: According to the safety organization Kids and Cars, for all ages the average number since 1998 is thirty-seven per year. This breaks down to thirty-four for ages zero to four, and two per year for ages five to fourteen; see section called "AGES" at http://noheatstroke.org/.

125 Congress settled on language: David Pimentel, interviewed by author, December 18, 2015, Chicago.

CHAPTER 6: WHAT A HORRIBLE MOTHER

148 "Those who can't afford camps": K. J. Dell'Antonia, "The Families That Can't Afford Summer," *New York Times*, June 4, 2016, https://www.nytimes.com/2016/06/05/sunday-review/the-families-that-cant-afford-summer.html?_r=0.

150 "Yes, sir," she answers: See transcript on *FreeRangeKids.com*, http://www.freerangekids.com/watch-police-interrogate-the-mom-jailed-for-letting-her-daughter-play-at-park/.

150 "What did it mean": Paula S. Fass, *The End of American Childhood: A History of Parenting From Life on the Frontier to the Managed Child* (Princeton: Princeton University Press, 2016), 55.

151 Fass describes how: Ibid., 83.

151 "Indeed, the middle classes defined": Ibid., 82.

152 She told me that: Diane Redleaf, interviewed by author, August 4, 2016, Chicago.

152 "And they are making"; Ibid.

155 "You don't have to be": Debra Harrell, interviewed by author, August 17, 2016, Amherst, Virginia.

156 David Pimentel explained it this way: Pimentel interview.

156 "When you make it a crime": Ibid.

158 "Does your husband know": Whitney Armstrong, interviewed by author, October 15, 2015, New York.

159 She notes how the columnist: Judith Warner, *Perfect Madness: Motherhood in the Age of Anxiety* (New York: Riverhead Books, 2014), 110.

161 "I'm not about to be intimidated": Julie Koehler, interviewed by author, September 21, 2016, Evanston, Illinois.

CHAPTER 7: QUALITY OF LIFE

170 "Motherhood has been elevated": Heather Havrilesky, "Our 'Mommy' Problem," *New York Times*, November 8, 2014, https://www.nytimes.com/2014/11/09/opinion/sunday/our-mommy-problem.html.

172 "A woman who was, perhaps": Judith Warner, *Perfect Madness: Motherhood in the Age of Anxiety* (New York: Riverhead Books, 2014), 15.

172 "It appeared normal to them": Ibid., 14.

179 "Anxiety is more about": Emily F. Miller, interviewed by author, August 14, 2014, Chicago.

CHAPTER 8: GUINEA PIGS

191 "Because of parental fear": Steven Mintz, *Huck's Raft: A History of American Childhood* (Cambridge: Belknap Press, 2006), 348.

203 Sarnecka didn't seem surprised: Barbara Sarnecka, interviewed by author, August 24, 2016, Chicago.

206 "This inability to cope": Julie Lythcott-Haims, *How to Raise an Adult: Break Free of the Overparenting Trap and Prepare Your Kids for Success* (New York: St. Martin's Press, 2016), 91.

208 "They have a right": Sarnecka interview.

209 "We are not teaching": William Deresiewicz, *Excellent Sheep: The Miseducation of the American Elite and the Way to a Meaningful Life* (New York: Free Press, 2015), 50.

216 "I mean, the experience": Erin Anderson, interviewed by author, 2016, Chicago.

216 Arendt argues that this: Hannah Arendt, *The Human Condition* (Chicago: University of Chicago Press, 1958), 247.